J. W. Baldwin
Baltimore
1974

IMPERIAL LIVES
AND LETTERS

OF THE ELEVENTH CENTURY

NUMBER LXVII
OF THE RECORDS OF CIVILIZATION
SOURCES AND STUDIES

IMPERIAL LIVES AND LETTERS

OF THE ELEVENTH CENTURY

TRANSLATED BY

THEODOR E. MOMMSEN AND KARL F. MORRISON

WITH AN HISTORICAL INTRODUCTION BY

KARL F. MORRISON

EDITED BY ROBERT L. BENSON

NEW YORK AND LONDON

COLUMBIA UNIVERSITY PRESS

Library of Congress Catalog Card Number: 61-15107

First printing 1962
Second printing 1967

Printed in the United States of America

THEODOR ERNST MOMMSEN

Grati Animi Monumentum

PREFACE

The death of Professor Theodor E. Mommsen on July 18, 1958, is deeply mourned by all who knew him as friend or colleague, scholar or teacher. Since this volume was one of the tasks which he left unfinished at that time, the appearance of his name both on the title page and in the dedication requires only a brief explanation.

The political and ideological struggles of the eleventh and early twelfth century formed one of Professor Mommsen's earliest and most durable historical interests. Indeed, as a student in Germany, for his doctoral dissertation he very nearly chose a topic from this period. As a professor at Princeton and later at Cornell, he devoted several of his richly rewarding seminars to the history of this conflict, and the conception of this book grew out of the last of these seminars. In 1957, Dr. Karl F. Morrison, then one of Professor Mommsen's graduate students, began a translation of three important sources for German imperial history in the eleventh century: Wipo's *The Deeds of Conrad II*, the anonymous *Life of the Emperor Henry IV*, and the Letters of Henry IV. Professor Mommsen agreed to collaborate in the revision of these translations, and he also intended to write an historical introduction to these sources, but at the time of his death, he and Dr. Morrison had completed only their translation of the two imperial biographies.

Anyone who has undertaken a translation or an edition knows the value of a co-worker's help in the solution of problems and in the discovery of errors. After July of 1958, deprived of Professor Mommsen's learning and judgment, Dr. Morrison finished their collaborative enterprise alone and wrote the historical introduction. In view of these circumstances, many of Professor Mommsen's friends and colleagues, as well as several of Dr. Morrison's friends, generously offered useful suggestions and criticism on the translation of Henry IV's Letters and on the Introduction. Dr. Morrison and I should like to express warm thanks to:

Professor Howard L. Adelson, The College of the City of New York
Professor Harry Caplan, Cornell University
Professor Craig B. Fisher, University of California at Davis
Dr. Charles Hamilton, University of Mississippi
Professor James Hutton, Cornell University
Professor Ernst H. Kantorowicz, The Institute for Advanced Study
Mr. Emile Karafiol, University of Chicago
The late Professor M. L. W. Laistner, Cornell University
Mr. William A. Percy
Dr. Doris Raymond, Mercer College
Dr. and Mrs. G. Wylie Sypher
Professor Brian Tierney, Cornell University
Professor Helene Wieruszowski, The College of the City of New York

Finally, special gratitude is owed to Mrs. Karl Morrison, who tirelessly typed and retyped the successive versions of the manuscript, and to the European Editor of the series in which this volume appears, Professor John H. Mundy, for much encouragement. Thanks are also due to Mrs. John Kotselas for the editing of the typescript.

Credit for the general plan of this book and for supervision of the two Lives belongs to Professor Mommsen. The book's very existence, however, and its merits are largely attributable to Dr. Morrison, who has amply justified his teacher's confidence. As Columbia University Press' special Editor for this volume, I worked closely with Dr. Morrison, particularly on the translation and preparation of the Letters. It is our hope that this book will serve as a suitable monument—one among many—to Professor Mommsen's memory.

Wesleyan University   ROBERT L. BENSON
Middletown, Connecticut
June 1, 1961

CONTENTS

"The authority of the ancients states quite clearly that those who are called kings now were termed tyrants in earlier days because of the cruel ferocity of their practices. But since the time zeal for the sacred religion began to increase, "kings" have been so called from their right ruling, since they repress bestial motives and through the power of discernment they show themselves men of the just cause. Of the former men, the Lord said: "They have ruled, and not by me; they have been princes, and I have not acknowledged them" (Hosea 8:4); but of these later ones: "Counsel is mine, and equity; prudence is mine, fortitude mine; through me kings reign, and the founders of laws decree just things; through me princes command, and the mighty decree justice" (Proverbs 8:14–16).

Bern of Reichenau to Henry III, in
C. Erdmann, Fr. Baethgen, ed.,
*Forschungen zur politischen Ideenwelt
des Frühmittelalters* (Berlin, 1951), p. 113.

IMPERIAL LIVES AND LETTERS

OF THE ELEVENTH CENTURY

ABBREVIATIONS

MGH	*Monumenta Germaniae Historica*
	Series:

AA.	*Auctores Antiquissimi*
Cap. Reg. Fr.	*Capitularia Regum Francorum*
Concil. Kar. Aev.	*Concilia Karolini Aevi*
Const.	*Constitutiones et Acta Publica*
Epp. Kar. Aev.	*Epistolae Karolini Aevi*
Ldl.	*Libelli de lite*
SS.	*Scriptores*

CSEL	*Corpus Scriptorum Ecclesiasticorum Latinorum*
Mansi	*Collectio Conciliorum*, J. D. Mansi, ed., vols. I–XIII (Florence, 1759 ff.), vols. XIV–XXXI (Venice, 1769 ff.); reprinted (Paris, 1901–1927)
Migne	*Patrologiae Cursus Completus*, J. P. Migne, ed. (Paris, 1844–1855)
	Series:

PL	Series Latina
PG	Series Graeca

MIÖG	*Mitteilungen des Instituts für Österreichische Geschichtsforschung*
ZfRG	*Zeitschrift der Savigny-Stiftung für Rechtsgeschichte*
	Series:

KA	Kanonistische Abteilung
RA	Romanistische Abteilung

INTRODUCTION

BY KARL F. MORRISON

"PONTIFICAL KINGSHIP" OF THE SALIANS

One major premise of conventional political thought was the intellectual battleground of the Investiture Controversy (ca. 1073–1122):
while strongly antagonistic, both Imperial and Papal writers shared the
classic view that God had divided the government of the Church between bishops, His spiritual, and kings, His temporal vicars. However,
both kingship and episcopacy, as the writers of the Controversy knew
them, were temporal and spiritual in character, and the nice distinction
between their duties implied by this principle could not, in fact, be
realized. Kings, on the basis of their material power and spiritual responsibilities, and bishops, by virtue of their spiritual authority and
temporal wealth and duties, each claimed supremacy over the other in
worldly affairs and correspondingly the right to intervene in the proper
administrative functions of the other. When the resulting practical and
theoretical difficulties were revealed in the contest of Empire and
Papacy, pro-Papal writers attempted to resolve them by arguing that,
though divinely bestowed, civil power was delegated to secular rulers
indirectly through the spiritual offices of the clergy. Consequently,
they maintained, all Christian government, while bipartite, was ultimately subject to clerical direction. This argument prejudiced the con-
verse ideological position described in the following essay: the concept
of the spiritual character and duties of the royal office held by the Salian
emperors (Conrad II, Henry III, IV, V). In the institutional context of
the imperial Church system, this concept was the theoretical warrant
for decisive intervention by the secular power in almost all ecclesiastical matters except the purely sacramental. For according to it, the
temporal ruler performed quasi-episcopal as well as royal offices in the

Church; indeed, he was a "pontifical" king, "the head of the Church." Between the "pontifical" king of the Salians and the "royal" pontiff of the reformed Papacy, there was no ground for amicable compromise; and after a struggle of fifty years, they were reconciled only at the cost of the secularization of the imperial office and the irreparable weakening of its administrative power.

"But Melchisedech, the king of Salem, brought forth bread and wine; and he was the priest of the most high God" (Genesis 14 : 18). Abraham himself, according to the author of the Epistle to the Hebrews, gave tithes to this King of Salem, who was "without father, without mother, without descent, having neither beginning of days, nor end of life; but made like unto the Son of God, abiding a priest continually" (Hebrews 7 : 2–3).

Melchisedech was regarded in the Middle Ages as a prefiguration of Christ in that kingship and priesthood were united in his person; in the political thought of the early Middle Ages, it was a commonplace that after the advent of the Christ, in whom those characters were perfectly and forever united, no mortal man might ever again hold them both. However, at their coronations, Saxon kings were told by the officiating prelates that they became sharers of the ministry of bishops.[1] And in the midst of the Investiture Controversy, Wido, later bishop of Osnabrück, wrote, "rightly the king is separated from the number of laymen in this fashion [in coronation], since as one anointed with the oil of consecration, he is acknowledged to be a sharer of the priestly ministry."[2]

Adversaries of the kings felt it necessary to discredit these claims to a dual character. Gregory VII, for example, drew a clear distinction between the priesthood and the laity when he vigorously asserted that the power of an exorcist, the fifth ecclesiastical grade below a priest, was vastly superior to that of any secular ruler in that he could govern spirits; priests, as the superiors of exorcists, were so much the greater

[1] P. E. Schramm, "Die Krönung in Deutschland bis zum Beginn des salischen Hauses (1028)," *ZfRG KA*, XXIV (1935), 319. The statement is prescribed at the imposition of the crown in the "Mainz" Coronation Order (ca. 961) and in its revised form (ca. 961–1000).

[2] *Liber de Controversia Hildebrandi et Heinrici*, MGH Ldl., I, 467. Cf. *Leodicensium Epistola Adversus Paschalem Papam*, MGH Ldl., II, 462: "Quis poterit discernere causam regni a causa sacerdotii?" See M. Bloch, *Les rois thaumaturges* (Paris, 1924), p. 189.

than temporal princes.[3] In the same tenor, Rangerius of Lucca and many others at the beginning of the twelfth century argued vigorously against lay investiture: "The ring and the staff are two sacred signs, nor are they to be received in any way from the hands of a layman."[4] Somewhat later, Honorius Augustodunensis remarked, "perhaps some praters contend with swollen arrogance that the king is not of the number of layman, since he has been anointed with the oil of priests." In fact, said Honorius, he was not a cleric—he was neither a monk nor a holder of priestly orders—but rather, he was wholly a layman, a spiritual subject of the pope in sacred matters.[5]

Both the claims of the royalists and those of their opponents could be amply supported from Scripture and tradition. The king did share the ministry of bishops; to that purpose he was consecrated by a quasi-episcopal unction. But he did not share the priestly dignity; he could not, by virtue of his unction, perform purely sacramental offices. He was, indeed, "separated from the number of laymen" by his unction; he was *non mere laicus*: and still, he was not a priest. Modern scholars have come to refer to this anomalous figure as the "pontifical king." By this term, one designates a king who enjoyed the temporal prestige of prelates and who was charged with their spiritual, but nonpriestly, functions—to rule, to judge, to correct, and, through these operations, to guard the doctrinal purity and, insofar as possible, the temporal well-being of the Church. One refers to a ruler whose office was both temporal and spiritual and, more specifically, to the king's ecclesiastical rather than his secular character.

Since this quasi-hieratic theory of kingship marks the works translated in this volume (and, indeed, since it was a major factor contributing to the Investiture Controversy for which these works are presented as illustrative material), it may be useful to make a few remarks on its origins, nature, and effects, although a full treatment is not possible here. The king who found it necessary to bow to the commands of the princes, the king who begged and bribed to gain support, the king who was more subject to his subjects than they to him, is not our theme, although this is the figure seen by one who looks for the facts of politics

---

[3] Gregory VII, *Das Register Gregors*, ed. by E. Caspar (Berlin, 1955), Epp. VIII, 21, pp. 555 ff. On the rank of the exorcist, see Honorius Augustodunensis, *Summa Gloria*, MGH Ldl., III, 69, chap. 9.

[4] *MGH Ldl.*, II, 509, vv. 1–2; 533, vv. 1159–1160.

[5] *Summa Gloria, MGH Ldl.*, III, 69, chap. 9.

alone. The figure presented here is that of the theoretical king, the king in abstract, the ideal counterpart of the king who dealt with reality. In viewing this figure one perceives the ideological basis for the actions performed by the real king; his concept of the source and character of his own power and of his proper relations to others who held power of a different nature; in short, his concept of the place in the world rightly due him.

Two elements were fundamental to this theocratic concept: the divine character of the kingly office itself, and the episcopal functions of the king. The first was founded essentially on the authority of Scripture; the second, also derived from Scripture, was even more fully warranted by tradition.

St. Paul gave the sanction of divinity to all offices, saying, "There is no power but of God; the powers that be are ordained of God" (Romans 13:1). The paradigm of Saul and David (cf. I Samuel 15:23, 28:17) illustrated this maxim by showing that the regal office was bestowed by God upon men whom He had elected and that those who lost His favor were cast down by the same power which had exalted them. Just as power was of divine ordination, so its exercise was by divine guidance. St. Paul, again, furnished the most familiar Scriptural authority: "For he [the prince] is the minister of God to thee for good. But if thou do that which is evil, be afraid; for he beareth not the sword in vain; for he is the minister of God, a revenger to execute wrath upon him that doeth evil" (Romans 13:4).

A natural corollary of these prescripts was that submission to established authority was a sacred duty. "Touch not mine anointed," wrote the Psalmist, "and do my prophets no harm" (Psalm 105:15, I Chronicles 16:22). The author of the first epistle of Peter admonished the Church: "Submit yourselves to every ordinance of man for the Lord's sake: whether it be to the king, as supreme; or unto governors, as unto them that are sent by him for the punishment of evil doers and for the praise of them that do well. Fear God. Honor the King" (I Peter 2:13,17). Above all, St. Paul also gave his support to submission, for, as he acknowledged the divine ordination of all powers, he condemned resistance to the exercise of those powers as a damnable sin (Romans 13:1–2). By submission, the governed would honor the divine origin and character of the government set over them.

Prior to the Christianization of the Empire, the Severi had claimed the aura of divinity for themselves by virtue of their service in the cult of the "Unconquered Sun." Their successor Aurelian elaborated their claims: in the Imperial cult, the emperor became "the vicar of God," a man who ruled by the grace of the sun-god, a man endowed with the majesty of his divine master. When the Empire became Christian, this semidivine pagan character, already grown conventional, was easily adapted to the Pauline figure; in its new role, the pagan concept, embroidered upon richly and heavily by Christian tradition, tended quite naturally toward regal pontificalism.[6]

St. Augustine, who strongly influenced the development of the tradition, offers a suggestion of this tendency. Not only did he maintain that when emperors ordered what was good Christ himself gave the order,[7] but even further, he wrote that the emperors should use this sacred power to perform quasi-episcopal functions. Christian emperors, he said, were in a peculiarly happy state if they were fosterers of the Church; if, among other things, they devoted their power most of all to spreading the worship of God among the peoples of the world; if, as men and rulers, they feared, loved, and worshiped God; and if they were not negligent in making sacrifices of humility, mercy, and prayer to God for their sins.[8] But the capacity in which the ruler was to be a "minister of God," in which he was to work constantly to spread the worship of God, in which he was to make his sacrifices, was but generally defined.

Before the days of St. Augustine, the biographer of Constantine the Great had been more specific; he acclaimed that Emperor as "Bishop of those outside" the Church and even as "Universal Bishop."[9] Constantine had earned this title, for, as though he were a "hierophant,"

[6] A convenient summary of the pagan antecedents is in E. Barker, *From Alexander to Constantine* (Oxford, 1956), pp. 346 ff. See also M. A. Canney, "Ancient Concepts of Kingship," in *Oriental Studies in Honor of Cursetji Erachji Pavry* (London, 1933); and N. H. Baynes, in the *Journal of Roman Studies*, XXV (1935), 83 f., partially reprinted in his *Byzantine Studies* (London, 1955), p. 343. For the persistence of the pagan notion into Christian times, see L. Cerfaux and J. Tondriau, *Un concurrent du christianisme: le culte des souverains dans la civilisation Gréco-Romaine* (Paris, 1957), and W. Ensslin, "Die Religionspolitik des Kaisers Theodosius des Grossen," *Sitzungsberichte der bayerischen Akademie der Wissenschaften* (phil.-hist. Kl. 1953), Heft 2, pp. 64 f.

[7] Ep. 105, 11, *CSEL*, XXXIV. 2, 603. Mr. William S. Barker kindly drew my attention to this passage.

[8] *City of God* V, 24.

[9] *Life of Constantine* IV, 24; I, 44. See W. Seston, "Constantine as a 'Bishop,'" *Journal of Roman Studies*, XXXVII (1947), 127–131. Professor E. H. Kantorowicz directed me to this article.

he had assumed the office of preacher on great occasions[10] and had sat among the bishops in synods and councils.[11] And, according to those jealous of the regal power, this was rightly done; for if, as Optatus of Milevis[12] had written, the Church was in the State, not the State in the Church, the ruler, as head of the State, was also in a position of dominance over the Church. It was natural then for his hegemony over secular affairs to be likened titularly and in other external respects to that of priests and bishops who held hegemony over spiritual affairs. His ecclesiastical functions were of one kind; those of the clergy were of another.

Thus, by the fourth century, the pagan attribution of a divine character and sacred responsibilities to the kingship had been Christianized and adopted by the Church. This attribution, in its new form, Caesaropapism, was adopted by Constantine the Great and maintained by his successors. To honor Omnipotent God, the author of Empire and the helmsman of the State,[13] Honorius and his Imperial brother Arcadius issued a remarkable series of edicts at the end of the fourth century in which their concern for the stability and orthodoxy of the Church was expressed in raising heresy to the status of treason, "for that which is committed against the divine religion redounds to the detriment of all."[14] Heresy had become treason, to be judged and punished by the secular power,[15] and consequently the maintenance of the purity of the orthodox faith fell to the same power. The Emperor Marcian, at the Council of Chalcedon, announced that, after the example of Constantine the Great, he was resolved to participate in the Council "to confirm the Faith" and to be sure that the members of the Council would not be moved "by the perverse suasions" of the people.[16]

In the next century, Justinian gave classic expression to this Caesaropapism in the *Prolegomena* to his *Novella VI*: The priesthood and the Empire, he wrote, were "the greatest gifts of God among men." The priesthood was to minister in divine affairs, and the secular power was to show protection and watchfulness in human affairs; both proceeded

[10] *Life of Constantine* II, 28, and IV, 22. See also Constantine's "Oration to the Assembly of the Saints," translated with some of the works of Eusebius, in Vol. I of *Nicene and Post-Nicene Fathers*, 2d series (New York, 1890).

[11] Rufinus, *Historia Ecclesiastica* X, 2, in *Eusebius Werke*, ed, by E. Schwartz and T. Mommsen, II (Leipzig, 1908), 161.

[12] Optatus of Milevis II, 3, *CSEL*, XXVI, 74.

[13] Honorius to Arcadius, *Collectio Avellana* 38, 4, *CSEL*, XXXV. I, 86.

[14] *Codex Theodosianus* XVI, 4, 4.   [15] E.g., *ibid.*, 1, 4, and *loc. cit.*   [16] Mansi, VIII, 130.

from the same divine source. Since it was the duty of priests to make continual supplication for rulers before God, Justinian professed that he, as emperor, rightly exercised "the greatest solicitude" to maintain "the true dogmas of God" and to confirm the honor of the priesthood, for thus he would merit the greatest divine gifts.[17] The emperor was established as judge of dogma and of the worthiness of priests; his province extended to all aspects of the Church, save for the actual spiritual content of its functions. The "regal pontificalism" of Constantine was now acknowledged to touch not only those outside the Church, but also all those within it.

The Church, though not always supinely acquiescent toward these imperial claims, tended, on the whole, to assent to them. In 448, at the Council of Constantinople, the emperor Theodosius was acclaimed by the assembled clergy as "Pontiff-Emperor";[18] and three years later, at Chalcedon, his successor Marcian was hailed as "Priest and King."[19] This attitude was known also in the West, and popes at least gave it lip-service. Pope Leo I wrote to Anatolius, the patriarch of Constantinople, urging him to prevail upon the Emperor to exert, "not only his regal, but also his priestly mind."[20] Pope Simplicius wrote to the Emperor Zeno, "exulting that within you is the spirit of the most faithful priest and prince.[21] "So widely was this position accepted that even Pope Leo I, stanch champion of the sacerdotal dignity as he was, not only acknowledged the Emperor Marcian as being both priestly and regal in disposition, but he also affirmed that God had preordained the Imperial power for the preservation of the Catholic truth and prayed that He "may confer upon you, besides the regal crown, the priestly rod [*palma*] also."[22]

His election being divine, his actions being directed toward the welfare of the Church, the secular ruler attained the greatest height of his pontificalism as "vicar of God." Ambrosiaster, at the end of the fourth century, wrote that the king was adored on earth as such;[23] and a cen-

---

[17] *Corpus Juris Civilis, Novellae,* I, 6, Prolegomena, ed. by R. Schoell and W. Kroll (Berlin, 1904), pp. 35 f.

[18] Mansi, VI, 733. A century earlier the Emperor Gratian had renounced the pagan title "pontifex maximus." See W. Ensslin, "Die Religionspolitik," pp. 9 f., 88.

[19] Mansi, VII, 177. For the contrary view, see below, pp. 34 ff.

[20] Ep. 155, Migne *PL,* LIV, 1126.   [21] Ep. 14, Migne *PL,* LVIII, 51.

[22] Mansi, VI, 217, 219. See W. Ensslin, "Valentinians III Novellen XVII und XVIII von 445," *ZfRG RA,* XXXVII (1937), esp. 378.

[23] *Quaestiones Veteris et Novi Testamenti* XVI, 8, *CSEL,* L. 157.

tury later, Pope Anastasius II tacitly recognized the Emperor Anastasius as holding a vicariate of God.[24]

By the fifth century, therefore, the functions of the ruler, like his office, were circumscribed with divinity and a quasi-sacerdotal character; he was the representative of God on earth. These concepts were widely dispersed in the West during the fifth and sixth centuries; and thenceforth they are met in the barbarian kingdoms of the West among the Ostrogoths, the Vandals, the Lombards, and finally the Franks.[25] Venantius Fortunatus even went so far as to write about A.D. 600 that the Merovingian Childebert I was "our Melchisedech, rightly King and Priest."[26]

This tradition, handed on to the Frankish kings, found ready acceptance and renewed vigor under Charlemagne. Alcuin hailed him as "son of God," as "chosen of God,"[27] and as "preacher in the instance of sowing the word of God,"[28] to whom bishops, as vicars of Christ, took second place. At the Council of Frankfurt (794), the Italian bishops, employing Byzantine hyperbole, prayed that he would be "King and Priest";[29] and others, more cautiously, called him "Bishop of bishops"[30] and a vicar of God, the King, "over all his members."[31] Charlemagne himself attributed divine inspiration to his own actions: "For we believe the heart of the king is in the hand of God [Proverbs 21:1] and that it is turned hither and yon by His will. And so we believe the lofty state of pastoral rule has been granted him, not by our judgment, but by that of God."[32] It was in this attitude, as "King by the grace of God" (a style

[24] Ivo of Chartres, *Decretum* XVI, 16. See A. von Harnack, "Christus praesens—Vicarius Christi," *Sitzungsberichte der preussischen Akademie der Wissenschaften* (phil.-hist. Klasse, 1929), pp. 436 ff.

[25] See W. Ensslin, "Das Gottesgnadentum des autokratischen Kaisertums der frühbyzantinischen Zeit," *Studi bizantini e neoellenici*, V (1939), 163 ff.

[26] *MGH AA.*, IV 40; *Carmina* II, 10.   [27] *MGH Epp. Kar. Aev.*, II, 241, no. 148.

[28] *Ibid.*, p. 294, no. 178.   [29] *MGH Concil. Kar. Aev.*, II, 142.

[30] Monk of St. Gall, *Gesta Caroli* I, 25. *MGH SS.*, II, 742.

[31] Cathwulf to Charlemagne, *MGH Epp. Kar. Aev.*, II, 503, no. 7. I am unable to find any substantiantion for the unsupported assertion made by Max Buchner that this letter is a ninth-century forgery. *Historisches Jahrbuch*, LV (1935), 604. For the most recent treatment of political thought at the court of Charlemagne, see L. Wallach, *Alcuin and Charlemagne* (Cornell, 1959).

[32] E. Munding, ed., *Königsbrief Karls des Grossen an Papst Hadrian* (*Texte und Arbeiten herausgegeben durch die Erzabtei Beuron*, I Abt., Hft. 6. (Beuron, 1920), p. 4. See also W. Levison in *Neues Archiv*, XLIII (1922), 464 f.; and W. Erben in *Neues Archiv*, XLVI (1925), 11, and in the *Historische Zeitschrift*, CXXIX (1923), 289 ff. Charlemagne refers to the bestowal of the bishopric of Pavia upon Waldo of Reichenau.

adopted by his father, but first given broad and consistent usage by Charlemagne himself), that he wrote to Pope Leo III that his duty was "to defend by force of arms the holy Church of Christ on every hand from incursion by pagans and from devastation by infidels without, and within to fortify it through knowledge of the Catholic Faith." As for the duty of the Pope, Charlemagne wrote only that he was to pray for the Emperor's military success.[33] The duty of the king, in short, was to superintend all affairs of the Church, to be truly a bishop, or "overseer," while the duty of the priest was through spiritual means to seek divine support for the king.

Although Charlemagne's successors were weaker than the great Charles, and some were deposed or otherwise abused, they were also revered by their supporters as vicars of God.[34] They themselves made the same claims to divine election and to "pontifical" functions as their illustrious forebear had made. Charles the Simple, for example, who saw the last great days of his house, styled himself "Charles, through the preordination of Divine Providence, the glorious king."[35] As for his kingly responsibilities toward the Church, he expressed his eagerness to extend the support of the regal office to the priesthood;[36] but he also stated his intention to follow the example of his ancestors "who always remained devoted in affairs of divine worship and strove with the most pious solicitude to correct whatever errors there were in the Holy Church."[37] For he maintained that whenever the ship of his Mother the Church was beset by enemy boarders and lacked a steersman, tradition counseled him to go to her defense; "for, indeed, the Church is strengthened by two universal persons—namely, the priestly and the royal—so that if one be inexperienced or too little provident, the other may not sleep in indolence."[38]

In the East Frankish kingdom, the same concepts are faintly traceable until the extinction of the Carolingian house, though not so distinctly as in the West Frankish realm. With the advent of Otto I and the Saxon dynasty, the theme revived, partially through the ecclesiastical tradition and partially through Byzantine influence, strong during the Ottonian campaigns in Italy and direct in the marriage of Otto II to

[33] *Ibid.*, p. 137, no. 93.
[34] See R. W. and A. J. Carlyle, *A History of Medieval Political Theory in the West*, Vol. I, chaps. 17 and 21, and Vol. II, chap. 7.
[35] F. Lot, ed., *Recueil des Actes de Charles III le Simple* (Paris, 1949), p. 165.
[36] *Ibid.*, p. 253, no. 106, and *loc. cit.* [37] *Ibid.*, p. 49, no. 24. [38] *Ibid.*, p. 85, no. 40.

the Byzantine princess Theophano. It received its most poignant expression in the futile efforts of Otto III to unite the Roman Empire and the Roman Church into a single power embracing the world. He envisaged himself as the spiritual son of the Church, but also as its rector; thus, he bestowed the Papacy upon his own candidates. By virtue of his secular office, "Emperor Augustus of the Romans by the will of God, the Savior, and our Liberator," he adopted also the more spiritual style, after the pattern of St. Paul, "servant of Jesus Christ," a title which he subsequently exchanged, however, for "servant of the Apostles."[39]

The concept of the sacred character of his office compelled him to endeavor to regulate the affairs of the Church; the same compulsion drove his successor, Henry II. Henry's zeal for the Church was revealed not only in the founding of the see of Bamberg through his own volition and labor, for which the obligatory Papal sanction was but an act of ratification, but also in the rigorous reforms which he prosecuted in Italy. There he removed unworthy bishops—to be sure, by the judgment of ecclesiastical courts, but by courts at whose head he sat—and secured the installation of at least forty-two new bishops, a number surpassed significantly among his successors only by Henry IV in the turmoil of the Investiture Controversy.[40]

This whole tradition of regal pontificalism, as at least one man saw it in the reign of Henry II, is epitomized in a very interesting portrait of Henry. In 1022 the Emperor presented to the monastery of Monte Cassino a codex of the Gospels in one of whose illuminations he was represented sitting in judgment. His figure occupies the center of the illumination; four figures at the corners of the folio represent Justitia, Pietas, Lex, and Jus; the figures at the left are connected with the word "Sapientia" (which names the figure between them) and those at the right, by the word "Prudentia" (which names their corresponding figure). Below him is represented the execution of a "tyrannus."

---

[39] P. E. Schramm, *Kaiser, Rom und Renovatio*, Part I (Berlin, 1929), p. 141. See also Menno Ter Braak, *Kaiser Otto III, Ideal und Praxis im frühen Mittelalter* (Amsterdam, 1928), pp. 102 f. and pp. 205 f. The parallel with the title "servus servorum Dei," used by the bishops of Rome from the days of Gregory I, is clear.

[40] H. L. Mikoletsky, *Kaiser Heinrich II und die Kirche* (Vienna, 1946), pp. 41 ff. Schramm, however, in "Sacerdotium und Regnum im Austausch ihrer Vorrechte," *Studi Gregoriani*, II (1947), 428, indicates that although Henry II did not abandon fully the traditional figure of the ecclesiastical king, he did withdraw somewhat from the extreme position of Otto III. See T. Schieffer, "Heinrich II und Konrad II," *Deutsches Archiv*, VIII (1951), 394 ff.

In the upper register, the dove, the usual representation of the Holy Spirit, descends upon his head.

There are two major observations which should be made about this illumination. First, Henry is shown wearing a tippet, arranged, as Schramm noticed,[41] like the stole of a deacon. The inscription around his figure declares: "Henry shines forth in his ancestral throne of Empire, Caesar and Augustus, worthy of the dignity of the garb of state." The reference "garb of state" probably relates specifically to the tippet, which is, according to Schramm, actually the *lorum*, or *pallium*, once the badge of the imperial or consular office, but adopted by high ecclesiastics before the composition of the Donation of Constantine (750–850). Thereafter it was worn by popes, patriarchs, archbishops, and, in the East, by the emperors. Its use by Western emperors, however, is neither well nor regularly attested. For this reason, Schramm was inclined to believe that Henry did not in fact wear the *lorum*, but that the representation was merely a concession on the part of the illuminators in the monastery of St. Emmeram at Regensburg, where the codex was made, to the Byzantine traditions supposedly familiar to the monks of Monte Cassino, for whom their work was destined. However, other sources, which Schramm discounted, affirm that the German emperor of Henry's day did wear the *lorum;* and there is no reason why the illuminators of St. Emmeram should have known that their Italian brethren were acquainted with the imperial use of the *lorum*, or should have cared enough about it if they had known, to alter an otherwise conventional portrait. Furthermore, the "Revised Mainz *Ordo*" prescribes the investiture of Saxon kings at their coronations with a *pallium*.[42] At any rate, one may suggest that the "garb of state" refers to the whole costume depicted and that the tippet is a badge of the ecclesiastical position received by the emperor through his imperial coronation, or of the clerical positions he held otherwise (for example, of his canonries).

The second feature to be noticed is specific. A vertical relationship exists between the representation of the Holy Spirit and Henry, and between Henry and the execution of the "tyrant" below him. The inscription above the Dove is "Clement Spirit, God, bless bounteously the King"; and that about the figure of Wisdom, "Through holy counsels, the wisdom of the King is fit." The inscription about "Prudentia" com-

---

[41] P. E. Schramm, *Herrschaftszeichen und Staatssymbolik*, (Stuttgart, 1954), I, 31 f.
[42] Schramm, "Krönung," p. 330.

memorates the advice of prudent men; and that about the execution, the condemnation of the victim as a tyrant by Law and Right, after the will of Henry. The symbolism of the illumination, therefore, may be interpreted as follows. The king is blessed by God and directly inspired by Him; in turn, "with holy counsels" as well as with human prudence, thus combining in himself elements of the divine and the human, he administers justice, not bearing the sword in vain, but being "a minister of God, a revenger to execute wrath upon him that doeth evil." By representing Henry with a tippet as well as with a crown and orb, the illustrator appears to have sought to emphasize this blending of the worldly character and the sacred in the kingship.[43]

Such was the ancestry of the Salian theory of kingship. Despite the impossibility of mortal man's reaching the perfection of Christ as king and priest, the kingly figure in this ideological heritage was a king-prelate. His power was the gift of God; it was bestowed upon him by divine cession, through which he became a representative of God on earth. The most important exercise of his powers was in protecting the Church from external enemies, and in strengthening it within through the maintenance of fitting order in doctrine and in the affairs of the clergy. The ruler was the head of the commonwealth of which the Church was the most cherished member; he regulated and corrected all affairs of the Church not purely spiritual in nature; in short, by virtue of his imperium, he was the head of the Church, but his office remained temporal in nature, although it was ecclesiastical by definition.

---

[43] See Herbert Bloch, "Monte Cassino, Byzantium, and the West in the Earlier Middle Ages," *Dumbarton Oaks Papers*, No. 3 (Harvard, 1946), pp. 177 ff., pl. 221. Bloch suggests with considerable weight that the specific case of Pandulf of Capua, a brigand who was overcome and executed by Henry, may be represented here (pp. 185 f.). But he overlooks the more general and theoretical interpretation given above. Cf. E. H. Kantorowicz, *The King's Two Bodies* (Princeton, 1957), pp. 114 f. and pl. 20, where Henry's figure in this illustration is interpreted as representing "a mediator between divine Reason and human Law. ... the mediator and executor of the divine will through the power of the Holy Spirit." This portrait, however, is singular. For example, a contemporary representation of Henry as king, rather than as emperor (in the Munich Staatsbibliotek Clm. 4456, made, like the Monte Cassino codex, at Henry's order), shows him without the *lorum* receiving a crown from Christ and a scepter and a sword from angels. Perhaps the most accessible reproduction of it is in A. Boeckler, *Deutsche Buchmalerei vorgotischer Zeit* (Königstein im Taunus, 1953), pl. 34. The thirteenth-century statue of Henry on the façade of the Bamberg cathedral bears no unusual marks. See A. Weise, *Die Bamberger Domskulpturen* (Strassburg, 1914), I, 239 ff., and II, pl. 124.

For the Salian kings, as for the Saxons who preceded them, the resources of Scripture and tradition were united to depict this image with the utmost clarity in the rite of coronation. Then, drawing upon the words of the Apostles and Fathers, the Church received the promise of the king-elect to remain orthodox in faith and to serve as its defender and fosterer; and it acknowledged him, after the act of coronation, as a sharer in the ministry of bishops, as a vicar of Christ.[44]

The order of the regal coronation itself, after the pattern of the Old Testament, was strikingly similar to the order followed in the consecration of a prelate.[45] Both orders began identically, with the ritual procession of the *electus* with holy relics to the Church where the service was to occur; with an identical formal interrogation as to his orthodoxy and intent; and with a solemn entry into the Church. The regal order continued with the unction of the king-elect's head, breast, shoulders, both upper arms, and, according to one service, both hands. The episcopal order prescribed in the corresponding place unction of the head and hands. For the king, there followed the imposition of the crown, the girding on of the sword of state, the investing with bracelets, *pallium*, ring, scepter, and staff. Similarly, the bishop in this place received the symbols of his office, the ring and the staff. Both ceremonies concluded with the "kiss of peace" and High Mass.[46] The acclamation of the people was as necessary to the proper elevation of the king as to that of the bishop. Both kings and prelates were anointed with the Holy Chrism, "this oil of unction whence Thou hast anointed priests, kings, and prophets,"[47] until in the twelfth and thirteenth centuries it became uniformly the practice for the king to be anointed only with the oil used in the unction of catechumens. In both cases, the infusion of the Holy Spirit was invoked at the unction. The regal symbols of office also largely matched the pontifical—the *pallium*, the staff, and the ring, an "episcopal" ring according to the "Salian Order" for the imperial coronation,[48] and a "pontifical" ring according to Benzo of Alba, a vigorous

---

[44] Schramm, "Krönung," p. 319.

[45] See the extensive citations in E. Eichmann, "Königs-und Bischofsweihe," *Sitzungsberichte der bayerischen Akademie der Wissenschaften* (1928, phil.-hist. Klasse), No. 6, pp. 3 ff.

[46] Schramm, "Krönung," p. 234 and *passim*.   [47] *Ibid.*, p. 316.

[48] P. E. Schramm, "Der 'Salische Kaiserordo' und Benzo von Alba," *Deutsches Archiv*, I (1937), 40.

champion of the royal prerogative.[49] So, too, the vestments and sandals worn by the king during his coronation were virtually identical with those worn by the bishop at his consecration.[50] Furthermore, the two services even held like prestige, as is indicated by the famous Sermon 69, (anonymous, though often attributed to Peter Damian), for there the regal unction is presented as the fifth sacrament of the Church, the episcopal consecration, as the fourth.[51]

Through this ceremony, the king was accepted by the Church as its defender, as one who held not only the symbols of wordly power—the crown, the sword, the scepter—but also some prelatical authority. The king was, so to speak, parallel in outward dignity to pontiffs, but superior to them in wordly power. They, on the other hand, were his superiors in purely spiritual matters, but his subjects insofar as their actions touched the visible world. The "Salian Order" for the imperial coronation illustrates well this dual relationship of the emperor of the Romans. After the coronation, "for another three days, he celebrates a synod with the pope to emend shortcomings of men in holy orders; and then, together with men well-versed in these matters, he treats of

---

[49] *MGH SS.*, XI, 602. Cf. the words spoken by the envoys of Henry V to Henry IV in 1105–1106, as recorded by Helmold: "Fac nobis reddi coronam, anulum, et purpuram ceteraque ad investituram imperialem pertinentia filio tuo deferenda." *Chronicon Sclavorum*, ed. by G. H. Pertz (Hanover, 1868), I, 64 f., chap. 32.

[50] The embellishments of Benzo show how suggestive they were to one contemporary. See Schramm, "Salische Kaiserordo."

[51] Migne *PL*, CXLIV, 899f. Mr. C. B. Fisher first directed my attention to the theory, long held by students of Peter Damian, that Sermon 69 was incorrectly attributed to Peter. W. Levison, for example, in his posthumous article "Die mittelalterliche Lehre von den beiden Schwertern," *Deutsches Archiv*, IX (1951), 28 f., was apparently not aware of this theory, and so too, among others, Schramm, in his *Herrschaftszeichen*, I, 72 n. 2. Cf. F. Kern, *Gottesgnadentum und Widerstandsrecht*, 2d ed. by R. Buchner (Münster, 1954), p. 76 n. 154. The work is generally attributed to Nicholas, the secretary of St. Bernard of Clairvaux, though on rather inconclusive grounds. See Migne *PL.*, CXLIV, 12; O. J. Blum, *St. Peter Damian* (Washington, 1947), pp. 26 n. 98, 43; J. J. Ryan, *St. Peter Damiani and His Canonical Sources* (Toronto, 1956), p. 154 n. 100; J. J. Ryan, "St. Peter Damian," *Medieval Studies*, IX (1947), esp. pp. 155 ff. See also the incisive work by K. Reindel, "Studien zur Überlieferung der Werke des Petrus Damiani: I," *Deutsches Archiv*, XV (1959), pp. 27 f. If this sermon is later than the time of Peter Damian, Letter 13 of Henry IV contains the earliest known exposition of the two-sword representation of Church–State relations. But see the related metaphoric usages of Alcuin (*MGH* Epp. IV, no. 136, pp. 205 ff.) and Pope Nicholas I (*MGH* Epp. VI, no. 123, p. 641).

the disposition of the commonwealth."[52] In other words, in matters of negligence in the performance of ecclesiastical duties, of slackness or outright heterodoxy in doctrine, or in other matters which touched the spiritual sphere, the emperor acted in conjunction with the pope, after the classic pattern in which the pope, as spiritual head of Christendom, defined the *via recta* and the emperor supplied the coercive power to compel adherence to it. In matters of the material world, "the commonwealth," however, the emperor resorted to his own advisers and followed his own counsels. But even in his treatment of wordly affairs he was not to disregard what Pope Leo I had called his "priestly mind," but as "the minister of God, a revenger to execute wrath upon him that doeth evil," as the ministrant of justice, he was to add the element of divine service, of sacerdotalism, to the performance of his office. As the auther of Sermon 69 wrote: "Happy, however, is he [the king] if he joins the sword of kingship with the sword of priesthood to the end that the sword of the priest may dull the sword of the king and that the sword of the king may sharpen the sword of the priest."[53]

Thus, the king had something of the character of the priesthood; and even the reformer Peter Damian wrote, "the king is in the Roman pontiff, and the Roman pontiff in the king... Moreover, he [the pope] may bring force to bear upon delinquents through the law of the public courts, when the cause dictates; and the king with his bishops may make investigation in regard to the state of souls, with the cited authority of the sacred canons,"[54] Kings and priests alike, he also said, despite the blame which might be attached to their personal habits, "are found to be called gods and christs [that is, anointed] because of the sacrament of the ministry which they have undertaken."[55]

The king became an ecclesiastic by the rite of coronation; the coronation order presents in detail the figure of the priestlike king. But the question remains, was the priestly character imparted to the king, to use Professor Kantorowicz's terms, "esoteric" or "clerical"?[56] The remarks above may serve to indicate that, in theory at least, it was "clerical" in all save the purely sacramental functions of the priesthood. In fact, although the kingship was the highest ecclesiastical position

---

[52] Schramm, "Salischer Kaiserordo," p. 390.   [53] Migne *PL*, CXLIV, 900.

[54] *Disceptio Synodalis*, Clausula, *MGH Ldl.*, I, 93.

[55] *Liber gratissimus*, chap. 10, *MGH Ldl.*, I, 31.

[56] E. Kantorowicz, "Mysteries of State," *Harvard Theological Review*, XLVIII (1955), 72 n. 23.

held by the kings, the kings from Henry II onwards appear to have enhanced the quasi-sacerdotal character of that office by serving as canons in divers cathedral churches. Henry II is known to have been an honorary canon in Bamberg, Magdeberg and Strassburg; Conrad II, in Worms, Neuhausen, and Eichstätt; Henry III, in Cologne, Basel, Freising, and perhaps Nivelles;[57] and Henry V, in Liége.[58] Henry IV was a suffragant in the monastic brotherhood of Echternach,[59] and by referring to the cathedral chapter of Speier as "our brethren" he identified himself with them.[60] Subsequent emperors held similar positions. Generally, the duties required of these royal canons were performed by proxies, but when the kings attended the churches in which they held canonries, it was the practice for them to perform the duties themselves.[61]

Thus, Henry II and his Salian successors, accepted as sharers of episcopal authority in the coronation service, also held the full dignity of clerics not ordained to the spiritual ministry. They were unconsecrated prelates, unordained ministers, and yet partakers of the power of the prelacy and "ministers of God." They united in their persons full secular power (for it was by virtue of that power that they were clerics) with ecclesiastical authority; they were fully kings and partially priests; Therefore, they were not "after the order of Melchisedech." Still, it is against this background of the kingly figure, elect of God, anointed of the Lord, vicar of God, ruler and cleric, that one must place the Salian concept of kingship.

The paucity of extant writings from the reign of Conrad II permits only general assumptions about his concept of the royal office. Little political theory may be gleaned from his official documents, and Wipo's biography of him, which may or may not represent the opinions of its subject, is the major and almost the sole nonofficial source for the reign.

In a recent article, Theodor Schieffer[62] ably contested the long-estab-

---

[57] Schramm, "Sacerdotium," p. 430. See also Aloys Schulte, "Deutsche Könige, Kaiser, Päpste als Kanoniker an deutschen und römischen Kirchen," *Historisches Jahrbuch*, LIV (1934), 174 and *passim*.

[58] Schulte, "Deutsche Könige," p. 143.   [59] *Ibid*., p. 170.

[60] *MGH Diplomata Heinrici IV*, p. 631, l. 25, no. 466. One cannot say whether German kings were also canons of St. Peter's in Rome before the time of Henry VI. See P. E. Schramm, "Die Ordines der mittelalterlichen Kaiserkrönung," *Archiv für Urkundenforschung*, XI (1930), 329 f.; and Schulte, "Deutsche Könige," p. 156. Cf. H. W. Klewitz, "Königtum, Hofkapelle, und Domkapitel im 10 und 11 Jahrhundert," *Archiv für Urkundenforschung*, XVI (1939), 134.

[61] See Appendix.   [62] Schieffer, "Heinrich II und Konrad II," pp. 405 ff.

lished theory to which this scarcity of information gave rise: that, despite his strong reverence for tradition in other matters of government (as shown most clearly in his recognition of the hereditary rights even of lesser vassals), Conrad cared little for the pontificalism of his predecessors. In fact, as Schieffer has shown, his actions indicate the contrary. Conrad himself declared: "Although we are bound to entertain an acute concern for gaining what is useful far and wide for the whole commonwealth, we are not ignorant of our greater obligation to be watchful for the state of the churches of God with even more diligent attentiveness."[63] And in his *Deeds of Conrad II*, Wipo affirmed (Chapter 6) the Emperor's probing and, perhaps, chastening interest in the affairs of his clergy: "Although he was ignorant of letters, nevertheless he prudently gave instruction to every cleric, not only lovingly and courteously in public, but also with fitting discipline in secret." He is known to have presided in 1027 at a synod in Rome together with Pope John XIX to settle Church affairs, dealing especially with the disobedience of Poppo, patriarch of Aquileia. As one of the two heads of Christendom, he presided at a second synod held at Frankfurt in the same year to resolve the dispute of Mainz and Hildesheim over possession of the convent Gandersheim and at a third in 1036, convened at Tribur to deal with general problems of ecclesiastical discipline. The punishments which he attempted to inflict upon Aribert of Milan, and which he effectually imposed upon the bishops of Vercelli, Cremona, and Piacenza,[64] are indicative of Conrad's lively determination to maintain his hegemony over the episcopal order. In addition, his benefactions to churchmen, and to ecclesiastical foundations, show that he was willing to purchase or liberally to reward the voluntary service, or even the subjection, of loyal clerical supporters.[65] As the lord of proprietary churches and monasteries, he acted with great freedom. Tenancy of properties belonging to other religious establishments was transferred to the monastery at Limburg, for example, which he founded and placed under the special protection of his family, and to the cathedral church of Speier, which he began to rebuild on a grand scale as the burial place of the Salians. Nor did Conrad condescend to religious sensitivities in giving the abbey of Schwarzach to the bishopric of Speier

---

[63] *MGH Const.*, I, 85, no. 39.   [64] See Wipo, "Deeds of Conrad II," chap. 35.

[65] Cf. L. Santifaller, "Zur Geschichte des ottonisch-salischen Reichskirchensystems," *Sitzungsberichte der Oesterreichischen Akademie der Wissenschaften* (phil.-hist. Klasse, 221, 1954), *I*, 69 f.

and Kempten to Ernst [II] of Swabia, for he disregarded completely the treasured liberties held by those two establishments as foundations traditionally subject directly, and primarily, to the Empire, not to lesser lords. Again, as lord of the imperial system of proprietary churches, he fostered the monastic reform movement, particularly the Lotharingian reforms advocated by Poppo, abbot of Stablo, which he imposed upon such proud institutions as Hersfeld and Tegernsee.[66] Thus, by virtue of his "worldly" office, he prescribed norms of conduct for churchmen, with ecclesiastical counsel; he inflicted punishments upon high ecclesiastics; he bestowed privileges upon religious establishments and took them away at will; and he imposed the reforms which found his favor upon foundations subject to him.

Bonizo, an enemy of Conrad's grandson, Henry IV, offers a tantalizingly indefinite suggestion of Conrad's position. According to Bonizo, Conrad sent to Rome during his struggle with the Hungarians asking "that ensigns *(vexilla)* be sent to him on behalf of St. Peter, with which he could be strengthened to subject the Hungarian realm to his overlordship." It was sent with two legates, who were ordered (if possible), to carry the ensign in the foremost battle line themselves; if Conrad forbade this (as he did), they were to say, "It is we, indeed, who bring you victory. See that you ascribe this not to yourself, but to the the Apostles."[67] The researches of Erdmann have shown convincingly that before the middle of the eleventh century, the word *vexilla* when mentioned as something sent out by the Roman See indicates not a banner, but a cross, emblematic of the Apostles Peter and Paul.[68] According to this interpretation, therefore, Conrad asked for and received such a cross, to be borne before him into battle.

Interestingly enough, the ceremonial use of the Imperial Cross dates from Conrad's reign. This cross was believed to be charged with vast spiritual powers, for it incorporated fragments of the Holy Cross,[69] "through which the Devil has been conquered, and the world has been saved by the working of God."[70] With the greatest confidence, Conrad had it inscribed: "Lo, the Cross of the Lord; let the side of the iniquitous

---

[66] Schieffer, "Heinrich II und Konrad II," pp. 407 ff.

[67] *Liber ad amicum* V, *MGH Ldl.*, I, 583.

[68] C. Erdmann, "Kaiserliche und päpstliche Fahnen im hohen Mittelalter," *Quellen und Forschungen aus italienischen Archiven und Bibliotheken*, XXV (1933), 42.

[69] Schramm, *Herrschaftszeichen*, pp. 511 f.

[70] Gerard I of Cambrai, *Acta Synodi Atrabatensis*, chap. 13, Migne *PL*, CXLII, 1305.

enemy flee. Here, O Conrad, may all enemies yield to you."[71] The uses
to which this cross was put are not clear, though its inscription and
Bonizo's remarks suggest that it may have been carried with the Emperor into battle as a standard. It is also assumed that "the Holy Cross
filled with the wood of the Lord," which Benzo of Alba relates was
borne before the Emperor-elect in the procession to his coronation,[72]
was the Imperial State Cross. It would be expected, in fact, for so po-
tent a treasure to be carried before the ruler on so great an occasion,
in conformity with the tradition which demanded that a German king
in procession to his coronation be preceded by ceremonial crosses.[73]
On the other hand, the processional usage of the Cross was generally
reserved for metropolitans and patriarchs.[74]

The biographer of St. Stephan of Hungary, against whom Conrad
was fighting when he received his ensign, offers a curiously parallel
incident: St. Stephan sent messengers to Rome, and the Pope "graciously bestowed all things, as many as were asked, and moreover he sent a
cross to be borne before the king, like a token of apostleship: 'I,' he
[the Pope] said, 'am apostolic; but he [St. Stephan] is deservedly an
apostle of Christ through whom Christ converts so great a people to
Himself.'"[75] It may be objected that the two cases are different, since
St. Stephan's "ensign" was bestowed upon him in return for his missionary activities, while Conrad's interests had no such claims to
"apostleship." Kirchberg, however, has suggested rightly that Conrad's
traditionalism extended not only to the maintenance of conventional
political relationships, but also to the furtherance of the missionary
activity to the East, begun under Charlemagne and prosecuted as state
policy from the time of Otto I. Wipo's account of Conrad's slaughter
of the Slavs (Chapter 33) is but one grim testimony of the activity;
there are other less sanguinary indications of it among Conrad's diplomata, in cessions to churches and the like. *Roma caput mundi tenet orbis
frena rotundi* was the device on his seals; and Kirchberg indicates clearly
that "Rome" for Conrad meant the Church as well as the city and that,
as Emperor of the Romans, he was earnestly resolved not only to keep
the "reins" in his hands, but also to extend the territory under the

---

[71] Schramm, *Herrschaftszeichen*, p. 483 n. 1.   [72] *MGH SS.*, XI, 602.
[73] Schramm, "Krönung," pp. 310, 324 f.
[74] See Letter 18 of John XIX, Migne *PL*, CXLI, 1152. Cf. *Liber Pontificalis*, ed. by
L. Duchesne- J. Bayet, 2d ed. (Paris, 1955), I, 88. *Vita Sergii II*, chap. 9.
[75] *Vita Sancti Stephani, MGH SS.*, XI, 234.

common control of himself and of the Church.[76] The parallelism between Conrad's *vexilla* and St. Stephan's "token of apostleship," therefore, is all the closer; and the similarity between the usage to which Conrad seems likely to have put his cross (though his use of the cross is still hypothetical) and the usage proper to the highest ecclesiastics is the more logically explicable.

Wipo's presentation of Conrad's reverence at his death for the "Holy Cross, together with relics of the Saints," of the Emperor as "elect of God,"[77] "vicar of God," "avenger of the Faith," "defender of churches and clerics," "a sharer of the will of God," as one before whom the Church made supplication,[78] and as a dispensor of ecclesiastical rights,[79] is also highly suggestive of a regal pontificalism which Conrad himself may or may not have attached to his office. It is unknown whether Conrad shared the conventional notion (which Wipo expressed with fitting conventionality) that the king was to consider, "with just judgment, the causes of the holy churches and of orphans and widows,"[80] to defend the widow, to champion the orphan, to comfort the poor.[81] Wipo would have had the king study the law and hear "what the law commands," for "to guard the law is to rule."[82] The king, he said, would punish those who spurn the law and defend those who observed its precepts.[83] It is unclear, however, what Wipo meant by "law." Possibly he had in mind a sort of common, or customary, law, as when in the *Deeds of Conrad II* he mentioned the "law of the Saxons."[84] But when he referred to specific laws which the king was charged to execute, as he did in the *Tetralogus*,[85] his references were to Scriptural precepts, particularly to those in the Books of the Law of the Old Testament. At any rate, one may conclude that Wipo especially charged the king with the sacred office of executing the "common law of Christendom," the injunctions of Holy Writ. Probably it can never be known whether Conrad conceived of his duties in this way, or whether he would have

---

[76] J. Kirchberg, *Kaiseridee und Mission unter den Sachsenkönigen und den ersten Saliern von Otto I bis Heinrich III* (Berlin, 1934), pp. 85 ff.

[77] Chapter 2 and *passim*.   [78] Chapter 3.   [79] Chapter 6.

[80] *Catilena* in H. Bresslau, ed., *Die Werke Wipos*, 3d ed. (Hanover, 1915), pp. 106, ll. 15–17.

[81] *Proverbia*, ll. 69–72, Bresslau ed., p. 71.   [82] *Ibid.*, ll. 1–3, p. 66.

[83] *Tetralogus*, ll. 137–139, Bresslau ed., p. 79.

[84] Chapter 6. See F. Kern, *Kingship and Law in the Middle Ages* (Oxford, 1939), S. B. Chrimes, trans., pp. 449 ff.

[85] Lines 222 ff., Bresslau ed., pp. 83 ff.

been pleased to be called "the head of the world"[86] or to be likened to Mount Sion, where "the Lord commanded the blessing and life for evermore,"[87] as Wipo addressed his successor. Yet his actions as king and emperor, his acquiescing in the unequivocal symbolism in his coronation, and his occasional service as a cathedral canon suggest that his position was not vastly different from that of his obscure chaplain, though perhaps it was the less ethereal of the two.

Although Henry III, Conrad's son and successor, by virtue of his zeal for ecclesiastical reforms, was more revered by churchmen than was his father, it is clear that he cherished and fostered much the same concept of the ruler's place in the Church as his father had held. Henry is reported to have said: "For those who govern laws are not governed by laws, since the law, as they commonly say, has a nose of wax, and the king has an iron hand, and a long one, and he can bend the law in whatever way it pleases him."[88] This was the same spirit which he manifested in his zeal for ecclesiastical reform when, as "lord of lords,"[89] as the ruler of the world after Christ,[90] as the "head of the Church,"[91] he presided in 1046 at Sutri over a synod which deposed two popes, secured the abdication of a third, and elected yet another. This, too, was his position when he presided with Pope Leo IX at the reform Council of Mainz in 1049 and when, in the same year at the Council of Constance, he ascended the very steps of the altar together with Leo and proclaimed a general pardon.[92] Again, as a "propagator of the orthodox Faith," he took up the sword in the East and enriched and strengthened the sees in that region.[93] These titles—"head of the Church," "propagator of the orthodox Faith," and the rest—were not empty trappings, as Henry's actions show; for they derived from Henry's own firm belief in the universal supremacy and in the spiritual character of his office. Indeed, he is reported to have said on one occasion, "I have been anointed similarly [to priests] with holy oil, and power of ruling before all others has been given me."[94]

[86] *Tetralogus*, l. 99, Bresslau ed., p. 78.   [87] *Ibid.*, Prologus, Bresslau ed., p. 75.

[88] Cosmas of Prague, B. Bretholz, ed., *Die Chronik der Böhmen* (Berlin, 1955), I, 94, chap. 8 (1040).   [89] Wipo, *Epistola ad Regem Heinricum*, in Bresslau ed., p. 3.

[90] *Tetralogus*, Bresslau ed., p. 76.

[91] B. Pez, *Thesaurus Anecdotorum Novissimus VI* (Augsburg, 1729), I, 235.

[92] *Annales Sangallenses Majores, MGH SS.*, I, 85.

[93] Kirchberg, *Kaiseridee und Mission*, pp. 94 ff.

[94] Anselm, *Gesta Episcorum Leodiensium*, chap.66, *MGH SS.*, VII, 229 f. Cf. G. Ladner, *Theologie und Politik vor dem Investiturstreit* (Vienna, 1936), p. 63.

By virtue of the unusually ample sources extant from his reign, one must look to Henry IV, who, according to a modern critic, "came to represent all that was autocratic and reactionary in civil and ecclesiastical affairs,"[95] for the most complete figure of the pontifical king among the Salians. Benzo of Alba wrote to Henry: "You are the vicar of the Creator"[96]; "after God, O Caesar, you are King, you are Emperor."[97] A variant reading in the decree of the Synod of Brixen (1080) provided by the version in the Hanoverian epistolary collection (see below p. 5) refers in a most suggestive way to Henry as "the catholic and pontifical King," while the accepted reading is "the catholic and pacific King."[98] Furthermore, it was not by chance that his partisans referred to him as "Your Blessedness";[99] or, like Abraham, "friend of God";[100] or, like Christ himself, "my hope."[101]

His contemporaries bear witness to Henry's personal devoutness. As mentioned above, he was a suffragant of the monastery of Echternach. Ebo, the biographer of Otto, bishop of Bamberg, recounts that his psalter became "wrinkled and almost unreadable" because of the frequency with which he used it.[102] And another author records the enthusiasm with Henry participated in the singing of psalms, especially the Penitentials.[103] He was particularly devoted to relics, and above all to those which formed a part of the imperial treasure. Of these, the most important were "the cross filled with the Lord's wood,"[104] perhaps the cross venerated by Conrad II, and the holy lance, the lance of St. Mauritius, which Conrad received as the symbol of his authority over Burgundy. When the lance was broken, Henry had it mended with a silver band bearing his name; and with the same band he also bound to the lance a nail reputed to have come from the Holy Cross.[105] Bearing these holy relics before him, Henry won his decisive victory over the

---

[95] Sister Agnes Bernard Cavenaugh, *Pope Gregory VII and the Theocratic State* (Washington, 1934), p. 23. Cf. pp. 38 f.

[96] *MGH SS.*, XI, 609.   [97] *Ibid.*, p. 608.

[98] C. Erdmann, ed., *Die Briefe Heinrichs IV* (Leipzig, 1937), p. 71 n.q.

[99] Peter Crassus, *Defensio Heinrici Regis, MGH Ldl.*, I, 439.

[100] Wido of Osnabrück, *MGH Ldl.*, I, 470. Cf. Isaiah 41:8 and James 2:23.

[101] *Vita Heinrici IV*, ed. by W. Eberhard, 3d ed. (Hanover, 1899), p. 9.

[102] *Vita Ottonis I*, VI, ed. by P. Jaffe, *Monumenta Bambergensia* (in *Bibliotheca Rerum Germanicarum*, IV [Berlin, 1869], 594).

[103] E. Dümmler, ed., "Ein Brief an König Heinrich IV," *Neues Archiv*, XXV (1900), 205.

[104] Schramm, *Herrschaftszeichen*, XXV, 461.   [105] *Loc. cit.*

Saxons on the Unstrut in 1075. So great was his trust in them that for the stability of his position he had his son Henry V make his vows of fidelity upon them in 1099,[106] and from the words of Benzo of Alba, it seems likely that they were borne before the King in his procession to the imperial coronation.[107] Thus, Henry's personal reverence was directed toward these particular relics as symbols of state as well as of religion; and the "context" of his attitude and devoutness, in this instance, is seen to be the sense of office which he entertained.

In general, it seems clear that Henry conceived of his office as being superior to all other ecclesiastical offices in his realm.

Gregory of Catino wrote during the Investiture Controversy, "The Divine Scripture admonishes that we ought to understand that the king is the head of the Church."[108] Henry's adoption of the ecclesiastical headship may have derived from a combination of practical knowledge with the zeal for the welfare of the Church which his personal devoutness prompted, for in practice, as Wido of Osnabrück observed, if wicked men do not fear secular vengeance, they certainly will not be recalled from their wickedness by spiritual censure.[109] The so-called "Laudes of Ivrea" sung about 1090 in acclamation of Henry's antipope, Clement, and of Henry himself, may illustrate the Emperor's position. They begin with the thrice-repeated *Christus vincit, Christus regnat, Christus imperat*, a reference to the Divine Ruler which, in the medieval political theology, was the origin of all wordly powers, and secondly, by inference, an acknowledgment of those powers. They continue with the orison and acclamation: "Give ear, O Christ. Life to Clement, bishop of the first see and universal pope." Then, after further orison, "Give ear, O Christ. Life and victory to Henry, Emperor Augustus, crowned by God, great and pacific." In a similar manner, they continue with an acclamation of the Empress, "crowned by God," of Ogerius, bishop of Ivrea, "elect of God," and finally with orisons for all the clergy and people. In this, there are two features worthy of note. First, Clement is acclaimed merely as bishop of the "first see," not of the "holy and

---

[106] *Loc. cit.*   [107] *MGH SS.*, XI, 602.

[108] *Orthodoxa Defensio Imperialis, MGH Ldl.*, II, 536. Paradoxically enough, Henry seems not to have claimed universal headship in ecclesiastical or in political matters, tacitly exempting other kings from his authority; nor do such claims seem to have been made on his behalf. Cf. Henry IV, Letter 39, and R. Rörig, "Heinrich IV und der Weltherrschaftsanspruch," *Deutsches Archiv*, VII (1944), 200–203.

[109] *MGH Ldl.*, I, 463.

Apostolic See," nor even of the "Roman see." The decree of the Council of Carthage (398) that "the bishop of the first see may not be called 'prince of priests' or 'supreme priest' or anything of this sort, but only 'bishop of the first see,'"[110] was here given expression in direct opposition to the Gregorian claims. This adherence to the ancient canon is regarded as evidence of a deliberate intent on Henry's part to consider the pope merely the head of the foremost church in an imperial system of churches.[111] Secondly, and in support of this view, all the other officials specifically named, even the bishop of Ivrea, are hailed as "crowned of God," or as "elect of God"; the source of Clement's authority is unmentioned. The question thus arises, what was to be the relation between "Clement, bishop of the first see and universal pope," and "Henry, Emperor Augustus, crowned by God"? If Henry were actually striving to assume effectual headship of the Church, as seems likely from these *laudes*, he could have claimed the earlier sanctions by reformers of the program he had adopted. Shortly after his accession, Peter Damian wrote urging him to use his regal power to depose Cadalus, bishop of Parma, the antipope Honorius II. The boy-king was reminded that he had succeeded to the rights and responsibilities of his father and of his grandfather[112] and admonished that, "unless you transfix the necks of those who stand in resistance to God, truly you carry the sword without cause, nor to him who does evil are you an avenger in wrath as long as you do not rise up against those who are corrupting the Church, and as long as you do not with Simon and Levi cast out the disgrace of a dishonored sister from the house of Israel."[113] Henry may have been reminded that when father ejected the archbishop of Ravenna for the abuse of his office, the same Peter Damian not only sanctioned the strong action of the secular ruler against erring ecclesiastics, but praised his action most extravagantly: "'Let the heavens rejoice, therefore, let the earth exult,' since truly Christ is known to reign in his king."[114] And later, when the young Henry had attained his majority, even his future enemy, Gregory VII, had given his support to this position,

---

[110] Mansi, III, 923, canon 25. It was repeated in the Concilium Africanum (Mansi, IV, 485, canon 6) and, more important for the present discussion, in the Pseudo-Isidorian Decretals (Con. Carth. III, canon 26, Hinschius ed., p. 298) and in the decretals of Burchard of Worms (I, 3).

[111] E. Kantorowicz, *Laudes Regiae* (Berkeley, 1946), p. 243. The text of the Laudes is in E. Dümmler, *Anselm der Peripatetiker* (Halle, 1872), p. 89.

[112] Epp. VII, 3, Migne *PL*, CXLIV, 437.   [113] *Ibid*., p. 440.   [114] *Ibid*., p. 436.

writing to Henry that if he were able to lead the crusade which he had proposed, he would leave the Roman Church to Henry, "after God," "so that you may guard her as your holy mother, and set your defense to her honor."[115]

Some of Henry's actions suggest regal pontificalism quite strongly and appear to have been practical expressions of his claims to supremacy in all ecclesiastical and secular affairs of the Empire. It was his frequent assertion on his own behalf, for example, that the kingly office was in the hand of God. Seemingly, therefore, as a "vicar of God" and as the head of the German episcopate, he imposed "with his own hand" the "regal circlet" on the head of Vratislav II of Poland and "ordered the Archbishop of Trier... to anoint him as king in his see, the metropolis, Prague, and impose the diadem upon his head."[116] A similarly prelatical action is obvious in yet another (alleged) act of Henry. It is said that when the approach of the Normans in 1084 forced him to retreat from Rome, "he bore with him the seal of the Lord Pope which he had stolen clandestinely."[117] However dastardly his methods, if the story is true, Henry took great pains to get into his own hands the official seal of Gregory VII, the instrument by which the "Lord Pope" gave life to his enactments, the key symbol of the temporal power of the Papacy. And this, one may believe, he did as "the head of the Church," just as in the same character he had summoned a solemn synod in Rome, presided over it, and secured the deposition of Gregory and the enthronement of his favorite, Clement.[118]

The reactions of the royalists to Gregory's attempts to remove Henry from political power through excommunication and through the absolution of his subjects of their allegiance are also instructive. First, they saw an intimate parallel between the process against Henry and that prescribed by canon law for action against bishops. Henry himself, as

---

[115] Gregory, *Register*, Epp. II, 31, p. 167.

[116] Cosmas of Prague, Bertholz ed., II, 140, chap. 37 (1086). See H. Spangenberg, "Die Königskrönung Wratislavs von Böhmen und die angebliche Mainzer Synode des Jahres 1086," *MIÖG*, XX (1899), 385 ff.

[117] Hugh of Verdun, *Chronica*, *MGH SS.*, VIII, 462 (1084). The importance of the seal in the transaction of ordinary affairs was considerable. For example, Bishop Hezilo of Hildesheim wrote to Henry IV, "I doubted, however, that this envoy had been sent by you to me... since, although I did not know him, he came to me without a letter, and without a seal." C. Erdmann, "Untersuchungen zu den Briefen Heinrichs IV," *Archiv für Urkundenforschung*, XVI (1939), 185 n. 7.

[118] Cf. the exhortations directed to Henry by Peter Crassus, *MGH Ldl.*, I, 438.

"one anointed the among anointed," asserted that "the tradition of the holy Fathers" taught that he was to be judged by God alone and that the only valid reason for his deposition would be his deviation from the Faith (Letter 13). The author of *De unitate ecclesiae conservanda* objected that Gregory had severed Henry from the body of the Church on the written evidence of his enemies and in his abscence, "whereas the holy canons establish that none can be accusers or witnesses who yesterday or the day before yesterday were enemies, and that the accusation of no one ought to be accepted in writing, and that the accuser is not to be heard while his opponent is absent."[119] The "tradition of the holy Fathers" to which Henry referred is rather plainly the same as the "holy canons" of his supporter; and both of the rulings of ecclesiastical law cited by the two authors, though different, pertain to the citing and judgment of prelates. The Pseudo-Isidorian Decretals provided the material for the assertion generally accepted by canonists, among them Burchard of Worms (fl. 1025), "that bishops are to be judged or removed by the Lord alone"[120] and that "the sheep cannot bring charges against their pastor unless he wanders from the Faith."[121] According to Burchard, a prelate's enemies could not be his accusers;[122] and he affirmed with the other major canonists that persons involved in criminal activities, such as the conspiracy which surrounded the presentation of charges against Henry, could not validly bring forth their accusations.[123] Finally, the canonists were in complete agreement that in proceedings against ecclesiastics "no one can be accused through writing, but [only] by the very voice of whoever moves the accusation, and in the presence of him whom he wishes to accuse. Nor in the absence of him whom he wishes

[119] Waltram of Naumberg (?), ed. by W. Schwenkenbecher, *Liber de unitate ecclesiae conservanda* I, 6, *MGH Ldl.*, II, 191.

[120] Burchard, *Decretum* I, 133; Pseudo-Isidore, Epistola Clementis Prima, chap. 38 (P. Hinschius, ed., *Decretales Pseudo-Isidorianae* [Leipzig, 1863], p. 42). Cf. Pseudo-Isidore, Epistola Anacleti Secunda, chap, 19 (Hinschius ed., p. 76); Gratian, *Decretum*, Pars II, C. II, q. VII, chap. 15 (E. Friedberg, ed., *Corpus Juris Canonici, Pars Prior* [Leipzig, 1879], p. 486).

[121] Pseudo-Isidore, Epistola Eusebii Secunda, chap. 9 (Hinschius ed., p. 237); Burchard I, 139; Gratian, Pars II, C. II, q. VII, chap. 13 (Friedberg ed., p. 485). Cf. Burchard I, 136.

[122] Vol. I, chap. 152.

[123] Burchard I, 169; Pseudo-Isidore, Epistola Felicis I Secunda, chap. 13 (Hinschius ed., p. 202); Gratian, Pars II, C. II, q. VII, chap. 22 (Friedberg ed., p. 488). Cf. Pseudo-Isidore, Epistola Calixti Secunda, chap. 8 (Hinschius ed., p. 138); Gratian, Pars II, C. III, q. IV, chap. 5 (Friedberg ed., p. 512).

to accuse is any accuser to be believed."[124] Thus, the legal objections of the royalists to the process Gregory instituted against Henry, the objections which Henry himself adopted in his own statements, appear to have found their bases in the order prescribed by canon law for the process against members of the episcopal order. [125]

And yet more generally, it was the royalist position that in attacking Henry, the pontifical king, Gregory had encroached upon prerogatives not rightfully his, and so had upset the peace of the Church and destroyed divine order.[126] "But it is a new thing, and unheard-of to all past ages," wrote Wenrich of Trier, "for pontiffs to wish so easily to divide the kingdoms of the nations, to shatter with swift-moving faction the name of kings—a name found amidst the very beginnings of the world and later confirmed by God—and to remove the anointed of the Lord like bailiffs, as often as they found it to their taste."[127] As for the absolution of the vows of allegiance, that was an attempt "to loose the Scripture of the Lord, and the mandates of the Lord, which pertain to the unity of the Church of Christ, which pertain even to the sacrament[128] of the Faith."[129]

Henry himself provided in his letters the clearest and most convincing affirmation of his regal pontificalism. Kingship and Empire, he said, were in the hand of God, and he upon whom God bestowed them was to be judged by God alone (Letter 17). Henry himself had been called to kingship and "ordained" of God (Letter 12), and the very power of God both preserved him from the assaults of his enemies (Letter 17) and gave him victory (Letters 16, 18). In view of all this, abuse of him

[124] Pseudo-Isidore, Epistola Calixti Secunda, chap. 17 (Hinschius ed., p. 141); Burchard I, 171; Gratian, Pars II, C. III, q. IX, chap. 3 (Friedberg ed., p. 530).

[125] Pseudo-Isidore, Epistola Felicis I Secunda, chap. 9, (Hinschius ed., p. 202); Gratian, Pars II, C. III, q. IX, chap. 18 (Friedberg ed., p. 533). Cf. Pseudo-Isidore, Epistola Calixti Secunda, chap. 18 (Hinschius ed., p. 141); Burchard I, 171; Gratian, Pars II, C. II, q. VIII, chaps. 1, 5 (Friedberg ed., p. 529).

[126] C. Mirbt, "Absetzung Heinrichs IV durch Gregor VII in der Publizistik jener Zeit," in *Kirchengeschichtliche Studien (Festschrift Hermann Reuter* [Leipzig, 1890]), pp. 106 ff.

[127] Wenrich of Trier, Epistola, *MGH Ldl.,* I, 289. The *villicus,* here translated "bailiff," was an agent of a lord who had put under his supervision one or more peasant settlements belonging to the lord. He was usually an unfree, or half-free, peasant himself and could be removed at the pleasure of his master.

[128] I translate "sacramentum" as "sacrament" on the basis of the author's own definition of "sacramentum" as a "holy sign." *De unitate ecclesiae conservanda,* I, 14. *MGH Ldl.* II, p. 206.   [129] *Ibid.,* I, 17, p. 209.

was in contempt of God, of right, and of justice (Letter 37). Of course, he acknowledged the duality of the priesthood and the kingship, and their common divine origin (Letter 13), but the function of the priesthood was to lead man to obey the king, "in the place of God," and that of the kingship was both to cast out the enemies of Christ from the Church and to produce obedience for the priesthood within it (Letter 13). Thus, the priesthood was considered, so to speak, an agency of the kingship, and the power of the kingship was capable of purging the Church and of forcing believers to obey the "priestly agency," or, in other words, to obey its own spiritual arm.

Obviously adopting the figure of Christ and the Church, Henry wrote that his bishops were joined to him "like most cherished limbs" (Letter 11); he was the head, against whom Gregory had presumed to rise up. In this character, as head of the episcopal order and as spokesman for the "Mother Church of Mainz," Henry composed a letter, truly a "pastoral letter" in tone, to the church at Bamberg, admonishing that church to act in such a way that, "just as she [the church of Mainz] embraces you before others with fidelity and love, so she may rejoice in your perseverance with her in that faith which is Christ's and ours" (Letter 33). Christ's faith and his, certainly, was to be preserved through the united effort of priesthood and kingship (Letter 5). But sufficient evidence exists to show that this union was intended to preserve the regal headship: Henry himself, as "king by the grace of God," was the only layman who, together with the imperialist bishops, signed the decree of the Synod of Brixen, which demanded the deposition of Gregory, Henry's enemy.[130] Crown and miter joined again with similar purposefulnesss on behalf of the royal prerogative in the letter to Theodoric, bishop of Verdun: "Pope Clement and Emperor Henry order you, as you love us, so to hasten quickly to consecrate the Archbishop of Trier" (Letter 18). So, too, although they may have been matched in themselves by the actions of purely temporal lords, Henry's actions as the lord of proprietary churches serve to illustrate his "pontificalism."

His deposition of Ulrich of Lorsch (Letters 2, 3, 4) indicates the potential harshness of his governance of the Church; his endorsement of the rights of the church of Osnabrück to certain tithes and rights of justice indicates his sense of duty toward his churches (Letter 19).

Unquestionably Henry felt a keen responsibility for maintaining the

---

[130] Similarly, Henry III's subscription to the decrees of the Council of Mainz preceded those of the German bishops. *MGH Const.*, I, 99, no. 51.

welfare of the Church. His early confession of misdeeds to Gregory (Letter 5), and his later confession to Hugh of Cluny that ecclesiastical affairs had gone to ruin through his sins (Letter 31), as well as other remarks, are clear indications of this. Yet, despite his acknowledgments of guilt and shortcomings, one must observe that it was he who was to set things aright. It was he who (with counsel, to be sure) was to "gather the things which have been scattered and bring together with the adhesive of union the opening made by the wedge of schism . . . to reassemble the kingship and the priesthood into one" (Letter 31). It was he who suggested to Paschal II that together they compose fully, "in the presence of God, that peace which the world can not give" (Letter 34).

Although he professed himself willing to render "all due obedience to Rome and to the Roman pontiff," he took away with one hand what he gave with the other, by insisting that "reverence and due honor be shown also to me by the Apostolic See as it was shown to my predecessors" (Letter 39 and *passim*). Agreement to this stipulation would have meant Papal recognition of him as head of the episcopal order in all affairs appertaining to this world, as one with superior ecclesiastical functions within and without the Church. For all practical purposes, it would have meant the acknowledgment by the Church of a king as its head. This the reformed Papacy of Gregory VII and the stronger among his successors could never have granted, although in other times, even in then-recent times, other rulers, among them Henry III whom even stanch reformers praised for the use to which he put his powers,[131] had enjoyed that position in fact and in title.

The last of the Salians, Henry V, seems to have cherished similar beliefs about his regal position. The rebellion he undertook against his excommunicate father, as a "minister of God" against an evildoer, and his insistence when negotiating with the Papacy upon his right to lay investiture of the higher clergy, together with the fact that he entered the cathedral chapter of Liége the year after his father's death, strongly suggest this. As for the proper relations of the priesthood and the kingship, he wrote conventionally of their common origin and of the necessity of their cooperation: "For since God preordained the beginning of priesthood and empire for his people from one and the same line of flesh and blood, He has warned us solicitously to take heed that we be

---

[131] See Humbert of Silva Candida, *Adversus Simoniacos*, III, 7, *MGH Ldl.*, I, 206, and Peter Damian, *Liber Gratissimus*, chap. 38, *MGH Ldl.*, I, 71.

salutary both for God and for His people."[132] Yet he broke notably with convention in his modification of the "pontifical kingship" of his predecessors. To be sure, he styled himself "Henry, through the favor of Divine Clemency, the fourth, Emperor Augustus of the Romans."[133] At the same time, he allowed Paschal II openly to affirm that "Divine Majesty through the ministry of our priesthood" had advanced him to the imperial office,[134] thus interposing an agent between God, the bestower of the regal power, and its recipient. Henry's surrender, in the Concordat of Worms, of the investiture of the higher clergy with the ring, which symbolized the devotion of the recipient to the Church and his marriage to the establishment which he received under his supervision, and with the staff, symbol of chastening power, is also of paramount significance. These emblems were no longer his to bestow. Yet, despite restrictions, he did retain, first, the right to be present, in person or through his representatives, at major ecclesiastical elections and, second, the power of investiture. That investiture was to be *per sceptrum*, by means of "the rod of virtue and equity, wherewith you know to succor the pious and to smite the reprobate with terror, to lay open the way to those who wander, and to stretch forth your hand to those who have slipped, and likewise, to destroy the proud and to raise up the humble."[135] In accepting the *regalia* through such an investiture, one recognized these powers of the king, which, after all, are not vastly different from those previously ascribed to other kings.

This concept of the pontifical king, so highly cherished by the Salians, was theoretical in origin and in written exposition, but its practical ramifications were of the utmost significance. If the king were actually "head of the Church," he could be certain of benefiting directly from the vast material resources of the Church. These were, in fact, central to the protection of the royal prerogative. So Conrad II, with the cooperation of Bishop Warrmann of Constance, had Ernst [I] of Swabia excommunicated by the spiritual authority of the Church and then hunted down by its material power. So, too, Henry IV found ecclesiastical resources indispensable in the Investiture Controversy, as his own letters witness. It was in the ceremony of investiture that the king, bestowing the symbols of ecclesiastical power, and receiving vows

---

[132] *MGH Const.*, I, 162, no. 109.

[133] *Ibid.*, p. 152, no. 102. Since Henry I of Germany never became emperor, Henry V of Germany was the fourth emperor of his name.

[134] *Ibid.*, p. 145, no. 96.   [135] Schramm, "Krönung," p. 318.

of fidelity from those upon whom the symbols were bestowed, received also his greatest claim to ecclesiastical support.

A contemporary of Henry IV defended lay investiture on the grounds that the king acted during the ceremony in a purely secular capacity, as "head of the people," and that as such he deserved, for the sake of the common interest, to know the man to whom he had entrusted the defense of his city;[136] after all, this same thing had been done long before by "kings who were not anointed and by mayors of the palace."[137] This position, however, would probably have been distasteful to the Salians themselves and to their more "reactionary" supporters. Henry IV, for example, was fully aware of the pontifical significance of his title when he wrote as "King by the grace of God to Udalrich the monk" and demanded that the former abbot of Lorsch give to his envoy his staff of office (Letter 3); the authority which had made the abbot unmade him. Wenrich of Trier went yet further and claimed "pontificacies and priesthoods" for his ruler;[138] the Scriptures, he wrote, showed that among the Maccabees, Alexander had established Jonathan high priest, and Demetrius, Simon. In what way, therefore, were the claims of Henry excessive?[139] And even more telling is the account given by Radulf Glaber of the show of confidence Henry III rendered to an abbot, anonymous in the chronicle. Henry said to the abbot, "'Set aside the staff of pastoral rule, which you believe ought to be used at a mortal man's giving.' When the abbot had cast it from him, the King took it up, and placed it at the right hand of an image of the Savior. 'Go,' he said to the abbot, 'and receive it from the hand of the Omnipotent King, and nevermore be the debtor of any mortal for it, but use it freely, as befits the exalted height of so great a name.'"[140] If the account be true, and it seems to represent Henry's opinions well, it is clear that Henry believed generally that when he invested ecclesiastics with the ring and the staff he acted as a representative, a vicar, of the "Omnipotent King" and as the head of the worldly affairs of the Church. And the recipients of those symbols were his "debtors." His handling of the staff indicates that he believed that, just as power was delegated to him by the King of Kings, so he, and he alone, might return it to its source, and thus, with the good pleasure of God, the power was fully his as long as he chose to retain it. The concept of the pontifical king,

---

[136] *Tractatus de Investitura Episcoporum, MGH Ldl.,* II, 502.

[137] *Ibid.,* p. 500.   [138] *MGH Ldl.,* I, 297.   [139] *Ibid.,* p. 298.

[140] M. Prou, ed., *Les cinq livres des ses histoires, 900–1044* (Paris, 1886), V, 133.

the king as the temporal head of the spiritual order as well as of the secular State, therefore, received its practical expression in the ceremony of lay investiture, just as it received its theoretical expression in the rite of coronation.

Although the scope of its aims and dissatisfactions was vast, on this precise point of practical expression the reformed Papacy, insisting on the purely lay character of kings, the spirituality of investiture, and the sinfulness of mixing the two, chose to join battle. The weapons it used were drawn from that province peculiar to itself upon which temporal powers might not encroach, the province of spiritual authority.

Its arsenal of tradition was fully as strong as that of the kingship. St. Paul, with curious impartiality, furnished essential Scriptural support for the spiritual as well as for the temporal power, for he wrote: "But he that is spiritual judgeth all things, yet he himself is judged of no man" (I Corinthians 2:15). Patristic weight was also given to this position. Hosius of Cordova, for example, had vehemently admonished Constantius II that the Empire and the Church were two distinct institutions, though both were of common divine ordination, and that each had its own sphere of interest. In sacred things, the emperor was to be instructed by the Church, and not to be its master.[141] St. Ambrose, gainsaying Optatus of Milevis, maintained that the emperor was within the Church as its son, not over it as its lord.[142] And St. John Chrysostom affirmed that the spiritual power stands as high above the secular as the heaven does above the earth, or even higher.[143]

Kings were special objects for the exercise of the spiritual censure; for it was generally maintained with St. Isidore of Seville that "the name of king is held...by virtue of upright action; it is lost through sinning."[144] The spiritual arm, according to those jealous of its power, as judge of right-doing and of sinning, was also capable of judging when a king had forfeited his office through his sins. These wicked kings, who inflicted "the greed of spendthrift government and very cruel dominion" upon their peoples, were "tyrants"[145]. Such rulers, consumed by vice, were inflicted by God upon peoples for their shortcomings, according

[141] Athanasius, *History of the Arians* XV, 44.

[142] Sermon against Auxentius, chap. 36; Letter 26, 4.

[143] In Ep. 11 ad Cor., Homil. XV, 4, Migne *PG*, LXI, 508.

[144] W. M. Lindsay, ed., *Etymologiarum sive originum Libri XX* (Oxford, 1911), IX, 4–5, chap. 3. Cf. the prefatory quotation in this volume.

[145] *Ibid.*, pp. 19–20.

to St. Augustine, and were to be endured as divine chastisement.[146]

Subsequently, however, the attitude of the Church inclined toward the subversion of tyrants, rather than toward submission to them. Of kings, Pope Nicholas I wrote to Aventius, bishop of Metz, "See whether they govern according to right; if they do otherwise, they are to be considered tyrants, rather than to be regarded as kings. We are bound to resist these men, and to rise up against them, rather than to be subject to them."[147] Shortly before the time of Nicholas, Louis the Pious had been deposed for his sins and for leading his people "to their common destruction, although he ought to have been a leader of salvation and peace for this very people."[148] His judges were bishops, "vicars of Christ and key-bearers of the kingdom of Heaven."[149]

This was the tradition adopted by Gregory VII, who divided kings into two classes: those who "are the body of Christ, the true King," that is, those who serve the Church; and those who are "the body of the Devil," or those who seek their own good and engage in oppression of the Church.[150] It was in the vigorous maintenance of this position, which made the Church the judge of which kings were worthy and which were not, that Gregory "ruffled and bestirred himself very notably."[151]

The Salians had certainly been forewarned that their concept of kingship would not be acceptable to all persons in all places. When Henry III, for example, had affirmed that through his priestlike unction, he had received power to govern "before all others," Wazo, bishop of Liége, answered him in the tones of an adversary. "This unction of yours," he said, "is other than you affirm it to be, and far different from the priestly; for through it you have been arrayed for slaying, but we, through the action of God, for vivifying; wherefore, by as much as life is more excellent than death, by that much, without doubt, our unction is superior to yours."[152] And while Henry IV envisaged himself as David, Gregory VII held before him the alternate figure of Saul, who was "cast aside by the Lord."[153]

St. Stephan of Hungary had written: "It is not fitting for any save men of faith, and imbued with the Catholic Faith, to accede to the order of

---

[146] *City of God* XIX, 12, 15; V, 19, 21, 24. [147] *MGH Epp. Kar. Aev.*, IV, 299, no. 31.
[148] *MGH Leges*, II (*Capit. Reg. Fr.*, II), 54 f., no. 197.
[149] *Ibid.*, p. 21, no. 197. [150] Gregory, *Register*, Epp. VII, 21, p. 557.
[151] John Overall, *Convocation Book* (Oxford, 1844), III, 241. [152] See note 91.
[153] Gregory, *Register*, Epp. III, 10, p. 267.

regal dignity."[154] And Henry IV confessed that deviation from the Faith was the sole reason for which he could be deposed.[155] Gregory, too, adopted the position that orthodoxy (which meant for him obedience to the Roman Church) was the major criterion for receiving and for losing royal power; and from this position he launched his attack upon Henry. When, despite continued warnings, Henry insisted on preserving his rights of investiture in Milan and elsewhere, Gregory took the unprecedented steps, first, of declaring lay investiture heretical and sacrilegious, and thereafter, of excommunicating a king of the Romans, an emperor-designate, because he persisted in the practice.

Because he would not sacrifice that position as the head of the episcopal order which tradition had handed down to his forebears, and which, cherished by them, was transmitted finally to him, Henry became for Gregory, a "member of Antichrist,"[156] a fosterer of heresies; he had deviated from the true Faith. He had betrayed the trust of that position as defender of the Church which he had accepted with the kingship; he was an enemy of God and the Holy Church, a tyrant to be resisted, not obeyed. He was cut off from the living body of the Church.

The political effects of this action were immense even though it was completely within the spiritual sphere, for the excommunication of Henry, as Mirbt has shown, was in itself the equivalent of formal deposition;[157] and further, the "civil" deposition of 1080, Schmeidler has demonstrated, was actually nothing other than ecclesiastical proceedings against a king who because of his official functions had been excommunicated as unjust[158] and tyrannical, and so unworthy to rule.[159] The denial of the Eucharist and of "Christian communion" to Henry, the charges of injustice brought by the Papal legate against him, the extortion of the holy relics (the imperial insignia) from him, and his own eagerness to be reconciled with Rome strongly support this view.[160]

---

[154] Migne *PL*, CLI, 1236.

[155] See E. Eichmann, "Das Exkommunikationsprivileg des deutschen Kaisers im Mittelalter," *ZfRG KA*, I (1911), 167 ff.

[156] E.g. Gregory, *Register*, Epp. IV, 1, pp. 289 f. Cf. the astonishment still shown by Otto of Freising at this event even at the distance of almost a century. G. Waitz, ed. *Gesta Frederici* (Hanover, 1884), I, 10 f.

[157] Mirbt, "Absetzung," p. 104.   [158] Cf. Henry IV, Letter 39.

[159] B. Schmeidler, "Heinrichs IV Absetzung 1105/6, kirchenrechtlich- und quellenkritisch untersucht," *ZfRG KA*, XII (1922), 168–221.

[160] *Ibid.*, pp. 174 ff. I do not wish to treat the question whether the Gregorian reformers actually would have claimed for the Papacy the power to dispense the king-

In the decrees against lay investiture, Gregory had claimed for the priesthood that shadowy region where the temporal mingled with the spiritual, so long claimed and held by the pontifical kingship; and from this action there ensued the turmoil and the bitter conflicts in which Henry IV and his son passed their reigns, the conflicts in which the strength of the kingship was ruinously spent.

Still, in these conflicts, the Pope was only striving for supremacy in the Church, and the King, for surpemacy in the State. Their aims were reasonable; indeed, except in the most unusual circumstances, it had always been agreed in Western Europe, that the pope was the spiritual head of the Church, a spiritual institution, and that the king was the temporal head of the State, a temporal institution. New factors were introduced in the eleventh century, however, and from them arose the Controversy. The first of these new elements was the equal strength of the two political entities, the Papacy and the German kingship. In earlier times, the moral and, to a greater degree, the material weakness of the Papacy had invited intervention in Papal affairs by the German king, the "emperor [or emperor-designate] of the Romans." By advancing their program of ecclesiastical reforms, by allying with the Normans on their southern borders, and by consolidating their control of Papal estates, however, the reformer popes had brought the Roman Church to a high level of moral and material strength; the conditions which once gave the secular arm opportunity for intervention in its affairs had been removed. At the same time, the German kingship was restored through the assiduity of Henry IV to a remarkable vigor, after its decline during his minority. This restoration was facilitated by two major elements, the introduction of certain feudal relationships between lord and liegeman, and the

ship. However, the strength of the affirmative is suggested both by Gregory's own writings and by those of his contemporaries. See, for example, the letter attributed to Nicholas II by Gratian (D. 22, chap. 1, Friedberg ed., col. 73; cf. Peter Damian to Hildebrand, Mansi, Vol. XIX, col. 888), another of Alexander II (P. Ewald, "Die Papstbriefe der Brittischen Sammlung," *Neues Archiv,* V [1880], 332, no. 22), and the letters of Archbishop Siegfried of Mainz (in M. Stimming, ed., *Mainzer Urkundenbuch,* Vol. I [Darmstadt, 1932], Nos. 315, 317, 328, 329, pp. 203, 205, 219, 221). Aside from the many clear statements Gregory made in his letters (for example, in his bulls of excommunication against Henry), one may recall that, according to Otto of Freising, the crown he sent to Rudolf of Rheinfelden bore the inscription "Roma dedit Petro, Petrus diadema Rudolfo" (Rome gave the diadem to Peter, Peter, to Rudolf). *Gesta Frederici* I, 7. Cf. Schramm, *Herrschaftszeichen,* pp. 62 ff.

existence of the Ottonian State-Church system; the second is generally considered to have been of greater importance than the first. This ecclesiastical system in which prelates were regal (or Imperial) vicars, in which their officials were officials of the State, in which their material resources were at the service of the temporal ruler, in which the king was "the head of the Church," was a central element of the restored regal power. On the one hand, there was the Papacy with its new concepts and power; on the other, the German kingship, with its power revived largely through the instrumentality of tradition. Their positions were largely (though not irreconcilably) antagonistic, and for the first time each had the material resources with which to defend its proper position.

The second new element was the redefinition of the "Church" by the reformers in such a way as to conflict sharply with the Ottonian State-Church system, and their attempt to implement their new definition. According to the theories fully expressed by Pope Gelasius I (492–496), and grown axiomatic by the eleventh century, man consisted of two parts, the soul and the body. The soul, as the vivifying element, was superior to the body; so the institution whose province was the spiritual was superior to that whose province was the physical. The Roman Church, by divine ordination, was at the head of that spiritual institution. To this concept, Gregory VII and his followers added the refinement that the province of the spiritual power extended to whatever affected the spirit; therefore, by logical extension, it included the material world and the governing of states. By this extension, Gregory claimed supremacy over all secular rulers, and indeed, the supremacy of any exorcist or priest over an emperor. By this redefinition, all ecclesiastics were in all matters subject primarily to their spiritual Lord, the Christ, and to His earthly vicar, the Roman pontiff. No longer were prelacies and abbacies to be at the disposal of the temporal lord and their resources at his services.

To Henry, this new attitude presented very considerable peril. If the imperial churches were taken from him, it was certain that the supreme authority in his kingdom would fall to the princes, as, in fact, it threatened to do at any rate. But while the Church of his realm with its immense resources remained as his support, there was good hope for the effectual maintenance of the ancient character of the king as the head of the State. Clearly, then, Henry opposed the Gregorian reformers for his own political and economic survival. He readily acknowledged the spiritual supremacy of the priesthood over nonpriests; he did not oppose ecclesiastical reforms, but to the contrary, he showed some zeal for them. On the point of the subjection of the Church to the temporal ruler in material affairs alone he could not afford to yield.

In Italy, where some of the richest parts of Henry's realm lay, the Papacy, with its new material strength and its refurbished theoretical weapons, and the German kingship, with its newly regained power and its traditional concepts, first met in conflict. Battle was joined on the long-festering issue of the Milanese archepiscopacy. In 1071, when Henry seemed to have gained victory over his chief enemies in Germany, the Saxons, Guido, the archbishop of Milan, died, and the aristocratic party, nobles and clergy, elected a certain Godfrey as his successor. Godfrey was invested by Henry and consecrated in 1072; but the "popular" party, the Patarini, had also elected an archbishop, Atto, who was consecrated by Pope Alexander II, without investiture by imperial agents. Because Henry refused to abandon Godfrey, five of his intimate advisers were excommunicated in 1073, charged with responsibility for their master's action and attitude. In the same year, a grave revolt by the Saxons forced Henry to make conciliatory gestures toward the new Pope, Gregory VII, so as to be able to devote his attention and resources fully to his problems in Germany; consequently, he renounced Godfrey and acknowledged Atto. Henry's victory over the Saxons on the Unstrut in 1075, the reascendancy of the aristocratic party in Milan, and the death of Atto made possible Henry's reassertion of his prerogative in Milan in 1075. The aristocratic party elected Tedald the new archbishop, and, in direct defiance of the decree against lay investiture which Gregory had issued from his Lenten Synod earlier in the year, Henry conferred investiture upon him through a deputized legation. He went even further and instructed this same legation to appoint and to invest bishops for Fermo and Spoleto, both of which lay within Papal territory, and then to seek to win Norman support away from the Papacy. The new principles of the reformed Papacy and its new material strength were thus simultaneously challenged by the conventional prerogative of the German king; the challenge was vigorously accepted, and the two powers came into bitter conflict.

Yet there were many central points upon which Henry and his foes agreed: the divine institution of the kingship, the obligation of rulers to undertake the defense of the Church, the interdependence of kingship and priesthood, the secular occupation of rulers, and the spiritual occupation of priests. The violence which Henry suffered and that which he perpetrated followed, however, from a struggle for headship in the Church, from a basic difference in concepts of the proper world order.

Pontifical kingship, in which the ruler had control of those aspects of the Church which appertained to this world, agreed ill with the position of the reformers that restrictions imposed upon any aspect of the activity of the Church limited also the freedom with which the Church might serve its spiritual function and, in fact, distorted that very function. In their view, the influence of the ruler in the internal affairs of the Church was untoward and must be removed; his claims to such influence, based on his position as "a sharer of the priesthood," must be destroyed. He must be seen as a layman, crowned as king as much through the ministry of priests as by the will of God; his unction must be clearly nonpriestly; his position, nonecclesiastical. His mind must no longer be both kingly and priestly. And stripped of all traces of pontificalism, he must be unequivocally a son, a spiritual subject of the Church—its defender, its liegeman. In this way, the supremacy of the spiritual authority would be vindicated.

Nothing could have been more unacceptable to the royalists. The Scriptures and the tradition of the Fathers pronounced the king, elect of God, crowned of God, vicar of God, the anointed of the Lord, bearer of the episcopal ring as well as of the material sword, one whose power was ordained of God, whom the very Scripture called a "minister of God." They prescribed obedience to him as a religious duty. How, therefore, could the king rightly be stripped of his ecclesiastical character? By the very command of God, one might not lift one's hand against the Lord's anointed. The kingship was unalterably an ecclesiastical, a pontifical office, as well as, or rather because it was, the supreme temporal office; and the king, in whose person the character of temporal power was joined with that of ecclesiastical authority, was rightly the "head of the Church."

In the last analysis, though they held much in common, the two positions were irreconcilable; there could be but one head, the regal pontiff or the pontifical king.

THE TEXTS

In the literary tradition of Western Europe, the biographies represented in this volume are, depending on one's point of view, either the continuation of an ancient genre or the first products of a new one. There had been numerous *vitae* of saints and prelates; yet between Einhard's day and Wipo's no secular person had had a biographer who wrote of him in purely secular terms. After the early eleventh century the secular biography was by no means a novelty; Otto of Freising's *Deeds of Frederick Barbarossa*, though only a partial treatment of Frederick's reign, and the biography of Henry II of England are but two examples. Between the time of Einhard and that of Wipo, however, one may count only eight biographies of laymen: two lives of Louis the Pious; Asser's *Life of Alfred;* two biographies of Queen Matilda, the wife of Henry I of Germany; Gumpold of Mantua's life of Wenceslas of Poland; Adalbold of Utrecht's now-fragmentary biography of the Emperor Henry II; a monk of St. Omer's *Deeds of Canute;* and Helgand of Fleury's biography of Robert II of France.[161] One should, perhaps, also mention the verse *Gesta Berengarii imperatoris* and Hrothsuitha's *Carmen de Gestis Oddonis.* In all but one of these works, the saintly character, the zeal for the true Church, the good works of the subject, and, even more, the special blessings extended by God to him are of paramount importance, and the actual happenings of political life assume decidedly secondary significance. While not denying his subject the aura of divine favor, however, Wipo's contemporary, the biographer of Canute describes him as a man of action rather than a man of God. The narratives of all these works are sketchy, and but slight attention is paid to detail save for descriptions of miracles. It should be added that an anonymous biography of St. Stephan of Hungary, composed about 1085, is like them in character.

Wipo shared with the authors of these works their eagerness to write for the spiritual edification of his readers and auditors (in those days when it was the custom to read works aloud to gatherings). Although in his prologue he asserted that a biographer should recount the unpleasant characteristics of his subject as well as the laudable ones, giving weight to this conviction by criticizing Conrad II sharply on several occasions, he was prone to "correct" what he considered faulty in order to attain "a higher pedagogical effect, a more meaningful mystical exposition."[162] His treatment is, in general, an honest if not penetrating

---

[161] See M. Manitius, *Geschichte der lateinischen Literatur des Mittelalters*, II (Munich, 1923), 128; III (Munich, 1931), 575 ff.

[162] G. M. Stahl, *Die mittelalterliche Weltanschauung in Wipos Gesta Chuonradi II Imperatoris*, Diss. Bonn (Münster, 1925), pp. 53 f.

annalistic account of a secular ruler in unecclesiastical, unsanctimoni-
ous terms. Although the anonymous biography of Henry IV differs
markedly from the *Deeds of Conrad* (it is considerably more emphatic
in praise of Henry's good works and holy character than Wipo's was of
Conrad's; in style, it is more rhetorical and in organization, less annalistic), the two works are similar in that the subject of each is un-
mistakably a temporal Christian prince.

Wipo's *The Deeds of Conrad II*

In presenting the most important information about Wipo and his
work, one can but paraphrase Bresslau's conclusions.[163] Of Wipo's own
life, we know only what he himself has told us in his writings, although
some suppositions may be fairly based on what seems to be implied
there. His homeland was probably in the Swabian-dialect area of
Burgundy, as his name, his special interest in Burgundy, and his ac-
quaintance with Bishop Henry of Lausanne suggest. He was probably
born late in the tenth century. His education seems to have included
readings of the classics in addition to the conventional studies of the
Scriptures and apocryphal writings, as his numerous allusions to Sallust,
Virgil, Horace, Lucan, Suetonius, Statius, and Persius (as well as Macrobius and Sulpicius Severus) show. He may also have read some of
Cicero and Boethius's *Consolation of Philosophy*. Any readings he may
have done in the Fathers seem to have left little impression on him;
for even Bresslau's keen sight was unable to detect any patristic citation
in Wipo's work, although it is permeated with the Augustinian positions conventional throughout the Middle Ages.

If he was an Alamannic Burgundian, it is unknown when he left his
homeland and went to the northern parts of Germany. He was present,
however, at the election of Conrad II, one of whose chaplains he became, perhaps even before the election; and he may have accompanied
his lord on the 1033 winter expedition to Burgundy and on the 1035
expedition against the Slavs, both of which he described with unusual
fullness in the biography and in his verse. As for his nonecclesiastical
functions at court, the position of adviser and exhorter which he adopted in his metrical works, *Proverbia* and *Tetralogus*, and to which he
alludes at the end of Chapter 1 in the biography, suggests a close rela-

[163] H. Bresslau, "Einleitung" to *Die Werke Wipos*, pp. i–lix.

tionship to Henry III, perhaps that of tutor to pupil. Though he seems to have remained in the court after the death of Conrad, he did not attain to high ecclesiastical office, for he wrote the *Gesta Chuonradi II* as a common priest. He lived to know of Henry III's Imperial coronation (1046), but how much longer is unknown.

It was to poetry that Wipo seems to have devoted his major literary efforts. In the *Gesta Chuonradi*, he mentioned with considerable pride his metrical works and the fact that he presented some of them to reigning emperors. Three of them—verses on the winter expedition to Burgundy, *Gallinarius* (probably on the gaining of Burgundy), and verses on Conrad's expedition against the Slavs—are no longer extant. Four surviving poetic works are attributed either definitely or with great certainty to Wipo: the most widely known is the Easter sequence, *Victimae paschali*, which is still heard frequently during Easter week; the others are the work on the death of Conrad, which he appended to the biography; *Tetralogus*, a panegyric for Henry III; and *Proverbia*, a series of pithy maxims composed for Henry, probably not long after his coronation as coregent in 1028, and after *Victimae paschali* his best-known work in the Middle Ages.

The historical importance and pedantic artistry of these writings pale beside the importance and the workmanship shown in Wipo's biography of Conrad. The form in which this work survives is the result of some revision, due to a change in its writer's aims which become clear in a comparison of the dedicatory letter to Henry II with the Prologue of the *Deeds* itself. In the Prologue, Wipo expressed the intention to write as one work the "Gesta" of Henry III and those of Conrad; the resulting *opus* would naturally consist of two parts, one devoted to each of the rulers. If he should die before Henry, as he said, the work would lack the second part, but he hoped that it would be completed by another writer. The reference to Henry as "King" indicates that the Prologue was written before his Imperial coronation (1046). In the dedicatory letter, on the other hand, the *Gesta Chuonradi* is presented as an *opus* complete in itself, although Wipo had not abandoned his intention of composing an account of the deeds of Henry. Here the acts of Henry are not thought of as being distinct from those of Conrad, but are intermingled with them. This position is obviously the later, for since Henry is addressed as "Emperor" as well as "King," the letter was composed after the Imperial coronation. The alterations in the biography required by the change do not seem to have been many or important, and their primary purpose seems to have been to relate the deeds of Henry to those of his father. One may cite as examples, in Chapter 1, the mention of Henry's valiant deeds in Burgundy and Hungary; in Chapter 8, the praise of Henry "King and Augustus" who made good Conrad's vow not to foster simony; the statement at the end of Chapter 29, that Casimir served "our Emperors" "until this very day"; the account of Henry's actions against the Poles in Chapter 33; and the statement that Henry made his daughter by Chunelinde abbess of Quedlinburg, an event which occurred in 1046. There are no references to subsequent occurrences. The date of the biography's first composition, therefore, is between 1039 and 1046; and that of its revision 1046–1047, or shortly thereafter.

In addition to the classical authors already mentioned, who served for literary embellishment, Wipo drew upon his own memory, the memories of others, and a world chronicle written at the abbey of Reichenau, which had the character of an official Imperial history in the eleventh century. This chronicle was used also in the composition of the *Annales Sangallenses majores*, of the chronicle of Herman of Reichenau, and of other similar works. Wipo used it for all but the first nine chapters of the *Gesta Chuonradi*, in which he described the election and coronation of his subject.

The biography was not widely read during the Middle Ages, although it is known to have been used on four occasions. The first was in 1125, when it served to prove a forgery the document which the bishop of Basel had produced to prove his lordship over the abbey of St. Blasien. Subsequently it was used by Otto of Freising in the composition of his *Chronicle*, by a monk of Zwettl at the end of the twelfth century in his revisions of the *Annales Mellicenses*, and in the fifteenth century by the anonymous author of a Swabian Chronicle.

The only surviving manuscript dates from the sixteenth century and is preserved in Karlsruhe in the Badesches Landesarchiv. It is full of errors, and portions of it are utterly nonsensical, apparently because the copyist could not accurately decipher the manuscript before him. For the establishment of a text, therefore, the most authoritative source is the 1607 *editio princeps* by Pistorius, apparently made from an eleventh-century manuscript. The Zwettl revision of the *Annales Mellicenses* is also of great importance, since the reviser copied freely and accurately, though eclectically, from the *Deeds*.

The Life of the Emperor Henry IV

Three extant works celebrate the deeds of Henry IV: the *Carmen de bello Saxonico* (composed about 1075/6), verses in praise of Henry's victory over the Saxons in 1075; the *Conquestio Heinrici IV imperatoris ad Heinricum filium* (ca. 1106), a brief poetic work in defense of Henry against his rebellious son; and the *Vita Heinrici IV imperatoris*, the most important and reliable of the three, despite errors in chronology, neglect of causal relationships, and what appears to be the bias of strong partisanship.

There is little definite knowledge of the provenance of the *Vita*, and even suppositions well-founded on the text itself are few. The author is unknown; the place of writing is uncertain; and even the time of composition is only generally determinable.

Bernard Schmeidler maintained on philological grounds that the author was a member of the Imperial chancery, the so-called Mainz *Dictator* ("supervisor" on the chancery staff).[164] This man, whose style Schmeidler found so similar to that of the biographer of Henry, entered the royal service in 1076 after some activity at Speier, and later served his master well by writing various "propaganda" letters, among them Letter 39, to Philip of France.[165] Schmeidler, after studying the sole surviving manuscript of the *Vita*, found it to have been written in a hand used by the Würzburg scriptorium early in the twelfth century, and because of the apparent urgency of the author's grief, he dated the composition shortly after Henry's death, late in 1106 or early in the following year. The place of composition, he said, was Würzburg.[166]

Some years after the publication of Schmeidler's findings, Hellmann showed the uncertainty of conclusions drawn from stylistic comparisons such as those with which Schmeidler presented his case. Similar training would account for similar style.[167] The theory that the author was a member of the Imperial chancery was based on extremely tenuous evidence, since the comparison between the literary form of the biography and the legal form of the chancery documents is in itself both

[164] B. Schmeidler, *Kaiser Heinrich IV und seine Helfer im Investiturstreit* (Leipzig, 1927), p. 362.

[165] B. Schmeidler, "Über den wahren Verfasser der Vita Heinrici IV imperatoris," *Papsttum und Kaisertum* (*Festschrift P. Kehr*, ed. by A. Brackmann, Munich, 1926), pp. 234, 243.

[166] *Kaiser Heinrich IV*, pp. 368 f.

[167] S. Hellmann, "Die Vita Heinrici IV und die kaiserliche Kanzlei," *Historische Vierteljahrschrift*, XXVIII (1943), 284 ff.

difficult and deceptive.[168] The philological approach adopted by Schmeidler and others, however, was the only one open, since the author covered his identity so completely. However, since that approach could not be accurate, nor its results free of uncertainty, Hellmann concluded that while the author may have been, and probably was, a member of the wider circle of the Imperial chancery,[169] no proofs were conclusive; the provenance of the manuscript itself (Würzburg, early twelfth century) was unhelpful; all results were negative.[170] The dating of the *Vita* remained about 1106/7.

In the most recent treatment of the *Vita*, Haefele has brought even this last remaining measure of certainty into question. For he has rightly observed that the apparent urgency of the author's grief may simply be another manifestation of the expert use to which the writer put his rhetorical training. The work may merely have been a rhetorical exercise composed at an indefinite time after the death of Henry IV, though its stylistic characteristics indicate that it was probably written during the reign of Henry V.[171] The character of the manuscript itself makes possible this sole (relatively) reliable conclusion.

The work is generally regarded as "a virtuoso piece of rhetorical style."[172] In construction, a significant break with the annalistic method represented by Wipo, it is, in fact, a product of the rhetorical movement given impetus in the mid-eleventh century by Marbod of Rennes, Onulf of Speier, and others of their school.[173] Classical embellishments from Horace, Terence, Livy, Sallust, Lucan, Cicero, Virgil, and Ovid are scattered throughout; direct citations of the Scriptures and, even more often, allusions to them are frequent. But it was the rhetorically elegant letters of Sulpicius Severus which supplied the author with a basic pattern for the work, as well as with some precious turns of phrase. As for other sources, the sources from which he drew his information other than memory may have included official documents issuing from the Imperial chancery—encyclicals, summonses, and the like[174]

[168] *Ibid.*, pp. 301 f.   [169] *Ibid.*, p. 326.   [170] *Ibid.*, p. 334.

[171] H. Haefele, *Fortuna Heinrici IV imperatoris* (Cologne, 1954), pp. 20 ff.

[172] Hellmann, "Die Vita Heinrici IV," p. 280.

[173] See L. Wallach, "Onulf of Speyer, A Humanist of the Eleventh Century," *Medievalia et Humanistica*, fasc. 6 (1950), pp. 35–36.

[174] Erdmann is probably right in condemning the "official" exchange of messages between Henry IV and his son given in the "Life of Emperor Henry IV" as "literary fiction." "Untersuchungen zu den Briefen Heinrichs IV," *Archiv für Urkundenforschung*, XVI (1939), 228 n. 1.

—and he is also known to have used Sulpicius Severus's widely read biography of St. Martin of Tours. Attempts to show that he used Sulpicius's seldom-met *Chronicle* are indifferently conclusive.[175]

Haefele has shown that two motifs are central to the *Vita*: first, and predominantly, the *Fortuna* motif, a nonhuman, mystic element which relates to the whole career of Henry IV, and secondly, the *Fides* motif, an element under the control of man, which colors most transcendentally the conflict between Henry IV and Henry V. Since *fides*, however, was the sole bond between ruler and ruled, the *fides* of the princes comes into discussion often even in the earlier portions of the biography, and with the greatest clarity in Chapter 3, where a charge is laid against Gregory VII for his absolution of Henry's subjects of their vows of fidelity. The two motifs are intertwined throughout the work, coming together most neatly in its turning point, Chapter 7, where it is told how Henry stationed troops in Rome "lest she should change her fidelity toward him," and the grim hint of future calamity is given—"But no fortune is long-lasting." Henry's misfortune reached its height in the infidelity of his sons; his fortune returned in death.[176]

The *Vita* consists of four parts; the first is a description of Henry's character (Chapter 1); the second, an account of his early acts as king in his own right, culminating in the capture of Rome (Chapters 2–6); the third, a sort of plateau on which the old troubles are laid to rest through Henry's *Landfrieden* and other good works, and from which new troubles arise in the discontent of the nobles (Chapters 7–8); and the fourth, a recounting of the rebellion of Henry V (Chapters 9–13).[177]

As has been mentioned above, only one manuscript of the *Vita* survives, the elegant work of an expert copyist of the early twelfth century.[178] It was discovered in 1518 by Johannes Aventinus, the state historian of Bavaria, and was subsequently published by him and again by Johannes Cuspinian in 1540.[179] Since the character of Henry IV until that time had been analyzed merely on the testimony of those ecclesiastical sources which were true to the tradition of the Gregorians and flagrantly hostile toward the royalists, this publication opened sud-

---

[175] W. Gundlach, "Die Vita Heinrici IV und die Schriften des Sulpicius Severus," *Neues Archiv*, XI (1886), 299 and *passim*.

[176] Haefele, *Fortuna Heinrici IV*, pp. 92 ff.

[177] Cf. *ibid.*, pp. 90 f.; Hellmann, "Die Vita Heinrici IV," pp. 274 ff.

[178] W. Eberhard, "Praefatio" to *Vita Heinrici IV*, p. 8.

[179] E. Schirmer, *Die Persönlichkeit Kaiser Heinrichs IV im Urteil der deutschen Geschichtsschreibung* (Jena, Diss., 1930), pp. 27 f., 31.

denly a new interpretation of the Investiture Controversy as a whole, as well as of Henry's character.[180]

The Letters of Henry IV

The letters of Henry IV represent an old literary genre which re-appears at the end of the eleventh century—the epistolary collection. Other such collections of the period are the letters of Peter Damian, Gregory VII, Lanfranc and Anselm of Canterbury, and somewhat later, Ivo of Chartres. Although it is clear that conventional methods of communication were in use at this time, letters from earlier periods are excessively rare; for example, only four survive under the name of Henry III. But suddenly, and it would seem, largely through the zeal of letter collectors, from the mid-eleventh century they become avail-able in numbers gratifying to students; in place of the four letters of Henry III, we have the forty-two letters of his son.[181]

The question of authorship, of course, is rather different from that presented by the two biographies just described. One wonders what part Henry himself took in the composition of the letters, and what part was taken by or assigned to the members of his chancery. Ebo, the biographer of Otto of Bamberg, who, as said in the general introduc-tion, testifies that Henry read his psalter with great diligence, affirms in addition that "the Emperor was so imbued with letters that he was able by himself to read and to understand documents, by whomever they were directed to him."[182] And Ekkehard of Aura, no friend of Henry, mentions that he delighted in the company of clerics and men of letters, and that "he employed them in his company in a rather friendly way, now with psalms, now with reading or collateral reading, or with investigation of the Scriptures or of the liberal arts."[183] Cosmas of Prague bears witness that Henry could also wield a pen, whether merely to make his monogram at the end of a document or to write more, one cannot say[184] One may conclude with certainty that Henry could read and understand Latin documents, regardless of the hand in which they were written, and that he had attained at least mediocre competence in literary pursuits.

[180] *Ibid.*, p. 6.
[181] C. Erdmann, *Studien zur Briefliteratur Deutschlands im elften Jahrhundert* (Leipzig, 1938), p. 1, and "Einleitung" to *Die Briefe Heinrichs IV*, p. 1.
[182] Ebo, *op. cit.*, I, 594, chap. 6. [183] *Chronicon, MGH SS.*, VI, 239 (1106).
[184] *Op. cit.*, II, 37 (1086), 140

This does not mean, to be sure, that every work in the letters proceeded from the hand or from the mouth of Henry. It is probable, however, that Henry dictated many of the extant letters, in German or in Latin, and that a *dictator* of his chancery polished or translated them into Latin, if necessary.[185] Erdmann, their editor, saw in them a unity in tenor and in personal references to Henry himself which, he believed, made it certain that Henry did, in fact, have a considerable part in their composition.

Admittedly, many of the letters were expressions of Imperial policy the writing of which Henry entrusted largely or wholly to his chancery. The Worms and Brixen decrees, though not numbered among the letters, are the clearest representatives of this portion of the correspondence, produced as they were completely by professionals in the *ars dictaminis*.[186] Letters 10, 12 13, and 17, in which the royalist position in the Investiture struggle was placed upon theoretical grounds, are attributed to a master *dictator*, Gottschalk of Aachen, and Erdmann and Gladiss have argued that the Letters 6, 9, 15, 18, 19, 32, and 33 also show his hand.[187] The power which the *dictatores* held as "spokesmen" for their ruler obviously was great. But it was not so great as Schmeidler has suggested in hypothecating an ideological struggle within the chancery during Henry's last years. According to his theory, the *dictatores* in charge of the major letters in that period were two, whom he terms "Ogerius A" and the "Mainz *dictator*" (the suggested author of the *Vita Heinrici IV*). "Ogerius A" was responsible for Letters 34, 37, 40, 41, and 42; the "Mainz *dictator*" for Letters 31, 38, and 39.[188] "Ogerius A," he affirmed, represents the idealistic party, dedicated to effecting a reconciliation between the Empire and the Papacy, "believing the best of all men"; the "Mainz *dictator*" was "a sharp *Realpolitiker*, reckoning with power elements, heedless, sly, and in the highest degree untruthful and unreliable in his statements."[189] In view of the concerted and well-directed propaganda effort which Erdmann has proved Henry made through his chancery, such a divergence in sentiment and disposition would have been inconceivable. In fact, the two characters are not so clearly separated as Schmeidler suggests, but on the

[185] Erdmann, "Untersuchungen," p. 248.

[186] Erdmann, *Die Briefe Heinrichs IV*, pp. 2 ff.

[187] C. Erdmann and D. v. Gladiss, "Gottschalk von Aachen im Dienste Heinrichs IV," *Deutsches Archiv*, III (1939), 116, 170 ff.

[188] Schmeidler, *Kaiser Heinrich IV*, p. 315.   [189] *Ibid.*, p. 331.

contrary they are mingled in these last letters. It is probable that they merely reflect two parts of the same policy in which idealism and the desire for reconciliation with the Papacy were united with slyness and a keen political sense, all of which were necessary to Henry's maintenance of the regal prerogative. Schmeidler's suggestion, however, is instructive in that it reminds one forcibly that the majority of the letters of Henry IV—those which dealt with affairs of state—were not merely the products of one man's disposition and capacity, but the common fruits of a regal will and a devoted, powerful, and highly competent chancery.

Although many of the letters relate to other matters, by far their greatest bulk pertains to Henry's two major struggles; that against Gregory VII and that against his own son, Henry V. These two sections of his correspondence comprise the earliest known propaganda literature in Germany.[190] The letters against Gregory speak for themselves, but it may be useful to mention the pattern made by the letters against Henry V. Five major propaganda letters survive from this second struggle: Letter 34, to Paschal II; Letter 37, to Hugh of Cluny; Letter 39, to Philip of France; and Letters 41 and 42, to the princes. It will be seen how neatly these letters fit Henry's aim to remove his son's ideological basis for rebellion (his own unreconciled state with the Roman Church) and to muster the strength sufficient to crush his enemies. The readiness for reconciliation which he expressed in the first two letters would win, he hoped, the first goal; his appeal to Philip, but, far more, his appeals to his princes, would gain the second.[191] These letters, and especially Letters 37 and 39, were given wide circulation in the obvious attempt to win support. Erdmann considered the second the masterpiece of Henry's propaganda effort,[192] and Otto of Freising mentions it as a letter which "could soften minds of stone."[193]

Since they were preserved as individual works, the letters are scattered in several sources. Four of them survive in the original; Letters 31, 37 and 38, from the Cluny collection, are now in the Bibliothèque

---

[190] See Erdmann, "Untersuchungen," pp. 218 ff., and "Die Anfänge der staatlichen Propaganda im Investiturstreit," *Historische Zeitschrift*, CLIV (1936), 491–512.

[191] See P. Rassow, "Der Kampf Kaiser Heinrichs IV mit Heinrich V," *Zeitschrift für Kirchengeschichte*, XLVII (1928), 462 f.

[192] "Untersuchungen," p. 227.

[193] *Chronica*, VII, 12. But Erdmann ("Untersuchungen," p. 227) denies that the letter was written with any material goal in mind.

Nationale in Paris; Letter 19, the only public rescript existing in the original, is in the cathedral archives of Osnabrück.[194] Of some letters, several copies survive; as mentioned above, Letter 39, preserved in five copies, is an outstanding example of this fortuitous duplication; Letter 17, which exists in an English manuscript, probably written in the twelfth century at Canterbury, is the only letter surviving in but one copy. Some were incorporated into chronicles; for example, Letter 39 was copied by Sigebert of Gembloux,[195] and Bruno of Merseburg, who transcribed twenty-one letters in his *Liber de bello Saxonico*, included among them Henry's two manifests of 1076 (Letters 11, 12, 14).[196] Hugh of Flavigny, Ekkehard of Aura, and others made similar use of them.

It is, however, in the epistolary collections, closely akin to this sort of historical work, that most of the letters are found, a fact which, as already mentioned, gives them a special place in the history of literature. Twenty-three of them exist, for example, in the so-called Codex Udalrici, a collection made by Udalrich of Bamberg (died 1147) in the decade after 1120 and dedicated to Gebehard, count of Henneberg, who was made bishop of Bamberg in 1122 by Henry V. A second basic source is the "Hanoverian Collection" (*Codex epistolaris imperatorum, regum, pontificum, episcoporum*) which, although it survives only in a sixteenth-century transcription, was originally made in the last five years of the eleventh century. And many of the letters survive in the monastic collections of St. Emmeram and Tegernsee.[197] Two of them, Letters 5 and 7, are found in the Register of Gregory VII.

Thus it was largely through the apparently new interest in collecting letters of political import[198] that the letters of Henry IV survived to show to future generations in the most authoritative form possible his concept of the kingly office and his position in the great struggles which marked his reign.

The texts used in making the following translations were the following: for "The Deeds of Conrad II," the third edition by Harry Bresslau (Hanover, 1919); for "The Life of the Emperor Henry IV," the edition by Wattenbach, as revised in a third edition by W. Eberhard (Hanover, 1899); and for "The letters of Henry IV," the edition by C. Erdmann, *Die Briefe Heinrichs IV* (Leipzig, 1937).

[194] "Untersuchungen," pp. 186 f., 193. [195] Erdmann, *Die Briefe Heinrichs IV*, p. 2.
[196] Erdmann, "Die Anfänge," p. 507. [197] Erdmann, *Briefliteratur*, p. 2. [198] *Ibid.*, p. 3

THE DEEDS OF CONRAD II

BY WIPO

While censuring Conrad II for his simoniacal practices, arbitrary deposition of bishops, and oppression of free monasteries, Wipo did not condemn the concept of royal supremacy which seemed to sanction those acts. He warmly approved Conrad's bestowal of ecclesiastical dignities—among them, the episcopacy itself —together with temporal honors, and he commended Conrad's instruction and discipline of clerics, just as he also praised the elevation of Bamberg to the status of bishopric by Conrad's predecessor, Henry II. In the coronation sermon which he attributes to the Archbishop of Mainz, and again in his own conclud- ing verses, Wipo affirms that the model for exercising royal power in this world is the exercise of power by God Himself: for God is a King, he writes, the King of kings, and the earthly king is His imitator, the vicar of Christ. The king- ship is "the highest dignity": like his divine prototype, the king is "the lord of lords." In addition to his political thought, Wipo's observations upon contem- porary institutions, especially those upon feudal relationships, are worthy of close attention.

Letter to King Henry, Son of the Emperor Conrad

To the most glorious Emperor, Henry, the third king of that name, well-suited to peace and war—Wipo, priest by the grace of God, sends what the servant of royal servants in this world owes the lord of lords.[1]

I have thought it fitting, Lord Emperor, to write the illustrious life and the glorious deeds of the Emperor Conrad, your father, lest the light hide under a bushel,[2] lest the ray of the sun be hid in a cloud,[3] lest memorable valor be overcast by the rust of oblivion. For if his deeds did not go before, brilliant and most radiant as they were, they would appear somewhat darkened by the immeasurable splendor of your

[1] Deuteronomy 10:17 and *passim*.   [2] Matthew 5:15.   [3] II Maccabees 1:22.

deeds of valor following. However, God granting, I, your lowly servant, intend to tell those acts of both of you which took place during
my lifetime, so as to say truly, distinguishing between you thus, that
the one performed an operation with good effect upon the commonwealth, that is, the Roman Empire, and that the other, according to
the dictates of reason, restored it to health. But if I write or have here
said more or less or other than the whole story, it will not be the fault
of the writer, but of whoever bore the tale; for many was the time
when I was ill and therefore unable to be present in the chapel of Conrad, my lord.[4] Concerning those things, however, which I myself have
seen and those which I have received from others, supported by the pen
of truth, I shall publish the fruit garnered by us who have been willing
to gather it. And since there are certain things worthy of praise which
you did while your father was alive, I thought that they should be placed
among the acts of your father; those, however, which you have done glo-
riously after his death must, I have decided, be set in order by themselves. If, however, some faultfinders object to me that this work is quite
superfluous, since others also have written on the same subject (although
I have not yet seen anything else written about it), I shall answer: "In
the mouth of two or three will stand all testimony,"[5] and that the
words of Christ in the Gospel are set forth in the Church, not through
one alone, but through four worthily qualified witnesses.

To you, most exalted Emperor, I dedicate this work, to you I represent the deeds of your father, so that as often as you consider doing
very distinguished things, you will picture to yourself first, as in a mirror, the valorous deeds of your father; and so that that which you have
inherited from your father's roots may flower more abundantly in you.

As you have surpassed all your predecessors in divers divine and worldly affairs, so may you deserve to hold your kingdom and Empire far longer
than all of them, through the favor of Omnipotent God. Farewell.

The Prologue Begins

Because a useful example is wont to render the spirit of one who im-
itates it the more ready and strong in action,[6] I have thought it apt and

---

[4] The word is *senior;* the diplomata of Conrad II indicate that this term denotes a
"dominus" or lord, of unusually high station. Cf. *MGH Diplomata Conrad II,* p. 336,
no. 244.

[5] Deuteronomy 19:15.   [6] Cf. Sulpicius Severus, *Life of St. Martin* I, 2.

fitting to connect with chains of letters the fleeting memory of passing affairs. [It has been my purpose], in particular, not to pass over the merits of the Christian Empire in sluggish silence,[7] not only that from this [work] a certain glory may endure through the perpetuation of their memory for those who administered the Empire well in this life, but also that a design of right living may be at hand for coming generations if they wish to emulate their forebears. Again [I have written these things as a lasting admonition for men yet to be], since it often comes to pass that shamefacedness and perturbation of mind on the part of descendants is born easily from praise of their ancestors, if, although they have praised their [forefathers'] deeds with repute as their teacher, they have not at least equaled them:[8] for just as valor enobles many common men, so nobility without valiant deeds degrades many from their noble estate.

Besides, it seems impermissible to be silent as regards the victories of Catholic princes and to publicize with loud voices the triumphs of infidel tyrants. It is ill-advised enough to write and to read about Superbus Tarquinius, Tullus and Ancus, father Aeneas,[9] fierce Rutulus,[10] and some others of this sort: [and], on the other hand, to neglect entirely our Charleses and three Ottos, our Emperor Henry II, Emperor Conrad, father of the most glorious king, Henry III, and the same King Henry, triumphing in Christ. Modern writers ought to fear to become vile before God through the vice of indolence, since the primordial authority of the Old Testament, which sets down diligently and with fruitful labor the histories of the Fathers, teaches in a prefigurative fashion that fruit of recent affairs ought to be hoarded in the storehouse of memory. Thus we remember that Abraham freed Lot, his cousin, in war; thus we discover that the sons of Israel overcame divers enemies. Thus we have before our eyes through the fullness of [these] writings the struggles of King David, the counsels of Solomon, the inventions of Gideon, the battles of the Maccabees.

But ancient philosophers advised the commonwealth in a different way[11] [that is, not by historical narrative]. They often related credible dreams,[12] by which they might attract the minds of hearers to that which they had undertaken to affirm. Sometimes, to the same purpose,

---

[7] Cf. Sallust, *Cataline* 1, 1.   [8] Cf. Sallust, *Jugurtha* 4, 6.

[9] Cf. Horace, *Carmina* IV, 7, 15.

[10] Turnus, king of the Rutules. *Aeneid* VI, 409.   [11] Sallust, *Catiline* 37, 8.

[12] Macrobius, *Interpretatio in somnum Scipionis* I, 3, 12.

they devised fabled narrations,[13] veiled with noble affairs and names, since images of this sort gainsay no philosophical question.[14] By frank discussions based on reason,[15] they gave assurance[16] to the rulers of the commonwealth[17] that human souls are eternal and—as Macrobius relates that Socrates said—that the soul (*anima*) does not perish after the body [literally, creature, *animal*].[18] And almost all philosophers have taught unhesitatingly that the fruit of human effort is not ended with one's life,[19] but that all who aid their country and preserve the law endure happily forever;[20] [and] that for those who detest justice, punishment is reserved by the judgment of a just creator. In truth, they have proven with many rationales that the human soul is immortal. Then, from this proposition, [they proved] that [the soul] while enclosed with the bonds[21] of the body uses the liberty of scanning with the lively movement of thought, now the secret places of the stars, now those of the earth, [and] sometimes the hidden things of the sea, which it never saw corporeally.[22] [They taught that] sometimes with the body wakeful, sometimes with it resting,[23] it [the spirit] assembles many things which are yet to be, with no sight other than its own, and retains them with memory; and that, shaken off from the nebulous veil of flesh, it enjoys them far more freely with the same vigor. And they said that to believe, nay more, to know this would be of the greatest use to princes, who often, growing slothful through insolent pride,[24] pay too little heed to the rewards of the life which follows. For this reason, the ancients erected statues and the amplest monuments possible to victors (whose spirits, they believed, lived forever) and thought that their acts ought to be inscribed so that after they had died honor might be manifest to the perpetual memory of posterity. Although with human wisdom alone they made their investigations in regard to the immortality of the soul, which had not yet been promised or revealed to them by Christ, nonetheless, led on by this investigation, they cultivated justice themselves and diligently inculcated it with their writings upon the rulers of their land as well. They thought that the accomplishments

---

[13] *Ibid.* 2, 9.   [14] *Ibid.* 11.

[15] Wipo may have had in mind Cicero's *Tusculan Disputations* I, 11 ff. Cf. Macrobius, *Interpretatio in somnum Scipionis* II, 13, 6.

[16] Macrobius, *Interpretatio in somnum Scipionis* I, 1, 5.

[17] *Ibid.* 8, 4.   [18] *Ibid.* 1, 7.   [19] *Ibid.* 5.   [20] *Ibid.* 4, 4,   [21] *Ibid.* 1, 5; 10, 9.

[22] This passage is patterned on the dream of Scipio.

[23] Cf. Macrobius, *Interpretatio in somnum Scipionis* II, 16, 26.

[24] Cf. Sallust, *Jugurtha* 2, 4; *Catiline* 16, 3.

of the commonwealth would die simultaneously with its rulers unless what had happened were noted and that a very great disaster would ensue from slothful silence, if the thing that any man now dead pursued during his lifetime should not be apparent from surviving writings.

Why should we suffer that to be denied to Christian princes and to champions of the Gospel Faith which pagans on their part offered to theirs, we from whom the utterance of Truth has sundered the torpor of taciturnity, saying: "What I say to you in darkness, say in light; and what you hear in the ear, proclaim above the housetops"?[25] For if our catholic kings, defenders of the True Faith, oversee without danger of error the law and peace of Christ, which He has transmitted to us through His Gospel, what other than the Gospel of Christ will those men preach who are to make manifest in their writings the things done well by those rulers?

Although the spirit of the writer hesitates to approach difficult undertakings [which are] completed with mature counsel, moral gravity,[26] and the greatest constancy, and although all those things in which the writer should busy himself be marked by improper extravagance, or dissembling audacity, or flagrant cupidity—even in the acts of those whom he mentions—yet those things which were done as well as those not done must be made public as far as the writer's intellectual faculties permit. For thus the good are incited to virtue,[27] but the evil are set aright through a censure which commands respect. This, then, is the end of writing, which no religion forbids[28] and intent commends, and which will benefit the fatherland; and something said well is of advantage to posterity.

What passes is manifest; whatever is to come, however, is not [known] beforehand.

Led on by this motive and by this hope,[29] I have wished to write for the common use of readers something which would be pleasing [also] to hearers. For if something deserving of respect be transmitted here, the reader will be able to imitate it openly.[30] Furthermore, I do this at my advanced age in order that, in spite of the pressure of many bodily failings, occupied with these affairs by the summons of God, I may be able to avoid idleness as the enemy of the soul.[31]

Prepared, then, as I am to speak of acts of state, I shall encompass the

[25] Matthew 10: 27.   [26] Macrobius, *Interpretatio in somnum Scipionis* I, 1, 6.
[27] Cf. Sulpicius Severus, *Life of St. Martin* I, 6.   [28] Virgil, *Georgics* I, 269.
[29] Sallust, *Jugurtha* 29, 3.   [30] Cf. Sallust, *Catiline* 13, 3.   [31] Cf. Ecclesiasticus 33: 29.

acts of two kings, primarily—namely, those of Conrad the Emperor and of his son King Henry III, whom almost all the wiser men name Henry, the Fine Line of Justice. With the art of the pen, I shall draw for unknown men yet to be the deeds of the father [Conrad II] which happened in my times, as far as I myself saw them or learned of them through the account of others. But as long as I shall live, I shall not cease from assembling the most famous accomplishments of his son, since he has survived until now, by the grace of God, to rule. But if it happen, just as it fell my lot to enter this life before the King, that I should depart before him, and thus leave my work incomplete, I beseech whoever writes after me not to be ashamed to superimpose his walls upon my foundations, not to disdain to take up the falling pen, not to look invidiously at my beginning, just as he does not want anyone to look invidiously at his conclusion. If, indeed, [it is truly said that] he who begins does half the work,[32] then it is not fitting for someone who finds the beginning of this work provided to be thankless when he brings it to its goal.

These things I have set forth by way of preface; now I shall come to the deeds of the Emperor. But first I have told a few things about how suitable his election was, so as to be able to write the more acceptably thereafter, if I recollect first who were the pontiffs or other princes then at the defense of the kingdom.

I. On the Assembly of Princes

In the year 1024 from the incarnation of the Lord, the Emperor Henry II, although sound of mind, was taken with an infirmity of the body, the which prevailing he departed this life the III of the Ides of July [July 13]. The Empire was sound, its affairs well ordered;[33] and after long labor, he had finally begun to reap the ripe fruit[34] of peace. His body was taken for burial from Saxony[35] to a place which is called Bamberg [Pabenberg], where he himself had founded with good zeal and industry an episcopacy distinguished with every ecclesiastical appurtenance. At its dedication, he associated with himself the Apostolic Lord Pope, Benedict [VIII] by name, by whose authority he confirmed with a state covenant charters for the protection of the place. In a short time after the death of the Emperor, the commonwealth, so to speak,

---

[32] Horace, *Epistles* I, 2, 40.   [33] Cf. Sallust, *Jugurtha* 43, 5.

[34] Cf. Sallust, *Catiline* 35, 3; Ecclesiasticus 1:22; James 3:18.

[35] That is, from the palace complex of Grone, in the vicinity of Göttingen.

desolate through the loss of its father, began to stagger. From this happening all the best men had fear and anxiety that the Empire was in danger, but the worst prayed that this were so.[36] Divine Providence, however, gave the anchors of the Church into the charge of bishops and such steersmen as were needed at that time to take command in guiding the fatherland without jettison into the harbor of quiet. For when the Emperor died without children, every man of very great power among the secular princes strove by force rather than by the qualities of his character either to become the first man [of the state] or by some pact or other to become second to the first. Consequently, discord fell upon almost the whole kingdom, to such a degree that in many places there would have been slaughters, arsons, and plunders,[37] had this fury not been checked by the resistance of eminent men. The Empress Chunegunda, though deprived of her husband's strength, nevertheless by the counsel of her brothers, Theodoric, bishop of Metz, and Hezzilo, duke of Bavaria, succored the commonwealth to the best of her ability and with serious thought directed the power of her talents and mind to the restoration of the Empire.

This state of affairs[38] demands that I mention the names of some of the greatest men, bishops as well as secular princes, who thrived then in the kingdom—

By whose counsels the realm of the Franks was wont to elect kings

—so that those things which I am about to say may not seem to have come about as if by chance, but rather in order that that which is seen to have been done by the advice of the most prudent men be believed useful, honest, and the best thing.

At that time, Aribo ruled the archdiocese of Mainz, a Bavarian by birth, noble and wise, apt in royal councils; Pilgrim held the archdiocese of Cologne, a relative of Aribo the archbishop, provident and fit for that office. Poppo governed the archdiocese of Trier, a brother of Duke Ernst [I], a pious and humble man, who at that time had under his guardianship Duke Ernst [II], a son of his brother, with the dukedom of Alemannia. Theodoric, noble and valiant in virtue, possessed the episcopacy of Metz. The generous Bishop Werinhar was in charge of the bishopric of Strassburg, zealous in divine and secular duties. Mazelinus, wise and faithful in ecclesiastical offices, sat in the see of the

---

[36] Cf. Horace, *Satires* II, 6, 1.   [37] Sallust, *Catiline* 5, 1.

[38] Cf. *ibid.* 9; 52, 3. Indented phrases, like the following, are verse lines in the original.

church at Würzburg. Eberhard ruled the episcopacy of Bamberg, the first bishop of that church, a man in character and customs most indispensable to the commonwealth. Heimo was leader of the church at Constance, a man wise in God, modest and provident for the affairs of this world. Bishop Bruno ruled Augsburg, brother of Emperor Henry, useful and outstanding in character, if it [that is, his good character] had not been obscured by the hate with which he opposed his brother,[39] the Emperor. Archbishop Gunther of good memory,[40] gentle and good before God and men, brother of Counts Ekkehard and Herman,[41] ruled the church at Iuvavenia, which they call in the vernacular Salzburg. Gebhard, outstanding because of his benevolence, was bishop of the church at Regensburg. Bishop Eigilbert, provident governor of his clergy and people, ruled the church at Freising.

Together with these men, many other bishops and abbots from these same regions were present [at the election of Conrad] to name each of of whom would produce distaste for this work.[42] I have avoided mentioning the prelates of Saxony, since biographical information which may appropriately be added to their names is hidden from me, although I have assumed without any doubt that they, too, were present at those supreme affairs and that they gave counsel and succor. I pass over Italy, because her princes were unable to come to the regal election on such short notice. Afterwards, meeting the King in the city of Constance with the Archbishop of Milan and other princes, they were made his men and vowed fidelity to him with a ready spirit.

These were the dukes, on the other hand, contemporaries of the above-mentioned men: Benno, duke of Saxony; Adalbero, duke of Histria; Hezzilo, duke of Bavaria; Ernst, duke of Alamannia; Frederick,[43] duke of the Lotharingians; Gozilo, duke of the Ribuarians; Cuono of Worms, duke of the Franks;[44] Udalric, duke of Bohemia.

[39] Bruno was put under the ban of Empire in 1024.

[40] Gunther died in 1025.

[41] Margrave of Meissen.   [42] Cf. Macrobius, *Interpretatio in somnum Scipionis* I, 11, 7.

[43] The reigning duke of Lorraine at the time of Conrad's election was Theodoric, who died in 1026 or 1027. Either Wipo was confused, or Frederick was coruler with his father.

[44] The duchy of Franconia as a political entity ceased to exist at the death of Duke Eberhard in 939, when the land was claimed by Otto I for the crown. Thereafter, the crown continued to control the lands, granting the title "Duke of the Franks" or "Duke of Franconia" with some property as marks of special favor and trust. See B. Schmeidler, "Franconia's Place in the Structure of Medieval Germany," in G. Barraclough, ed. and trans., *Medieval Germany*, 911–1250 (Oxford, 1938), II, 79 ff.

Of course, Burgundy was not yet dependent upon the Roman Empire, as it is now. The fact, however, that it has now been subjected is credited to the glory of three kings. Emperor Henry II first sought to subject it and persevered successfully in this effort. Then Emperor Conrad with a spirited onslaught ejected the Latin Franks [that is, the French] from it and subjected it. Finally, King Henry III, pious, pacific, the Fine Line of Justice, governed magnanimously the same Burgundy in war and peace. I shall commemorate in another place the things which he did there by Divine Providence in the counsels of peace, as in those of war, in councils and assemblies which I myself occasionally attended.

Now I return to the principal subject.[45] We hear nothing of Hungary in the stated time, however, which the same King Henry III subdued with a noble and wondrous victory and, after the victory, made secure for himself and his successors with very wise counsel.

The above-mentioned bishops and dukes and the other powerful persons, thinking that in no other way could they avoid the threatening peril better or more quickly, strove with the greatest resourcefulness[46] and with memorable industry to the end that the commonwealth might totter no longer without a ruler. The expedient of letters and envoys made it possible to weigh private counsels[47] and the opinions of individuals as to the man to whom each would consent, to whom he would object, or whom he wanted for his lord; nor was this done in vain. For it is the part of foresight to prepare within for that which is needed without; and counsel before action is the seed of the following fruit.[48] That is to say, you wait for help from another in vain if you do not know what you want. Taking counsel secretly in difficult affairs;[49] deliberating by stages, from one point to the next; acting swiftly will have a good outcome. At last, the day had been agreed upon, and the place designated; there was a public assembly the like of which I do not remember ever having seen before. I will not put off writing about that thing worthy of memory which was done in this assembly.

II. On the Election of the King

Between the confines of Mainz and those of Worms, there is a place which could accommodate a very large crowd by virtue of its size and

---

[45] Cf. Sallust, *Jugurtha* 4, 9; Jordanes, *Chronica* 311; *Gothic History* 39; 75; 172.
[46] Sallust, *Catiline* 1, 1; 38, 2.   [47] *Ibid.* 29, 1.   [48] Cf. Ecclesiasticus 37:20.
[49] Cf. Horace, *Carmina* II, 3, 1.

flatness;[50] and some island retreats were nearby, thus making it safe and suitable for the consideration of secret matters. But I leave it to the topographers to speak more fully of the name and situation of the place, and I return to [my] undertaking.

While all the magnates, and, so to say, the valor and the vitals of the kingdom, had convened there, they pitched camps on this side and in the region about the Rhine. As it [the Rhine] separated Gaul from Germany[51] the Saxons, with their neigbors, the Slavs, the eastern Franks, the Bavarians, and the Alamanni, convened from the German side; and from Gaul, the Franks who live above the Rhine, the Ribuarians, and the Lotharingians were joined together. An affair of supreme importance was in question; there was hesitation in view of the possibility of an indecisive election. Hung between hope and fear,[52] as relatives together, so, too, members of the same households long explored alternate desires among themselves. For there was to be deliberation, not about a middling matter, but about one which, unless considered with very great zeal in a fervent breast, might be terminated to the ruin of the whole body of the kingdom. And, to use common proverbs: "Food cooked well delights the mouth; food taken raw leads to peril." And, as they say, "Medication to be put in the eyes has to be seen to carefully." When, in this fashion, a long disputation took place as to who ought to rule; and when age—too immature or, on the other hand, too greatly advanced—rejected one, untested valor, another; and a proven state of insolence, some others, few were chosen among many, and from the few two only were singled out. On them rested at last, in an instant of unity, the final examination of the greatest men, long contemplated with the utmost diligence.

Two Conrads were there, of whom one, since he was of the greater age, was named Cuono the Elder; but the other was called Cuono the Younger. Both were very noble men in German Francia, born of two brothers, one of whom was called Hezil and the other Cuono. We learn that these [latter] were born of Otto, duke of the Franks, with two others, Bruno and William. Of these, Bruno, become pope of the Apostolic See of the Roman Church, was called by a changed name Gregory [V]; and William, made bishop of the Strassburg church, exalted it in a wondrous way. Although the two aforesaid Cuonos were, as has been said, very noble on their fathers' parts, they were not at all

[50] Kamba (?).   [51] Cf. Caesar, *Gallic Wars* I, 1.
[52] Cf. Virgil, *Aeneid* I, 218; Livy VIII, 13.

less outstanding on their mothers' sides. Mathilda, the mother of Cuono the Younger, was born of the daughter[53] of Conrad, king of Burgundy. Adelheid, mother of Cuono the Elder, sprang from a very noble family of the Lotharingians. This Adelheid was the sister of Counts Gerhard and Adelbert, who, always contending with kings and dukes, to the end scarcely gave assent to the cause of their relative, King Conrad. Their forefathers, it is said, came from the ancient family of the Trojan kings, who submitted their necks to the yoke of the Faith[54] under St. Remigius the Confessor.

The rest of the nobility vacillated long between these two men—that is, the elder and the younger Conrad. And although almost everyone chose the elder Conrad by hidden counsel and eager desire because of his valor and probity, nevertheless everyone dissembled his opinion cleverly because of the power of the younger, lest they [the two men] come to strife through their ambitious desire of the honor. But finally by Divine Providence, it happened that they came into common agreement with the stipulation, fitting enough in such a doubtful matter, that if the greater part of the people should acclaim one of them, the other should yield to him without delay.

I think it a worthy thing to say by what method

the elder Cuono disclosed his character,

not because he despaired of ruling, as he already perceived that the assent of God was breathed into the hearts of the princes, but so that he might strengthen the spirit of his kinsman that it might be less perturbed amidst the new state of affairs. Therefore, he addressed him with this most outstanding speech:

"In prosperous affairs, the most becoming happiness neither exceeds the measure of gravity nor allows anyone to be ungrateful for benefices received; and, just as in adverse affairs pernicious pusillanimity draws man to the worse things, so in favorable affairs honorable pleasure leads him to the better: the fruit of felicity once borne, is of little value if it does not feed with joy well-tempered the spirit of the one who tends it.

"Thus, I feel that the vigor of my spirit is increased with great rejoicings, since in so great a gathering the common consent looked first to us two alone, to us, one of whom it may place in the regal dignity.

[53] Gerberga, wife of Herman of Swabia.
[54] Cf. II Esdras 3:5; Ecclesiasticus 51:34; Matthew 11:30.

But we ought not to think that we surpass our relatives either in nobility or possessions or that we have especially merited something worthy of such great veneration. It ill behooves us to extol with empty words ;[55] our ancestors preferred to advance their glory with deeds rather than with pronouncements.[56] Among equals

"It will become any men to be content in the common life.

But whatever that is, in which we are thought more competent for some undertaking than others, let us render thanks for it to God, its author. We must take thought, therefore, lest we who, by consent of others, are thought worthy of so great an honor seem unworthy of this favor through our own—indeed, through familial—discord. For it is exceedingly foolish to make use of the power of others instead of one's own.

"In any election, no man is allowed to pass judgment on himself, although [he may pass judgment] on another. If, indeed, anyone were permitted to pass judgment on himself, how many kinglings, not to say kings, might we see? Ours was not the power to narrow the choice for this office from many to two. Prayers, zealous efforts, the consensus of Franks, Lotharingians, Saxons, Bavarians, and Alamanni gave to us their good will, so to speak, as to the shoot of one root; just as to one house, so to an indissoluble friendship. No one will suppose that men bound together by so many reasons can be separated by enmity.

"It befits as many things as nature has bound together to be in harmony—nature who joins to herself the friendship of kinsmen.

But if, on the other hand, we reject because of some obstacle the things offered by others—that is, if we come into mutual discord—it is certain that the people will then wish to desert us and to seek for themselves some third man. And not only will we be deprived of the supreme dignity, but—and this is more detestable to all good men than death—we will fall into the reputation of baseness and jealousy, as though we were unable to uphold the high character of so great a position of command and—this I think a great crime among relatives—as though one were unwilling to yield for the honor of the other.

"The greatest dignity, therefore, the supreme power, will abide as yet about us, and it has so come to us that, if we wish, it may rest upon

---

[55] Ephesians 5:6.   [56] Sallust, *Catiline* 8, 5.

one of us. For this reason, it seems to me, if this dignity remain joined on one of us, that the other is not deprived in any way of sharing this same honor. For just as to the forebears of kings, although they may not all be kings, a certain derivative honor is transferred, so also those who are chosen and nominated before others for a position of power, although they may not come into it, nevertheless will not lack entirely a certain honor born from the fact that they were not accounted unworthy of the greatest dignity. Besides (if kinsmen of kings be honored because of their royal relations), since every one wishes to regard us as we, in the spirit of harmony, would regard each other, and since the advancement of the one depends upon the other in this fashion: who could be more happy than we, if one reign, and the other through his good will, step forth as though alone to aid the one ruling the commonwealth? Let us, therefore, be careful that we not give preference to an outsider instead of to a relative, to something uncertain instead of to something certain,[57] lest this day, hitherto happy and joyful enough because of such a judgment freely given, bear a long time of misfortunes for us, if we begrudge between us the favor conceived by so great a people.

"So that this may not come to pass on my part, most beloved of all my kinsmen, I want to say what I think concerning you. If I learn that the spirit of the people wants you, that it earnestly desires you for a lord and king, by no perversity will I divert this good will from you. Rather I shall elect you as much more avidly than the others as I should hope to be more pleasing to you than they. If, however, God should look to me, I do not doubt that you will render in turn what is due to me."

To these words, the younger Cuono answered that this whole resolve would be agreeable to him, and he promised in the most certain terms that he would render all fealty owed to the King, to him as to his dearest kinsman, if the call to the supreme power should come to him. Amidst these words, the elder Cuono, with many looking on, leaned forth a little and kissed his kinsman. By this kiss it was first discovered that each of them had made his peace with the other. Hence, after the affirmation of this token of concord, the princes sat down together, and a very large crowd stood immediately at hand:

Each man rejoiced that the time was at hand when he was allowed to bring forth openly what he had long covered in his heart.

[57] *Ibid.* 20, 2; Sallust, *Jugurtha* 83, 1.

The Deeds of Conrad II   65

The Archbishop of Mainz, whose opinion had to be taken before all, asked by the people what was seemly to him, with a full heart and a happy voice, acclaimed and elected the elder Cuono as his lord and king, and rector and defender of the fatherland. The other archbishops and the remaining men of holy orders unhesitatingly followed him in this vote. The younger Cuono, who had been negotiating for a short time with the Lotharingians, returned suddenly and elected him as lord and king with the greatest good will. The King, taking him by the hand, made him sit beside him.

Then, one by one, men from each of the several realms repeated the same words of election again and again; there was a shout of acclamation by the people; all consented unanimously with the princes in the election of the King; all eagerly desired the elder Cuono. On him they insisted; him they placed without any hesitation before all the mighty lords; him they judged to be most worthy of the regal power; and they demanded that there be no delay of his consecration. The above-mentioned Empress Chunegunda graciously brought forth the regal insignia which the Emperor Henry had left to her and supported him for governance as far as lay within the authority of her sex. I believe that the good will of heavenly powers, indeed, was not absent from this election, since among men of singular power, among so many dukes and margraves, he was elected without malice, without controversy; he, who, although he was inferior to no one in family and in valor and in allodial goods, nevertheless in comparison with such men held of the state but little in fief and in power.

Although the Archbishop of Cologne and Duke Frederick, with certain other Lotharingians, departed belligerent, as was said, on the younger Cuono's account (but, in fact, at the instigation of the Devil, the enemy of peace), they, nevertheless, returned swiftly to the favor of the King, with the exception of those whom the common state of death had caught. Whatever he ordered, they accepted gratefully. And Archbishop Pilgrim, as if in emendation of his former wrong, besought the King that he be allowed to consecrate the Queen in the church at Cologne.

Of her I am going to speak subsequently. Now I shall return to the King. Truly, by the assent of God was he elected whose later acknowledgment by men as king had been foreseen by God. For he was a man of great humility, provident in counsel, truthful in statements, vigorous in deeds, not at all greedy, the most liberal of all kings in giving.

I shall speak afterwards more fully of his habits. This, however, must be said here, that he could never have failed to become a prince—and the greatest prince—in whom was the strength of the greatest virtues. For since it has been written, "Humility surpasses glory,"[58] he to whom the queen of virtues adhered surpassed rightly the glorious of this world. It was not, therefore, in accord with divine law for anyone on earth to fight against him whom Omnipotent God had predestined to govern all.

III. On the Consecration of the King

When the election was over, everyone, with the greatest eagerness, hastened to follow the King to Mainz, where he was to receive the most holy unction. They went rejoicing;[59] the clergy chanted psalms, the layfolk sang, each in his own fashion. At no time have I found that God received such great praises from men on one day in one place.

If Charlemagne had been present, alive, with his scepter, the people would not have been more eager, nor could they have rejoiced more at the return of so great a man than at the first coming of this King. The King arrived at Mainz. And there, received with due honor, he waited devoutly for his consecration, [as one] desirable to all. When the Archbishop of Mainz and all the clergy solemnly prepared themselves to bless him on the day of the birth of St. Mary, the Archbishop delivered this sermon to the King during the sacred offices of regal unction:

"All power of this transient age is derived from one most pure font. It is usually the case, however, that when several rivulets spring forth from the same source, at one time they are turbulent, at another, clear, while at their head, the font stays fast in its purity. In the same way, inasmuch as the human state dares to set Creator and creation side by side for comparison, we have the power to conjecture in a similar way about God the Immortal King and about earthly kings. For it has been written: 'All power is of God.'[60] When this Omnipotent King of kings, the author and the beginning of all honor, pours the grace of some dignity upon princes of the earth, insofar as it is in accord with the nature of its origin, it is pure and unstained. When, however, it has come to those who wield this dignity unworthily and pollute it with pride, malice, lust, avarice, wrath, impatient willfullness, and cruelty,[61] they will serve the perilous potion of iniquity to themselves and to all subject

[58] Proverbs 15:33.   [59] Cf. Acts 5:41.   [60] Cf. Romans 13:1.
[61] Cf. Sallust, *Catiline* 10, 4.

to them,[62] unless they purge themselves by doing penance. O let the whole Church of the Saints pray and intercede before God that the dignity which is offered pure today by God to our present lord and king, Conrad, be preserved inviolate by him as far as is humanly possible.

"Our sermon is with you and for you, O Lord King. The Lord, who elected you to be king over His people,[63] has wished first to test you and to have you rule afterwards. For he scourges all whom He received[64] He sees fit to assail the one whom he has wished from an earlier time[65] to receive; it pleases Him to humble him whom He has designed to exalt.[66] So God tried Abraham his servant and glorified the one tried. So He permitted David, his bondman, to suffer the wrath of King Saul, persecution, injuries, the haunts of the desert, flight and exile—David whom afterwards He made the most glorious king in Israel. Blessed is he who suffers trial, since he will receive the crown.[67] Not without cause has God exercised you; He has sweetened that which was to come to fruition within you. He permitted you to lose the favor of your predecessor, the Emperor Henry, and to receive the same again, that now you may know how to be merciful to those who lose your favor; you have suffered injuries that now you may know how to be merciful to those who sustain injuries. Divine Piety has been unwilling for you to be without preparatory discipline, so that after this instruction from Heaven you might take up the Christian Empire. You have come to the highest dignity: you are the vicar of Christ.

"No one but his imitator is a true ruler. It is necessary that in this 'throne of the kingdom' you reflect on the perpetual honor. It is great felicity to rule in the world, but the greatest is to triumph in Heaven. Although God requires many things of you, He wishes most of all that you render judgment and justice,[68] and peace for the fatherland, which always looks to you; and [He wishes] that you be the defender of churches and clerics, the guardian of widows and orphans. With these and other good [works] your throne will be firmly established here and forever.[69]

"And now, Lord King, all Holy Church asks with us your favor for those who hitherto have transgressed against you and have lost your favor through some offense. Of these, there is one, Otto by name, a noble man, who offended you. We pray your clemency for him and for all the rest, that you may grant pardon to them for the love of God

[62] Cf. Jeremiah 25 : 15.   [63] I Kings 8 : 16.   [64] Hebrews 12 : 6.   [65] Cf. Proverbs 3 : 12.
[66] Cf. Luke 14 : 11.   [67] James 1 : 12.   [68] I Kings 10 : 9.   [69] Proverbs 29 : 14.

which has changed you today into another man[70] and has made you a sharer of His will,[71] to the end that He may deign to repay you in kind for all your transgressions."

During this sermon, the King, moved by compassion, sighed and, even more (how could it be believed?),[72] broke into tears. Thereupon, as the bishops and the dukes with all the people petitioned, he pardoned all whatever transgressions they had done against him.

The whole people received this gratefully. All cried out for joy when the piety of the King had been manifested:

> Beastlike would have been the man who could not be moved to tears that such great power ignored such great wrongs.

And although he would have been able to avenge his wrongs, even if he had never become king, nevertheless he was not led by reliance in such great power to reserve anything for vengeance.

When the divine offices and the regal consecration had been performed most fittingly, the King began the procession. And, as is read of Saul the king, he returned with the holy company to his chamber with an eager countenance and a noble step, as though he went higher "than any of the people from his shoulder and upward"[73] and as if he had been transformed into a bearing not seen before in him. After that he was received with regal magnificence at dinner and consumed this first day of royal splendor as was most suitable for his office.

IV. On the Disposition of Offices and On the Queen

I think it rather unnecessary to speak of the fealty rendered to the King, because of the evidence borne by frequent practice that all bishops, dukes, and the other princes, vassals of primary rank and those of ordinary rank, indeed, all free-born men if they be of any moment, render fealty to kings. At any rate, all submitted themselves to him quite sincerely and willingly by oath.

Similarly, in the disposition of offices, one need not dwell long on whom the King established mayor of the palace, whom he ordained chamberlains, whom, stewards and cupbearers and other officials,[74] although I can say briefly that I neither remember nor have read that

[70] Cf. I Samuel 10:6.   [71] Cf. Hebrews 6:4.   [72] Cf. Sallust, *Catiline* 5, 3.

[73] I Samuel 10:23.

[74] The omission of the marshal, or constable, from this list of state officials is notable.

the ministries [that is, the offices of State] of any of his predecess6rs were provided for more suitably and honorably. In this matter, the ingenuity of Bishop Bruno of Augsburg and the advice of Bishop Werinhar of Salzburg availed much; so, too, that of the vassal Werinhar, whom the King through long association had found cautious in counsel, bold in wars.

The beloved wife of the King, Gisela, was held in esteem above all these because of her prudence and counsel. Her father was Herman, duke of Alamannia; her mother, Gerberga, daughter of Conrad, king of Burgundy, whose forebears had proceeded from the stock of Charlemagne. One of us,[75] because of this, set forth two verses, among others, in this fashion in a book which he called *Tetralogus* and afterwards presented to King Henry III, when he celebrated in Augsburg the birth of the Lord:

"When the fourth line after the tenth is numbered, prudent Gisela proceeds from Charlemagne."[76]

Although she was characterized by such great nobility and by a most becoming appearance, she was marked by no arrogant pride; fearful in the service of God, assiduous in prayers and almsgiving (and in this acting as secretly as possible, attending that Gospel precept that one not do one's acts of justice before men).[77] She was liberal of character; distinguished by ingenuity; avid of glory, but not of praise; loving of modesty; patient of womanly labor; not at all extravagant in useless matters, but abundantly generous in the honorable and useful; rich in estates; qualified through experience to administer well the highest dignities. She was for some days kept from her consecration by the malice of certain men,[78] which often goes up like vapor from inferiors to superiors. For the rest, whether she suffered that hatred justly or unjustly remains even now in question; at any rate, the manly probity in the woman was victorious, and by the consent and petition of the princes, she was consecrated and followed the King as his necessary companion. This much have I briefly inserted about the Queen, interrupting the account of the deeds of the King; now I shall return to the latter.

[75] Wipo's usual way of referring to himself.

[76] Wipo alludes to the design of a geneological table.   [77] Matthew 6:1.

[78] Aribo of Mainz refused to crown Gisela because her marriage to Conrad was within the forbidden limits. The ground for his objections is unclear, although they may have lain in Gisela's second marriage, to Herman II of Swabia.

V. Of the First Deeds of King Conrad

Turning our pen to the deeds of the excellent King Conrad, certain things must be told which he did on the very day of his consecration. For although they may seem small, nonetheless they are eminently significant in a mystical way. But since this is written as a state history [*historia publica*] which makes the spirit of the reader more attentive to the new turns of events than to the figurative meaning of words, it seems more fitting simply to follow this affair through in its entirety instead of mixing in some comment with mystic reasonings.

During the very procession of the King, three persons came before him, each with his own complaints. One was a tenant farmer of the church of Mainz; another was an orphan; and the third was a certain widow. When the King began to hear their cases, certain of his princes turned him aside, saying that he should make no delay of his consecration and that he should attend the divine offices as quickly as possible. Looking toward the bishops, he responded like a vicar of Christ in a most Christian way: "If it is my part to apply myself in government, and if it is the part of the constant man never to put off what can be done suitably, it seems to me more upright[79] to do what I ought than to hear from another what should be done. I remember that you have said often that not the hearers of the law, but the doers are made just.[80] If, however, one must haste to the consecration, as you say, it behooves me to set my footsteps firmly in the work of God so much the more carefully as I know that I draw near to that exacting dignity." Saying these words, he stopped at that spot where these unfortunates had first met him,

With feet unmoved, he set the law before them.

When he had proceeded thence somewhat, a certain man came before him saying that he had been expelled from the fatherland entirely without fault on his part. The King, taking him by the arm, drew him along to his throne, above all those standing around, and there he diligently commended the cause of the poor man to one of his princes.[81]

Happy is thought the inception of governance,

when more haste is made to do the law than to bless the King. The zeal

---

[79] Sallust, *Catiline* 1, 3.   [80] Romans 2:13.   [81] 1024.

for mercy was more abundant in the King than the desire for consecration; he advanced through the path of righteousness,[82] when he sought the regal honor. He was able to sing with the Psalmist: "My foot stands in the right way."[83] He strengthened himself through the good of grace, before he mounted the throne of the judge. He feared to be thrown down, should he not show equity in the regal loftiness. It was quite laudable, amidst the new joys, amidst the pleasurable ministrations of the king, to hear the complaints of so many paupers and to decide their cases. He was unwilling to neglect what he could swiftly put in order. He declined to defer doing justice, since that was the essence of ruling. He delayed his benediction for the sake of the royal honor; for it has been written: "The honor of the king loves judgment."[84]

In all affairs, nothing can be of such benefit
As the judgment of the king in his office.

Thus the King in such causes, for which the regal authority is wont to be solicited most of all—that is, for the defense of churches, widows, and orphans—prepared for himself that day the way to the remaining affairs of government.

VI. On the Journey of the King through the Realms[85]

I have thought it not too necessary to narrate all the journeys of the King and to mention the places in which he celebrated each year the festivals of the birth of the Lord, and those of Easter, with the exception of whatever must be said if at any place something outstanding and renowned occurred. For if I wished to notice everything, my own strength would run out before my material.[86] As soon as I can, I shall come to his most renowned deeds, in which he stood out in so much glory that silence concerning his lesser deeds cannot be displeasing to any one.

When the regal entourage had been assembled, King Conrad first went through the region of the Ribuarians to the place which is called

---

[82] Psalm 23:3 and *passim*.   [83] Psalm 26:12.   [84] Psalm 99:4.

[85] "Iter Regis per Regna," which, as Klewitz has shown, denotes the solemn "progress," the ritual journey of the king with the symbols of his office, to announce his status to his subjects. H.W. Klewitz, "Die Festkrönungen der deutschen Könige." *ZfRG K. A.*, XXVIII (1939), 81.

[86] Cf. Sallust, *Jugurtha* 42, 5.

Aquisgrani palatium [that is, the Pfalz, or palace complex of Aachen], the place where the regal throne of state was set up by the kings of old, and especially by Charles [Charlemagne], and which is regarded as the archthrone of the whole realm. Sitting on it, he ordered most excellently the affairs of the commonwealth; and he held a popular assembly and a general council there, in which he distributed divine and human [that is, spiritual and temporal] rights with efficacious results.

His fame took strength from his virtues: every day he was held by all more outstanding than the day before, for the fastness of peace, more dear for the grace of benevolence, more honored for regal judgment. For although he was ignorant of letters, nevertheless he prudently instructed every cleric not only lovingly and courteously in public, but also with fitting discipline in secret. He disposed his vassals well toward himself in that he did not suffer the ancient benefices of parents to be taken away from any of their progeny. Besides, as regards the frequent gifts by which he constrained them to dare brave deeds, they thought that his like could not be found in the whole world. It would arouse suspicion to tell how munficent he was, how agreeable; of what a constant, of how undaunted a soul; gentle to all good men, severe to evil; kindly toward subjects, harsh toward enemies; effective in action; indefatigable in his effort to be of the greatest service to the kingdom—in brief, so proficient that no one could doubt that after the days of Charlemagne no other man more worthy of the regal seat had lived. Thus, there is still the proverb: "The saddle of Conrad has the stirrup of Charles." As regards this proverb, a certain one of us proffered this verse in the fourth satire of a book which he called Gallinarius:

Conrad steps upon the stirrup of Charles the king.

With such tokens the name or glory of the King transcends the regions of the heathen, transnavigates the sea floods. Everywhere was spread the valor which always flowed forth [from him] in unslackening force.

After his return from the Ribuarians, the King went to Saxony; there he confirmed by his unchanging authority the very cruel law of the Saxons, according to their desire. Then, exacting tribute payments from the barbarians who border on Saxony, he received all the income owed him.[87] From there he went to Alamannia, passing through Bavaria

[87] 1025.

and eastern Franconia. In this progress, he bound the realms very firmly in a bond of peace and in royal guardianship.

VII. How the King Held an Assembly with the Italians

In the first year of his reign, King Conrad celebrated the holy day of Pentecost in the city of Constance. There Aribert, archbishop of Milan, met the King with the other Italian optimates and became his man. And he faithfully promised to him, through the security of oaths and hostages, that when he [Conrad] came with an army to subject Italy, he [Aribert] would receive him and acclaim him publicly with all his men as lord and king and would crown him straightway. The remaining Lombards acted similarly, with the exception of the Ticinenses, who are also called by another name, Pavians. Their legates were on hand with gifts and patrons, striving to placate the King in the matter of an offense of their citizens. But they were in no wise able to obtain this [forgiveness] from the king according to their desire.

I shall relate briefly[88] how they had offended. There was in the city of Pavia a palace once built with marvelous workmanship by King Theodoric and afterwards much adorned by Emperor Otto III. When the death of Emperor Henry, the predecessor of King Conrad, became known, however (as men are wont always to be intemperate when placed in unfamiliar circumstances), the Pavians, running at once to the defenseless palace, ill-advisedly shattered with illicit daring the walls of the King and razed the whole palace to the last stone of the foundation so thoroughly that it was as if no king had ever decreed that a palace be set within that city. Because of this audacity, a great and lengthy disputation was held between the King and the Pavians. The Pavians said: "Whom have we offended? We were faithful and honored our Emperor [Henry II] until the end of his life. Since we had no king after he died, we will not be accused legally of having destroyed the house of our king." The King said in opposition, "I know that you have not destroyed the house of your king, since you had none at that time; but you cannot deny that you have rent asunder a regal house. Even if the king died, the kingdom remained, just as the ship whose steersman falls remains. They were state, not private, buildings; they were under another law, not yours. Those, however, who trespass against propor-

---

[88] Cf. Sallust, *Catiline* 4, 3.

ties of others are hateful to the king. You, then, trespassed against properties of others; therefore you are hateful to the king." After many words of this sort had been bandied about vehemently, the legates departed in failure, abandoning the attempt at peace. But the rest of the Italians were dismissed in peace, honored with very ample gifts by the King. And the King, when the realm of the Suevi had been put in good order, went to the castle of Zürich, and there he received into his overlordship some Italians who had not come to Constance. From there, after a few days, he came to the city of Basel.

VIII. That King Conrad Appointed the Bishop of Basel

The city of Basel is situated on a triple frontier—that is, that of Burgundy, Alamannia, and Francia.[89] But the city itself belongs to Burgundy. The King found this city devoid of a bishop, since its shepherd, Adalbero, had departed from this world three months before the King came.[90] There the simoniac heresy suddenly appeared and swiftly vanished. For while the King and the Queen received an immense sum of money for the episcopacy from a certain cleric, a noble by the name of Udalric who was then made bishop there, the King, afflicted later with contrition, obligated himself by solemn vow to receive no more money for any episcopacy or abbacy. He kept to this vow fairly well. But his son, the third Henry, who afterwards became King and Augustus, made good completely and without any hesitation his father's vow. For it is said that he has not accepted the price of one obol[91] for any ecclesiastical dignity through his whole life, until this very time.

When a regal assembly had been held at Basel, and the border regions of Burgundy had been occupied carefully, over the will of Rudolf, king of that same Burgundy, King Conrad went by the Rhine to Saxony.

I shall say briefly why I should remember King Rudolf. This Rudolf, king of Burgundy, as he administered his kingdom weakly in his old age, gave rise to very great ill-will among the princes of his kingdom.

---

[89] It is unclear whether Wipo means France or Franconia.

[90] Actually, scarcely a month and a half passed between Adalbero's death (May 12, 1025) and Conrad's entrance (June 23, 1025).

[91] The coin of the smallest value minted in the early Middle Ages. It was of silver, or silver alloys, and its value was one-half that of the denarius. In general, it weighed from 0.46 to 0.70 grams. Specimens from the pre-Hohenstaufen period are now quite rare. See H. Dannenberg, *Die deutschen Münzen der sachsischen und fränkischen Kaiserzeit* (Berlin, 1876), I, 261, no. 667, plate 29.

For he invited the second Henry, the Emperor, the son of his sister, into his kingdom, designated him king of Burgundy after his death, and made the princes of the kingdom render an oath to him.[92] Emperor Henry, to promote this affair, used often—indeed, very often—an infinite amount of money. But when Emperor Henry died, King Rudolf sought to invalidate his promises. King Conrad, however, intent on increasing the kingdom rather than decreasing it, and wishing to reap the labors of his predecessor, subjected Basel to himself, so that he could observe carefully whether King Rudolf would attend his promises. Afterwards, Queen Gisela, daughter of the sister of this same King Rudolf, made peace between them.[93]

IX. Of Boleslaus, Duke of the Slavs

In the same year [1025] which I have mentioned above, Boleslaus Sclavigen,[94] duke of the Poles, took for himself in injury to King Conrad the regal insignia and the royal name. Death swiftly killed his temerity.[95] But his son Misico, similarly rebellious, cast his own brother Otto out into the province of Russia, because he favored the partisans of the King. I shall tell in its proper place how King Conrad afterwards curbed the impudence of this Misico and the perfidy of a certain Udalric, duke of Bohemia.

X. Of the Enmity between the King and Duke Ernst

At the same time, by the suasions of that enemy of peace, the Devil, Ernst, duke of Alamannia, Cuono, duke of Franconia, and Frederick, duke of the Lotharingians,[96] came into agreement with many others against King Conrad. But although they attempted many things and prepared many strongholds, it was in vain; for they pursued nothing but calamity. Since King Conrad considered them all of little moment, he decided on a military expedition with his troops into Italy. Duke Ernst humbly followed his train to Augsburg where he was received into his favor, though with much difficulty—for the King refused for a long time—by the intervention of his mother the Queen and of his brother Henry, then a boy, and of other princes.

---

[92] In 1016 and 1019.   [93] 1027.   [94] That is, "of the Slavic nation."   [95] 1025.
[96] Frederick had not yet recognized Conrad as king.

XI. That the King Went to Italy with His Army

In the year of the incarnation of the Christ, 1026, King Conrad, by the counsel and petition of the princes of the realm, designated his son, the boy Henry, to be king after him and commended him in guardianship to Bruno, bishop of the church at Augsburg. And diligently placing snares for his above-mentioned enemies through the agency of his son and his other vassals, he himself set out for Italy with a copious army. During this expedition, the above-mentioned Ernst, duke of Alamannia, after he had fought for some time for the King, received from the King the abbey of Kempten, although it was against divine and mortal law that a free institution serve any way other than in freedom. And Duke Ernst was sent back honorably to guard the fatherland.[97]

XII. That the King Beset the Pavians

After the King had entered Italy, he came to Vercelli by way of Verona, passing between Milan and Pavia, and celebrated there the holy Easter. In those days of the Easter season, Leo, the bishop of that city,

A man of great wisdom, left the world in peace.

Harderic, a canon of Milan, succeeded him. Although the King had already subjected almost all the Italian plain to his governance, he was not able to take the city of Pavia with dispatch, since it was quite populous. He was unwilling to receive those Pavians into favor, since they still refused to rebuild the palace which they had destroyed in the place where it stood formerly. But he began in a remarkable fashion to press hard their defenders, Adalbert the margrave and William and the other princes within those regions. He laid desolate their castle named Orbe and demolished many other castles and very strong fortresses.

In this tempest, evil was done mightily in Italy because of the contentions of the Pavians; many of their churches in the surrounding region were burned with these castles, and the populace which had fled there perished by fire and the sword. Fields were laid waste; vines, cut off. The King prohibited exit and entrance; he stopped shipping by river;

[97] 1026.

he forbade the exchange of goods; and thus for two years he beset the Ticinenses, until, without any further delay, they complied with all his orders.[93]

XIII. Of the Uprising which Took Place at Ravenna

At this same time, King Conrad entered Ravenna and ruled there with great power. One day the wretched Ravennese provoked a struggle with the army of the King, and, trusting in their great number, they strove to expel the army from the city. Taking advantage of the narrowness of a certain gate, they prohibited those who were without from succoring those within. Once the rebellion had been stirred up, the battle began to grow serious in all quarters. Some assailed those billeted in their houses; others fought in the streets; still others obstructed the gates.

Many from the walls, many from the high turrets

were guilty of a dastardly kind of battle, with stones and sharpened stakes. On the other side, the Germans resisted with arms and ingenuity and, paring off detachments, beset the Ravennese from the front and from the rear. Making their way toward each other with raging swords, they left those who were between them dead, wounded, or fleeing. A certain count, Eppo by name, a very good knight from Bavaria, left the city with the banner and struck down those who stood upon the bridge. Most of those hurled down from the bridge by the sole effort of this man perished in the water. When King Conrad learned of this revolt, just as he was in his bedchamber, he seized his arms and demanded his horse. After leaving the hall, he saw the Ravennese overcome in the fight flee to churches and seek refuge everywhere, and he had mercy upon them, since those of both sides were his men. He recalled his army from the pursuit of the citizens, and he retired to the palace. In the morning, however, the Ravennese who were left came before the King, as he ordered—in sackcloth and bare feet and with unsheathed swords, as their law demanded of conquered citizens—and rendered satisfaction in all ways. There King Conrad displayed in his accustomed fashion the greatest munificence to a certain wounded

---

[98] 1027. No subsequent mention was made of a royal palace within the walls of Pavia, although in the twelfth century a palace stood outside them.

German, whose foot with a great part of the calf above the ankle was wholly cut away in the battle. The King ordered that his leather leggins be brought, and he had both of them filled with coins and placed upon the cot of the wounded soldier beside him.[99]

XIV. The King Withdrew to the Mountains Because of the Heat

At this time, very great heat vexed Italy, so great that the dumb animals and a great number of men were endangered by it. But King Conrad, yielding to no one save to God alone and to summer heat, withdrew into the mountains beyond the Etsch River because of the shady places and the moderate temperature of the air there. There for two months and more he was furnished sumptuously, through the purveyance of the Archbishop of Milan, with the supplies due a king. He departed from there at the time of autumn and traveled again through the Italian plain. By holding councils and regal assemblies in opportune places, and by committing rebels to chains, he pacified the kingdom. And by progressing thus through the land, he came to the border of Italy and Burgundy.

XV. That Legates of King Rudolf Came to King Conrad in Italy

At the beginning of the year of the nativity of the Christ, 1027, King Conrad celebrated in Ivrea the birth of the Lord. There legates of Rudolf, king of Burgundy, came, giving assurance that he would come to Rome to the imperial election and consecration of King Conrad. The King gratefully received this news, and when the legates had been sent back with gifts, he began to advance toward Rome, crossing the Po River. Coming, however, to Lucca, he found the city together with Margrave Reginhar in opposition to him. There the King, after a brief delay of a few days, received the surrender of the city and the margrave and within a short time subjected all Tuscany to himself.

[99] The earliest grant of the right of coinage to the Ravennese known is a grant by Henry III in 1043 to the archbishop. No Ravennese coins prior to 1232 survive, and it is probable that none were made before that time. From the Carolingian period, the chief Imperial mint in Lombardy was at Pavia, and it is probable that the coins mentioned here were taken from the Pavian mint, which struck for Conrad II. See *Corpus Nummorum Italicorum*, IV, 487; X, 682.

XVI. That King Conrad Was Made Emperor at Rome

Therefore, King Conrad, having entered Rome in the same year as above—that is, 1027 from the nativity of the Savior, in the tenth indiction—was wondrously received by Pope John [XIX] and all the Romans with royal honor. And on the holy day of Easter, which fell that year on the VII of the kalends of April, he was elected emperor by the Romans, and he received the imperial benediction from the Pope,

Called Caesar and Augustus by the Roman name.

And more, Queen Gisela received at the same time the consecration and the name of empress. After these things were done thus in the presence of two kings—of Rudolf, king of Burgundy, and of Canute, king of the Angles—and after the divine office was ended, the Emperor was led to his chamber in the place of honor between the two kings.

In those Easter days, a great conflict broke out between the Romans and the Germans because of a lowly matter. Two men contended for the hide of an ox, and when they had begun to strike one another with blows, the whole army of the Emperor was aroused, and armed horsemen and footsoldiers gathered from every side. A certain young man, Berengar by name, son of Liutold, a count of Alamannia, was killed there on our side, a man very noble and extremely warlike. After long resistance, the Romans fled, overcome at last, and innumerable of them perished. But the Emperor ordered that the aforesaid youth, since he had been dear to him and a member of his household, be buried beside the tomb of the Caesar Otto [II]. On the next day, the Romans who had provoked the rebellion came before the Emperor with bare feet—free men with naked swords, slaves with twisted plaits about the neck, as though prepared for hanging—and gave satisfaction, as the Emperor ordered.

XVII. That the Emperor Came to Apulia

After peace had been made, therefore, between the Romans and the Germans, the Emperor advanced into Apulia and subjected to himself Beneventum and Capua and the remaining cities of this region, either by force or by voluntary surrender.[100] And to the Normans, who, com-

---

[100] Sallust, *Jugurtha* 13, 2.

pelled by some necessity or other, had flocked together into Apulia
from their country, he gave permission to live there, and he established a union of them with his princes to defend the borders of the
realm against the treachery of the Greeks. When all other affairs came
to pass happily and in good order for him, the Emperor turned back
and went again through Italy, bypassing Rome.

XVIII. Of the Wicked Lord[101] Thasselgard

At that time in Italy, there was a certain wicked lord called Thassel-
gard, who had committed many crimes in the kingdom in the time of
Emperor Henry. But by seaside retreats and other fortifications, which
he kept immeasurably safe,[102] he had been able to evade the pursuit of
Caesar Henry. Noble though he was by descent, he was despicable in
person, reprehensible in habits, a great predator of churches and widows. The Emperor Conrad hunted him down most diligently and arranged ambushes for him on all sides and in every way. [At last] when
he wanted to flee from one of his castles to another, he was captured
by soldiers of Caesar.

When the Emperor heard this, he hastened with such great speed
that he transversed almost one hundred Latin miles in a day and a night.
For he thought that he might escape again in his accustomed way.
When the Emperor arrived, the wicked lord was presented to him.
When he saw him, the Emperor is reputed to have said, "Is this not
that lion which has devoured the game of Italy? By the Holy Cross of
the Lord, such a lion will eat no more of my bread." Thus he said, and,
with the other princes of the kingdom sitting in judgment, he straightway ordered that he be hanged on a gallows. After he had been hanged,
peace and security, which had long lain hidden, emerged at once
through all that province.

XIX. On the Conspiracy of Certain Germans

In the meantime, while the Emperor was staying in Italy, great malice, many plans, many factions arose among the Germans against the
the Emperor, though to no avail.

To begin with the lesser and to come to the greater: a certain count

[101] "Tyrannus." See general introduction, p. 34 f.
[102] The center of his activities was the region about Fermo.

in Swabia, named Welf, rich in estates, powerful in arms, and Bruno, bishop of Augsburg, clashed between themselves and produced many evils in the kingdom though their lootings and burnings. Finally, the aforesaid count invaded Augsburg itself, despoiled the treasury of the bishop, and laid waste the whole city. Later, under the constraint of the Emperor, he restored everything and made amends to the Bishop.

Cuono, duke of Worms, cousin of the Emperor, who was neither faithful to the Emperor nor, on the other hand, very harmful to him, remained quiet for the time being. Frederick, duke of the Lotharingians, stepfather of the aforesaid Cuono, was prevented by his own death from acting as an enemy of the Emperor.[103]

Ernst, duke of Alamannia, stepson of Emperor Conrad, only lately exalted by him with benefices and gifts, deserted him and, at the instigation of the Devil, promoted a rebellion again. By the advice of certain of his vassals, he devastated the province of Alsace and laid desolate castles of Count Hugo, who was a relative of the Emperor.[104] After that, he assembled a great army of young men, invaded Burgundy, and began to fortify a certain island above castle Solothurn with breastworks and ramparts. But because Rudolf, king of the Burgundians, was afraid to harbor an enemy of the Emperor, he forbade the undertaking to him. After [Ernst] had returned from there, he fortified a certain castle above Zürich and incurred no ordinary condemnation by the fatherland, by harassing to a very great degree the church of Reichenau and the abbey of St. Gall. With law and justice thus set aside, he stood fast in his iniquitous endeavors until the return of the Emperor.

XX. Where Duke Ernst Surrendered Himself Again

After peace had been confirmed through all Italy, Emperor Conrad returned to Alamannia in great prosperity and began to take counsel about those who had betrayed the fatherland, holding an assembly of the royal household with his vassals in Augsburg. Coming thence to the town which is called Ulm, he held there a publicly announced assembly.

Duke Ernst did not come here with a suppliant vow.

---

[103] Wipo here, as in chap. 1, has confused Frederick, who died in 1033, with his father Theodoric, who died in 1026 or 1027.

[104] The reference is to Hugh IV of Egisheim, father of Pope Leo IX. His father, Hugh III, was a brother of Conrad's mother, Adelheid.

But relying on the great number of the best of his vassals[105] whom he had with him, [he came] in order that he might either make peace with Caesar according to his own taste or leave from there [unimpeded] by virtue of his own power. And when an assembly with his own men had been held, he first reminded them of their sworn promise of fealty [to him]; then he exhorted them not to desert him, lest they lose their honor. [He added] that it would not be seemly for them to be mindless of the fact that in their ancestral histories the Alamanni had always borne witness of good faith and steadfastness toward their lords and that, if they were faithful to him, there would be rewards for themselves and glory and honor for their posterity.

To these words of his, two counts, Frederick and Anselm,[106] responded for the others in this fashion:

"We do not wish to deny that we promised fealty to you firmly against all except him who gave us to you. If we were slaves of our king and emperor, subjected by him to your jurisdiction, it would not be permissible for us to separate ourselves from you. But now, since we are free, and hold our king and emperor the supreme defender of our liberty on earth, as soon as we desert him, we lose our liberty, which no good man, as someone says, loses save with his life. Since this is so, we are willing to obey whatever honorable and just requirement you make of us. If, however, you will something which is contrary to this, we shall return freely into that position whence we came under certain conditions to you."

After hearing these remarks, the Duke realized that he was abandoned by his own men and therefore rendered himself to the Emperor without any negotiated agreement. Caesar made him go into exile in Saxony to a certain crag which is called Gibichenstein [Giebichenstein], so that, confined there, he might desist from any further rebellion once and for all.

XXI. That the King of Burgundy Came to Meet the Emperor at Basel[107]

The Emperor, transversing Alamannia, received in surrender all who had been rebels against him and cast down their bulwarks. Going through to Basel, he talked to Rudolf, king of Burgundy, who came to meet him there outside the city at a village which is called Muttenz.

---

105 Cf. Hosea 10: 13; Sallust, *Jugurtha* 13, 3.
106 Probably the counts of Riessgau and Nordgau.   107 1027.

And after a familiar discussion, the Emperor took the king with him into the city. When peace had been confirmed between them—the Empress Gisela mediating in all these matters—and the kingdom of Burgundy had been given over to the Emperor with the same sort of agreement as that by which it had been given earlier to his predecessor, Emperor Henry, the King [Rudolf], enriched again with gifts, returned with his own men into Burgundy.

But the Emperor, descending by the Rhine, came into Franconia, and there Duke Cuono, his cousin, formerly a rebel, gave himself up. The Emperor confined him for some time under light guard, and after his bulwarks had been destroyed—the best which he had—he received him into favor and restored his full honor to him. Shortly after, Adalbero, duke of the [H] istrians or Carinthians, convicted of lese majesty, was exiled with his sons by the Emperor,[108] and that Cuono just mentioned received from the Emperor his [Adalbero's] dukedom, which the father of this very Cuono is said to have had once. So Duke Cuono, as long as he lived,[109] remained faithful and one who strove well for the Emperor and also for his son, King Henry.

XXII. Of the Legation of the Bishop of Strassburg

At this same time, Werner, bishop of the city of Strassburg, was sent by the Emperor as an ambassador to Constantinople. While he pretended that he was going to Jerusalem to pray, he was thwarted in a wondrous way, as we think,

By the judgment of the Lord, whom no one will be able to deceive.

For while he led forth with him a large train of men, but a larger one of dumb animals—horses, oxen, sheep, pigs—and many worldly delicacies—all beyond measure—on coming into Hungary, passage was forbidden to him by King Stephan, something which at that time never happened to pilgrims. After he had returned thence through Bavaria, he went on with all his entourage and entered Italy. When he had tarried much about the territorial bounds of Verona, he reached with very great labor the Adriatic Sea through Venice and finally arrived in Constantinople after a calamitous sea voyage. And after he had been received honorably by the Emperor of the Greeks,[110] and he [the

---

[108] Actually this occurred in 1035. See Wipo chap. 33.
[109] He died in 1039.   [110] Constantine VIII.

latter] had associated with him in a very familiar way, he began to wish to go to Jerusalem with the assistance of the Emperor. Since some other affair always intervened, he was never able to realize this desire. But after the passage of some time, he died[111] and was buried in the same city [Constantinople]. William, a canon of Strassburg, received his episcopacy. Afterwards, the Emperor of the Greeks[112] reported to Emperor Conrad the condition of the legation, with a letter written in gold.

XXIII. *That the Emperor Had His Son Henry Consecrated King*

With the approval of the princes of the kingdom together with the whole multitude of the people, in the year of the Lord 1028, in the eleventh indiction, Emperor Conrad had his son Henry, a boy of great capacity and good disposition, aged eleven years, exalted to the highest regal honor at the palace complex at Aachen, by Pilgrim, archbishop of Cologne. Then, consecrated and crowned on the principal Sabbath of Eastertide, he trebled the Easter happiness. For while in former years the world venerated two crowns, that is, those of his father and mother, now a third had been added.

Hope increased for the peace which King with Caesar made,

especially as his age at the time of his coronation promised quite a long life. Then, going through divers realms, Caesar through his own efforts, and the King under his guardian and agent, Bruno, bishop of Augsburg, tamed all rebels and happily strengthened the bonds of peace on every hand.

XXIV. *Of the Death of the Bishop of Augsburg*

In the following year, the Emperor celebrated Easter in Regensburg. There, Bishop Bruno of Augsburg died. The Empress, together with her son King Henry, accompanied his body to Augsburg, his see, and had it buried honorably. This Bishop Bruno was noble indeed. For since he was the brother of the Emperor Henry [II], he was the son of the aunt of Gisela the Empress. The sister of this same Bishop,[113] through her marriage to Stephan, king of Hungary, was the first fos-

---

[111] 1028.   [112] Romanus Argyrus, successor of Constantine VIII.   [113] Gisela.

terer of Christianity in the Pannonian nation. Ebehard received the bishopric of Augsburg.

XXV. How Duke Ernst Received His Dukedom and Lost It at Once

In the year of the Lord 1030, Emperor Conrad celebrated Easter at Ingelheim. There Ernst, the above-mentioned duke of Alamannia, released from custody, received his dukedom, on the condition that, with all his men, he would pursue as an enemy of the commonwealth Wezelo, his vassal, who had disturbed the kingdom with many factious intrigues, and that he confirm with a solemn vow that he was going to do it. When the Duke was unwilling to do this, he was adjudged a state enemy of the Emperor, and, with the complete loss of his dukedom, he withdrew from that place with a few men. The Emperor gave the dukedom of Alamannia to Herman, the younger brother of this same Ernst, and commended him to Warmann, bishop of Constance. But, by the common counsel of all the princes of the realm, the Emperor had the same Ernst and all those resisting justice and peace excommunicated by the bishops and ordered their possessions to be sequestered by the state. The Empress Gisela herself—a thing pitiable to recount, but laudable to do—holding her ill-advised son[114] in less esteem than her wise husband, gave publicly official assurance that, whatever happened to him [Ernst], she would indulge no vindictiveness or animosity because of this affair.

XXVI. That the Emperor Came upon the Hungarians with His Army

At this same time, many dissensions arose between the Pannonian nation and the Bavarians, through the fault of the Bavarians. And, as a result, King Stephan of Hungary made many incursions and raids in the realm of the Norici (that is, of the Bavarians). Disturbed on this account Emperor Conrad came upon the Hungarians with a great army. But King Stephan, whose forces were entirely insufficient to meet the Emperor, relied solely on the guardianship of the Lord, which he sought with prayers and fasts proclaimed through his whole realm. Since the Emperor was not able to enter a kingdom so fortified with rivers and forests, he returned, after he had sufficiently avenged his injury with

[114] That is, the son of Gisela and Herman II of Swabia.

lootings and burnings on the borders of the kingdom; and it was his wish at a more opportune time to complete the things he had begun. His son, King Henry, however, still a young boy entrusted to the care of Eigilbert, bishop of Freising, received a legation of King Stephan which asked for peace; and solely with the counsel of the princes of the realm, and without his father's knowledge, he granted the favor of reconciliation. Acting justly and wisely, he received in friendship the King who had been wrongly wronged and who sought favor voluntarily.

XXVII. That Duke Ernst Sought Aid from Count Odo

Meanwhile, when this was going on, the aforesaid Ernst, deprived of the dignity of his dukedom, contemplating many things, attempting many things to the end that he might resist the Emperor, spent his great labors in vain. After he had gotten together his vassal Wezelo and a few others, he went into Latin Francia [France] to Count Odo, his relative. For the mother of Odo[115] and the mother of Empress Gisela[116] had been sisters. But this man from whom he sought counsel and aid— whether he did not want or did not dare to—gave him no succor against the Emperor.

XXVIII. How Duke Ernst Perished

Duke Ernst, having turned back, came again into Alamannia. There he stayed in the safest places, and he lived by petty brigandage in a certain wilderness which is called the Black Forest. Finally, when he was hemmed in on all sides by the soldiery of Caesar, some persons who favored the Emperor, by means of ambushes laid in the pastures, took away the best horses which the Duke and all his men had. After the horses in which he had placed great reliance had been lost, the Duke, no longer caring about anything,[117] did not know what to do in such perturbation. But after he had collected everywhere horses of whatever sort he could get, he left the forest with all the men whom he had then, considering it better to die with honor than to live in shame. And when they had come to woodlands in that region of Alamannia which is called Baar, they saw a deserted camp which their enemies had occupied the night prior. Straightway, they realized that ambushes were

[115] Bertha.   [116] Gerberga.   [117] Sallust, *Catiline* 12, 2; *Jugurtha* 41, 9.

prepared for them. For Manegold, a vassal of the Emperor, holding a great fief of the abbey of Reichenau, had been placed on guard by the Emperor and Warmann, bishop of Constance (who then governed Alamannia in the stead of Duke Herman), lest Duke Ernst make raids to plunder or pillage in the region. At once, Duke Ernst and his followers became all too cheerful, thinking that they were swiftly to avenge their wrongs upon their enemies; and taking to the road, they began to pursue their pursuers. With the same intent, Count Manegold and those who were with him advanced here and there and diligently observed the maneuvers of the Duke. With this occasion given on each side, they were so deployed in relation to each other that the one could see and accost the other. There were, however, many more knights on the side of Manegold than on the side of the Duke.

Without holding back, all who had come together fought bitterly; those on the side of the Duke, aroused by wrath, ferocity, boldness; those on the other side, driven on by desire for glory, for reward. Those who were with the Duke, since they thought nothing of life, all hastened to destruction. The Duke, since he spared no one, found no one in this battle sparing him, and after being wounded by many, at length he fell dead. There fell Count Wezilo, the vassal of the Duke on whose account all these things occurred. The noble men Adalbert and Werin, and many others, were slain there. On the other side, Count Manegold himself, author of this melée, fell and many others with him The body of Duke Ernst was brought away to Constance, and after an indulgence from the episcopal power had been obtained first [which was necessary] because of his excommunication, he was entombed in the church of St. Mary. The body of Manegold was buried in Reichenau.

This battle, forever most pitiable, occurred on the XV of the kalends of September.[118] When it was reported to the Emperor, he is reputed to have said,

"Rarely will rabid dogs [live to] multiply with offspring."

XXIX. Rudolf, King of Burgundy, Died, and Odo Invaded His Realm

In the year of the Lord 1032, Rudolf, king of Burgundy, the uncle of the Empress Gisela, died in peace. Count Odo Francigen,[119] son of his sister, invaded his realm, and took certain very well-armed castles

[118] Probably the true date is XVI kal. September (August 18).
[119] "Of the Frankish nation."

or cities by craft or battle. Neither did he dare to make himself king nor, indeed, did he wish to lose the kingdom. Some persons related that he had often said that he never wished to be king, yet always to be the master [*magister*] of a king. In this fashion, he drew away [for himself] a great part of Burgundy, although King Rudolf had already confirmed, not long ago, through a solemn oath that the kingdom of Burgundy should go to Emperor Conrad and his son, King Henry, after his death. But while Count Odo did these things in Burgundy, Emperor Conrad was in Sclavonia with his troops.[120] What he did there and how he afterwards repelled Odo from Burgundy, I shall tell in the following [passages].

When the afore-mentioned Boleslaus, duke of the Poles, died, he left two sons, Misico and Otto. Misico persecuted his brother Otto and expelled him into Russia. While Otto lived there for some time in a miserable condition, he began to ask the favor of Emperor Conrad, in order that through his intercession and assistance he might be restored to his fatherland. Since the Emperor was willing to do this, he decided that he himself would attack Misico with troops on one side and Otto on the other. Since Misico was unable to withstand this attack, he fled into Bohemia to Duke Udalric, against whom at that time the Emperor was enraged. But Udalric was willing, in order to please the Emperor, to give Misico up to him. Caesar renounced this dishonorable pact, saying that he did not wish to buy an enemy from an enemy. Otto was restored to his fatherland and made duke by Caesar; but since, after some time, he acted with too little caution, he was slain secretly by one of his household.[121] Then Misico sought in every way the favor of Empress Gisela, and of the other princes, that he might be found worthy to return to the favor of the Emperor. Caesar, moved by compassion, granted him pardon; and after the province of the Poles had been divided into three parts, he made Misico tetrarch and commended the remaining two parts to two other men. So, with his power diminished, his temerity was reduced. After the death of Misico,[122] Casimir, his son, has served our emperors faithfully until this very time.[123]

[120] In his expedition against Misico (Mesko), which was begun in 1031 and concluded with a treaty at Merseburg in 1032.

[121] 1032.   [122] 1034.

[123] From 1042 his relations with Henry III worsened, and in 1050 Henry readied an expedition against him. The expedition was canceled, however, by Casimir's voluntary submission.

XXX. That the Emperor Went to Burgundy with His Son, King Henry

In the year of the Lord 1033, Emperor Conrad with his son King Henry celebrated the birth of the Lord in the city of Strassburg. After he had collected an army, he went from there into Burgundy, by way of Solothurn, and coming to the monastery of Peterlingen on the feast of the purification of St. Mary, he was elected to rule Burgundy by the greater and lesser [feudatories] of the kingdom; and on the same day, he was crowned as king. Then he besieged certain castles which Odo had fought his way into, but because of the extreme bitterness of the winter[124]—for that was the season—he was much impeded. About this extreme cold, one of us made a hundred verses, which he presented to the Emperor. In them amazing things are told, such as [the following]. If the horses in the camp around the castle of Murten set their feet firmly on the ground after they had toiled during the day, during the night they became immobilized, so frozen that they could never be dragged away from the ground frozen around them except with axes and stakes. One man, however, who had no help killed his own horse, which was stuck in this way and pulled the hide away, from the shanks upward; the rest he left fixed to the frozen earth. Indeed, men were often confused one with another because of this cold; for the young and old looked alike; day and night, all were hoary and bearded because of the horrid rigor of the ice, although the majority were youths and unbearded men. Nevertheless,

Scarcely was this the reason that Caesar abandoned the wars.

On his return, the Emperor came to the castle of Zürich. A number of Burgundians—the widowed queen of Burgundy[125] and Count Humbert[126] and others—who had been unable to come to the Emperor in Burgundy because of the ambushes of Odo met him there, having traveled by way of Italy. After they had been made his men, through promising under oath fealty to him and to his son King Henry, they returned wondrously enriched with gifts.

---

[124] Cf. Sallust, *Jugurtha* 37, 3.

[125] Irmgard.

[126] Humbert Whitehands, from whom the House of Savoy descended. See C. W. Previté-Orton, *The Early History of the House of Savoy (1000–1233)*, (Cambridge, 1912), p. 10 n. 7, and *passim*.

XXXI. That the Emperor Came upon Odo with an Army

In the summer of this same year, the Emperor came upon Count Odo in the Gauls of the Franks [that is, France], saying if Odo sought unjustly in Burgundy things belonging to others, he ought, by the aid of God, to lose something of his own. Then the Emperor made such great ravaging and burning on the allods and benefices of Odo which were situated in the realm of Henry, king of the Franks, that Odo himself, compelled by necessity, came humbly and asked for pardon. He promised to relinquish Burgundy and to give him [Conrad] satisfaction, according to his command. So the Emperor returned with his own honor and Odo's fine.

XXXII. How the Emperor Expelled Odo from Burgundy

In the year of the Lord 1034, the Emperor celebrated the holy Easter in Bavaria at Regensburg. In the summer of this year, since the aforesaid Odo had not heeded his promises, but still held a certain part of Burgundy, which he had invaded unjustly, Emperor Conrad, bitter of heart, neared Burgundy with contingents of German and Italian troops. On one side, the Germans, on the other, Aribert, archbishop of Milan, and the other Italians under the leadership of Count Humbert of Burgundy, gathered at the Rhone River. When Augustus came to the city of Geneva, he subjected Gerold, prince of this region, and the Archbishop of Lyons[127] and very many others. Then, turning back, he besieged the castle of Murten, which was strengthened with the bravest soldiers of Odo, took it by force, and led away as captives those whom he found within. The other partisans of Odo fled on hearing this, solely through fear of Caesar. Caesar pursued them and drove them out entirely from the kingdom. After he had received many hostages from the princes of Burgundy, he returned to the Empress through Alsace.

For when he went into Burgundy, the Empress had followed him to Basel and retired thence to Strassburg to await the return of the Emperor. At that time, Mathilda, daughter of Emperor Conrad and Empress Gisela, a girl of extreme beauty who was betrothed to Henry, king of the Franks, died at Worms and was entombed there.

[127] Burchard III.

XXXIII. That King Henry Subjected the Slavs

In the meantime, while the Emperor was doing those things in Burgundy which have been recounted above, his son, King Henry, although still in the years of boyhood,[128] attended no less energetically the affairs of the commonwealth in Bohemia and in the other regions of the Slavs, where he vigorously subjugated Udalric, duke of Bohemia, as well as many other opponents of Caesar. When his father returned, he met him, and thus he gave to the peoples double joy because of the double victory.

Then, when troops had been collected from Saxony, the Emperor came upon those who are called Liutizi and who, once semi-Christian, now are wholly pagan through the wickedness of apostasy; and there he brought to an end an implacable conflict in an astounding fashion. For there were at that time many quarrels and border raids between the Saxons and the pagans. And when Caesar came, he began to inquire by which side the peace, which had long been inviolate between them, had been destroyed first. The pagans said that peace was disturbed first by the Saxons and that this would be proven through a duel, if Caesar so commanded. The Saxons, on the other hand, although they contended unjustly, similarly pledged before the Emperor their willingness to engage in single combat to refute the pagans. The Emperor, even though he took the counsel of his princes, did not act cautiously enough and permitted this matter to be adjudged by a duel between them. At once two fighters met, each elected by his own men. The Christian began to fight boldly, confiding in that faith alone which, however, is dead without works of righteousness,[129] and not diligently heeding the fact that God, who is Truth,[130] disposes everything in true judgment, He who makes His sun to rise over good and evil, who causes rain to fall on the just and the unjust.[131] The pagan, however, put up a stanch resistance, having before his eyes only the consciousness of the truth for which he fought. Finally, the Christian fell, wounded by the pagan. Because of this outcome, the pagans became so greatly elated and bold that, if the Emperor had not been present, they would have thrown themselves upon the Christians straightway. But, in order to curb their incursions, the Emperor constructed the castle of Werben in which he stationed garrisons of knights, and he constrained the

[128] Cf. Ovid, *Metamorphoses* II, 55.   [129] James 2:92.   [130] I John 5:6.
[131] Matthew 5:45.

princes of Saxony by solemn oath and imperial order to resist the pagans of one accord. Then he returned to Franconia.

But in the following year, the same castle was taken by the pagans through craft, and many of our men who were in it were killed by them. Disturbed by this, the Emperor again came with troops to the Elbe River. But since the pagans prevented a crossing, the Emperor sent part of the army across under cover through another ford of the river. When the enemies had been set to flight in that way, Emperor Conrad entered the region by the now-free bank of the river and laid them so low with immense devastations and burnings everywhere except in impregnable places that afterwards they paid to him the tax which had been imposed by emperors of old and which was now increased.

For both before and at that time, Emperor Conrad toiled greatly amidst the nation of the Slavs. Because of this, one of us composed a short account in verse, which afterwards he presented to the Emperor. There one may read how the Emperor sometimes stood in marshes up to the thighs, fighting in person and exhorting the soldiers to fight; and how, after the pagans had been conquered, he slew them with the greater ferocity because of a certain most reprehensible superstition of theirs. For it is said that at some time the pagans kept a wooden effigy of our crucified Lord Jesus Christ in shameful mockery and spat upon it and struck it with blows; finally, they tore out the eyes and cut off the hands and feet. To avenge these deeds, the Emperor in a similar manner mutilated a great multitude of captured pagans for one effigy of Christ and destroyed them with various deaths. Therefore Caesar is called an avenger of the Faith in these verses and is compared with the Roman princes Titus and Vespasian, who in avenging the Lord had exchanged thirty Jews for one coin since the Jews sold Christ for that many denarii.[132]

After his return, the Emperor imperiously cast aside whatever resistance he found in the kingdom. In the same year, Adalbero, duke of the Carinthians, lost the favor of the Emperor and was deprived of his dukedom and sent into exile.

XXXIV. Of the Covenant of the Italians

Also at this same time, a great turmoil, unheard of in modern times, was raised in Italy because of the covenants which the people made

[132] Wipo refers to a legend common in his day.

against the princes. For all the valvasores and subtenants of Italy had covenanted together against their lords, and all the lesser [feudatories] against the greater, not to suffer anything done to them against their own will by their lords to go unavenged. They said if their Emperor did not want to come, they themselves would make a law by themselves, for themselves. When this was reported to the Emperor, he is reputed to have said, "If Italy hungers now for law,

God granting, I shall sate it well with laws."

And preparing himself, he entered Italy with troops the following year. Meanwhile, the Italian princes, realizing that the ill-conceived covenant could lead to danger, came together with the lesser [feudatories] and strove first with exhortations and counsels to destroy this fresh evil. When this did not succeed, they attempted to gain the upper hand through war, but when battle was joined, the incredible multitude of the lesser [feudatories] was victorious through the mere pressure of their troops. There the Bishop of Asti[133] perished in unworthy circumstances;[134] the others fled, and, in great disturbance, they awaited impatiently the coming of the Emperor.

XXXV. That King Henry Married the Daughter of King Canute

In the year of the Lord 1036, King Henry, son of the Emperor, married the daughter of Canute, king of the Angles, Chunelinda by name, who was consecrated as queen during the regal nuptials. In the same year, as has been said, Emperor Conrad entered Italy in the company of his son King Henry,[135] with an army, and celebrated the birth of the Lord at Verona in the year of the Lord's incarnation 1037. Coming from there to Milan, he was magnificently received by Archbishop Aribert in the church of St. Ambrose. On the same day (we do not know by whose counsel), a near-grave tumult was made by the Milanese populace, which asked of the Emperor whether he was willing to favor their covenant. Disturbed by this, the Emperor commanded that all should come together in the city of Pavia to a general conference.

When this was held, the Emperor made a law for all those who were

133 Adelrich.   134 In battle.

135 Actually, Henry remained in Germany, and joined his father in Italy with military reinforcements only in the spring of 1037.

crying out in protest. In this assembly, a certain Count Hugo[136] and a great many other Italians brought charges against the Archbishop of Milan because of many legal proceedings in which he had offended them. After the Archbishop had been summoned, the Emperor ordered that he should give satisfaction to all. When the Archbishop refused to do this, the Emperor perceived that the covenant of Italy had been concluded entirely through the devices of that very man. He arrested him summarily and retained him in his power. Later he commended him into the custody of Poppo, patriarch of Aquileia, and Cuono, duke of Carinthia. By these two men, Aribert was led with the Emperor to the city of Piacenza. One night, one of the members of the household of the Archbishop[137] put himself in his place in the bed where he [Aribert] was accustomed to lie; and he pulled the blankets up and lay hidden, so to deceive the guards. The Archbishop fled on a horse which had been brought to him by someone, and on his coming to Milan, he was received with great joy by his own men. Thereafter, he left nothing undone which he could do against the Emperor.

The Emperor destroyed all the castles which had resisted him, and, after just law had been restored, he laid low the iniquitous covenant of Italy. Coming to Ravenna, he celebrated the holy Easter there. In the same year, three bishops in Italy, those of Vercelli,[138] Cremona,[139] and Piacenza,[140] were accused before the Emperor, who had them arrested and sent into exile. It displeased many that priests of Christ should be condemned without [formal] judgment. Certain persons related to us that our most pious King, Henry, the son of the Emperor, in all reverence for his father, secretly detested the presumptuousness of Caesar toward the Archbishop of Milan and toward these three. And rightly so, for just as after the judicial sentence of deposition no honor is to be shown, so before the judgment great reverence is due priests.[141] In the same year, the afore-mentioned Count Odo [of Champagne] came from France and invaded certain places in the realm of the Emperor. After battle had been joined with him by Gozelo, duke of Lorraine, and his son Godfrey and by Count Gerhard and the soldiery of the bishops of Metz, he was killed in flight. His banner, which was taken to Caesar in Italy, gave testimony that this enemy had been dispatched. At that time, the Emperor beset the Milanese heavily, and,

---

[136] Hugo, count of Milan, a member of the house of the Obertini.
[137] Albizo, a monk, later abbot of the Monastery of the Savior in Tolla.
[138] Arderich.   [139] Hubald.   [140] Peter.   [141] Cf. Sirmondian Constitutions 2.

since he was not able to take the city, strengthened as it was with ancient fortifications and a very great number of people, he consumed with fire and sword whatever was in the surrounding countryside.

XXXVI. Of a Miracle which Happened on the Day of Pentecost

At this same time, while the Emperor besieged a certain castle of St. Ambrose outside Milan, which is called Corbetta, something happened there which many held for a miracle. On the Lord's holy Pentecost, before the third hour, out of a perfectly serene sky, suddenly lightning bolts tore forth with thunder, of such great power that a great part of the men and horses in the camps died. So great was the terror of some men that they went mad, to such a degree that even after some months they had scarcely regained their senses. But when those who had been outside the camps returned, they said that they had neither seen nor heard anything of the sort.

At this time, Emperor gave the archepiscopacy of Milan to Ambrose, a Milanese canon, although that donation profited this man little. For the citizens of Milan demolished whatever that Ambrose had in their territory and retained their Archbishop Aribert with honor until his death.[142] But all that, with the approbation of King Henry, son of the Emperor, I shall describe more fully in the Deeds of the King, if God wills.

At this same time, the Pope came to meet the Emperor at Cremona, and, after he had been honorably received and dismissed, he returned to Rome. When the army had been dispersed over a wide territory, the Emperor himself withdrew to places in the mountains because of the coolness [there]; for the great heat was very oppressive that summer.

XXXVII. Of the Riot which Took Place in Parma

In the winter of this same year, when the army had been assembled, the Emperor crossed the Po and came to the city of Parma, where he celebrated the birth of the Lord at the beginning of the year of the Lord's incarnation of 1038. On this day of the nativity of the Lord, a great riot took place between the Germans and the citizens of Parma; and a certain very valiant man, Conrad, server of the food of the Emperor, was killed together with others. The army, stirred up by this, attacked the citizens with swords and fire; and the Emperor, after the

[142] 1045.

conflagration, ordered that a great part of the walls be destroyed, so that those ruins would indicate to other cities that the presumptuousness of those men [the Parmese] had not gone unpunished.

After that, the Emperor crossed the Apennine Mountains and went into Apulia. But the Empress went to Rome to pray and returned from there to the Emperor. The Emperor, however, going to the borders of his Empire, stabilized conditions in Trojo, Beneventum, and Capua, and other cities of Apulia, with law and justice. Solely by his command, he settled the dissensions which existed between the foreign Normans and the native peoples, and, when he had removed everything that gave offense to the realm, he returned happily and came to Ravenna. After decisions had been made there concerning sieges and strategems against Milanese, who were still rebels against him, and when all other affairs through the realm had been put in order according to his will, he resolved to see the fatherland again.

At this time, because of the extreme heat, an extremely contagious plague came upon the army with no regard either for age or for person. There on the XV of the kalends of August, Queen Chunelinda, wife of King Henry, as though standing on the threshold of life, fell at the doorway of death. She left only one little daugther by the King, whom the father later betrothed to Christ and had consecrated an abbess.[143] The son of the Empress, Herman, duke of the Alamanni, a youth of good disposition and vigorous in martial affairs, was stricken ill by the same plague and died amidst the hands of the most experienced physicians on the V of the kalends of August, not without great detriment to the Empire. In the same month, and the one following, a very large multitude of the army was touched by the disease and perished. The soft and delicate body of the Queen was preserved with aromatic substances and brought to Germany in the train of the King and the Empress. It was entombed in the collegiate church of Limburg. As to the Duke, it was decided that he should be taken to Constance, a city in Alamannia; but because of the adversity of extreme heat, he was entombed in Trent.

XXXVIII. That the Emperor Handed Over Burgundy to His Son the King

In the same year, Stephan, king of the Hungarians, died, and left the realm to Peter, the son of his sister. On his return to Bavaria, the King

[143] Beatrix, who became abbess of Quedlinburg in 1045.

restored the health of the sick army with medicines and good counsel. Since he found the whole realm resplendent with the serenity of peace, he went in the autumn of the same year to Burgundy. After all the princes of the realm had been called together, he held a general conference with them and made Burgundy then, for the first time, taste the law, long disused and almost wiped from the books. After three days of the general conference had been spent, on the fourth day, with the acclaim and at the request of the first men of the realm with all the people, the Emperor handed over the kingdom of Burgundy to his son, King Henry, and had the kingdom swear its fidelity again to his son.[144] The bishops led him [Henry] with the other princes into the Church of St. Stephan (which is considered to be the chapel of the king in Solothurn) and praised God with hymns and divine canticles, while the people were shouting and saying that peace would beget peace, if the King reigned with Caesar. The Emperor returned, descending through Basel, and he saw again eastern Francia [Franconia], and Frisia,

in confirming peace, in making law.

XXXIX. Of the Death of the Emperor

In the year of the Lord's incarnation 1039, when the Emperor Conrad was confident that now the actual state of the kingdom, nay "the hope for the Empire," had been set well upon his son, King Henry, and when he saw almost everything throughout the kingdom bent to his pleasure— in this year, he celebrated the holy day of Pentecost at Utrecht, a city of Frisia. There, while he was showing reverence magnificently to that most holy festival, going forth in procession, crowned, with his son and his Empress, he was seized with a moderate discomfort at the Table.[145] Nevertheless, he concealed the discomfort lest he disturb the happiness of so great a day. On the following day, when the mortal illness violently pressed on, he ordered the Empress to go out of the chamber to eat with his son the King. Meanwhile, the Emperor sensed that the end was near for him. And just as he was sound in life, always constant and vigorous in action, so at the very end the Emperor remained of a faith in no way less slack. After bishops had been called, he had the Body and Blood of the Lord and the Holy Cross borne in with relics of the Saints; and drawing himself up, with affecting tears in a pure confession and intent prayer, he received most devoutly the

[144] August 15, 1038.   [145] At Holy Communion or at a State dinner.

Communion of Saints and the remission of sins. After faithful admonition, he bade farewell to the Empress and to his son, King Henry, and departed this life on the II of the nones of June, the second day of the week in the seventh indiction.

The internal organs of the Emperor were buried at Utrecht,[146] and the King [Henry] enriched the place of the tomb with gifts and estates. The rest of the body, as best as could be devised, was shrouded and covered and brought to Cologne. It was carried through all the monastic establishments of that city and of Mainz and Worms and those [monastic establishments] situated in between, with all the people following and praying. It was conveyed with incredible prayer and great alms given for the redemption of his soul, and on the thirtieth day after his death it was honorably entombed by the Empress and his son the King in the city of Speier, which the Emperor himself, as his son also was to do afterwards, greatly exalted.

God added this favor to Emperor Conrad, that as far as we have seen or heard, such great lamentations of all men, so many prayers, such alms were never rendered any [other] of the Emperors while his body remained unburied. And (as we have heard, through the report of Bishop Henry of Lausanne and the other Burgundians who followed him from death to entombment),[147] the son of Caesar, King Henry, bent his shoulders under the body of his father [as pallbearer] with very humble devotion at every entry into a church and finally at the entombment. And the King showed most zealously to his dead father all this—not only what the son owes to the father in perfect love, but what the servant owes to his lord in holy fear.

We have written briefly this account of the deeds of the Emperor Conrad. If we have passed over anything and left it entirely untouched, let it be believed that we had not heard of it. If, however, something has been said in a more condensed fashion than the greatness of the matters would warrant, we will aver truthfully that this has been done for the convenience of the reader.

One of us made a canticle of lamentations on the Emperor, which he presented afterwards to his son King Henry in the city of Constance. We have thought it not unfitting to insert these lamentations here, since they are germane to this present work.

---

[146] Cf." Life of Henry IV," p. 136 n. 175; above, chap. 37; and Raynold of Lyon's *Vita Hugonis Abbatis*, Migne *PL*, CLIX, 905 chap. 4.

[147] Cf. Macrobius, *Interpretatio in somnum Scipionis* II, 3, 6.

XL. *Verses on the Death of the Emperor Conrad*

Let him who has a serene voice proffer this canticle
Of the lamentable year and the ineffable hurt
For which every man grieves publicly and in his home.
The populace sighs for [its] lord in vigils and through [its]
    sleep:
"O King God, guard the living and have mercy upon the dead!"

In the year one thousand nine and thirty,
From the nativity of Christ, nobility fell prostrate on all sides.
Caesar fell, the head of the world, and with him many of the
    greatest,
The Emperor succumbed, Conrad, lover of law.
"O King God, guard the living and have mercy upon the dead!"

But in that same time, there was a downfall of glory:
The morning star fell, Chunelinda the queen.
Woe, how cruel a year! Herman sank down,
Son of the Empress, a duke fearful to the enemy,
[Cuono fell, duke of the Franks, and a great part of the *seniores*.]
"O King God, guard the living and have mercy upon the dead!"

May the glory of the Emperor be in our memory,
And let the man of good disposition live in fresh remembrance.
Let the upright lord live anew in frequent song;
Let brilliant fame survive this, the consort of life, after death!
"O King God, guard the living and have mercy upon the dead!"

Born of the blood of kings, he excelled all by far.
Glorious in person, handsome under his crown,
The scepter, the kingdom, the Empire, to none were more
    becoming.
He adorned the commonwealth with honor—he labored to
    this end.
"O King God, guard the living and have mercy upon the dead!"

After he replenished Franconia with the abundance of peace,
He tamed the Alamanni and all the tyrants of the kingdom.
He imposed the bit of the law upon the Saxons and Bavarians.
Laudable Italy saw his mighty deeds.
"O King God, guard the living and have mercy upon the dead!"

First Rome subjected herself from the greatest to the least;
The Ravennese encountered his magnates in war;
The Veronese felt the blades of unconquered Caesar;[148]
Hesperia [South Italy] prostrated herself, made her humble
    entreaties to him who mastered her.
"O King God, guard the living and have mercy upon the dead!"

After returning to Alamannia, he found cavil.
Caesar dissipated this like as the wind, the trace of dust.
All who had been predators perished at once,
And the most eminent citizens were exiled therefor.
"O King God, guard the living and have mercy upon the dead!"

The Emperor never tarried, everywhere the giver of peace.
He carried war to the pagans lest they harm Christians:
The marsh did not defend them, nor was there safety in the
    waters;
Well he made the barbarian Slavs and all peoples depraved feel
    his force.
"O King God, guard the living and have mercy upon the dead."

[148] No extant reports mention Conrad's encounter with the Veronese. Since Wipo's reference seems to be to Conrad's first Italian journey, Bresslau suggests that the Veronese have been confused in it with the Pavians.

THE LIFE OF THE EMPEROR HENRY IV

The life of Emperor Henry IV, as presented by his anonymous biographer, illustrates Gregory of Catino's principle that "the king is the head of the Church." For Henry appears not merely as a generous patron of religious establishments and a careful guardian of the poor, but as a king established "by the hand of God" to whom bishops must faithfully submit in order to escape divine vengeance. The author's attitude toward Henry's part in the Investiture Controversy is clear, though cleverly veiled. For example, he admonishes Henry to withdraw his judicial sentence of deposition against Gregory VII, yet he openly condemns Gregory as deceiver and deceived, accepts Wibert of Ravenna as true pope, and praises his Emperor as "the light of the world," the establisher of order in the Church and in the Empire. The biography also contains much of value about the civil discords in Henry's reign, and particularly about the conflict between Henry and his son, Henry V, which darkened his last years.

1. "Oh, that my head were waters and mine eyes a fountain of tears,"[1] so that I might lament, might lament not the destruction of a captured city,[2] not the captivity of the base populace, not the loss of my own property, but the death of the august Emperor Henry, who was my hope and my only comfort,[3] nay more (to say nothing of myself), the death of him who was the glory of Rome, the splendor of the Empire, the light of the world![4] Henceforth will life be joyous to me? Will there be a day or an hour without tears? Or shall I be able with you,

---

[1] Jeremiah 9:1. [2] Cf. *Aeneid* II, 643.
[3] Cf. Psalm 70:5; Hebrews 6:18; Colosians 4:11; Wipo, *Sequentia Paschalis*, Bresslau ed., p. 65.
[4] Cf. Proverbs 20:27; John 5:35; II Peter 1:19.

most cherished friend, to speak of him without weeping?[5] Behold, as I write what unbearable grief has dictated, the tears fall,[6] the letters are wet with my weeping, and the eye washes away what the hand writes.

But you may protest my unrestrained grief and counsel me to hold back my weeping, lest perhaps it become known to those who rejoice at the Emperor's death. You counsel me rightly, I confess. But I cannot command myself not to grieve,[7] I cannot contain myself from mourning. Although they may whet their furor upon me, although they may long to tear me limb from limb,[8] grief knows no fear, grief feels no pains inflicted.

Nor do I alone lament his death. Rome bemoans it; all the Roman Empire bewails it; rich and poor in common (except the waylayers of his power and life) weep because of it. Nor is this a cause of private grief for me; a sense of duty forces me to lament this public calamity. For when he retired from the stage, justice left his lands,[9] peace departed, and deception crept into the place of good faith. The chorus of those praising God was hushed, the solemnity of the Divine Office fell silent, "the voice of rejoicing and salvation" is no longer heard in the "tabernacles of the righteous,"[10] since he who solemnly ordained all these things is no longer reached [by them]. The monasteries have lost their patron, the cloisters, their father. Now, indeed, that he is dead, and no longer to be seen, one comes to realize what emoluments, what honors he conferred upon them. And thus, a true reason for grief is at hand for all cloisters, for at his entombment their glory was entombed.

Woe, O Mainz, what great splendor have you forfeited, you who lost such a cultivator of the arts for the rebuilding of your minster, once in ruins![11] If he had survived to put the last touch to the work of your minster which he had begun, it would indeed contend with that famous minster at Speier, which he began from the very foundation[12] and brought to completion throughout with wondrous massiveness and sculptured work, to such a point that this work is worthy of praise and

---

[5] Sulpicius Severus, Letter 2 to the Deacon Aurelius on the Death of St. Martin.
[6] *Ibid.*   [7] *Ibid.*   [8] *Ibid.*   [9] Cf. Virgil, *Georgics* II, 474.   [10] Psalm 118:15.
[11] It burned in 1081, according to Marianus Scotus.
[12] It was actually begun by Conrad II in 1030 and completed by Henry IV at the end of his reign. See Otto of Freising, *Deeds of the Emperor Frederick*, I, x: "This church, as is seen today, he [Henry IV] himself constructed with wondrous and artful work."

admiration above all the works of the kings of old. It is difficult to believe how he adorned this minster with gold, silver, precious stones, and silk vestments unless one has the opportunity to see it.[13]

Your reason for grieving, O ye poor, is indeed the greatest, for you have been made poor now alone, when you have lost him who comforted your poverty. He fed you, he washed you with his own hands, he covered your nakedness.[14] Lazarus lay not before his door, but before his table; he looked not for crumbs,[15] but for regal delicacies. At this table, he did not shrink from the corruption and stench of the ulcerous man,[16] although the minister of his table [steward] contracted his nostrils into a wrinkle or stopped them up against the stinkard.[17] In his chamber lay the blind, the halt, and those consumed with divers illnesses. From these, he himself removed their foot-coverings;[18] to these he gave places to sleep; these, he covered, rising [from his bed] at night.[19] Nor did he shrink even from the touch of one whom illness had forced to soil the bed.

The poor preceded his entourage; they accompanied it; they followed it. Although he had commended the care of them to his intimates, he himself, nonetheless, cared for them as though they had been commended to no one. But everywhere throughout his manors, he set aside sustenance for the poor; and he wished to know personally their number and when they died, so that he could both care for the memory of the deceased and be sure that another had been substituted in his place.[20] Whenever the barrenness of a year inflicted a famine [upon the people], he undertook to feed many thousands, truly mindful of the word of the Lord, commanding: "Make to yourselves friends of the mammon of unrighteousness, that when ye fail, they may receive you into the everlasting tabernacle."[21]

With what grief do we think the poor are afflicted, when they consider that they have had, but no longer have now these good things which we have enumerated, and much more than we have enumerated. For who devotes this humanitarian care to them? Who serves more fully in these offices of mercy, in which Henry the Emperor served? O man, marked out with the praise of pious duty and humility! He commanded the world; the poor, him. The world ministered to him; he, to the poor.

[13] Cf. Sallust, *Catiline* 13, 1.   [14] Cf. Sulpicius Severus, *Life of St. Martin*, chap. 2.
[15] Luke 16: 20 ff.   [16] Cf. Sulpicius Severus, *Life of St. Martin*, chap. 18.
[17] Cf. Psalm 22: 24.   [18] Sulpicius Severus, *Life of St. Martin*, chap. 2.
[19] Cf. Joshua 3: 1.   [20] Livy II, 7, 6.   [21] Luke 16: 9.

These things about that goodness of mercy toward the poor, which he loved much and which he could not conceal from men, we have spoken of first, not in accord with the worth of [his] deed, but in accord with the capacity of [our] mind; for who could know what he did [secretly] with God alone as witness? About the other virtues for which he was renowned, indeed, we shall make few remarks, for we are in no position to tell everything.

Let no one wonder if I mingle the happy deeds of his life with the lament of his death, since it is the wont of those who grieve, when they lament a dead friend, to recount his whole life and habits to the increase of their grief.[22] And so I rejoice to write about him; I rejoice to indulge [my] grief[23] and to weep for the dead, who, while he lived, was my joy.

Now he acted the part of a commander; now, that of a common soldier[24] thus showing forth in the one that office which he had to bear, and in the other, humility. He was of so acute of mind and of such great discernment that, while the princes hesitated to make a decision in the case of a legal matter which had to be resolved, or in dealing with the affairs of state, he swiftly loosed the knot and set forth clearly what was the more equitable, what the more useful, drawing this, as it were, from the secret place of wisdom itself. He gave attention to the words of others; he himself spoke few; nor did he burst forth to be the first to make a decision, but awaited that of others. He perceived the workings of the mind of him upon whose face he fixed the sharpness of his eyes; and he saw as though with lynxlike eyes, whether he carried toward him hate or love in his heart. Nor is it unpraiseworthy that in a throng of the foremost men he seemed to stand out above the rest and taller than he actually was and that he presented a certain awesome splendor in his countenance with which he struck back the gaze of onlookers as though with lightning, while, on the other hand, among the members of his household and in a small number of companions he appeared placid of countenance and equal [in stature] to the others.

Not only did the powerful of his Empire fear him, but his repute terrified both the kings of the East and those of the West, so much that they became tributaries before they were conquered. The king of Greece himself, to dissemble his fear, earnestly sought his friendship and with gifts came before him whom he feared as a potential enemy, lest he become an [actual] enemy. The golden altar tablet in Speier

[22] Cf. Lucan X, 178.   [23] *Aeneid* II, 776.
[24] Sallust, *Catiline* 60. See Letters 2, 3, 4, pp. 139–141.

bears witness to this, admirable as much because of the novelty of its art as because of the weight of metal. The king of Greece sent that tablet when he learned that the good pleasure and zealous concern of the Emperor was hot toward the Speier minster, a noble gift most worthy both of him who sent it and of him to whom it was sent. But also the king of Africa added greatly to his fisc since he feared greatly the power of the Emperor.

He oppressed the oppressors of the paupers; he gave despoilers to the spoil;[25] he beat back those who were abusive of him and rose up against his power, to such a degree that even today traces of his royal vengeance are seen among their posterity. After he had done this, he provided both for the state of his own affairs in the present and for the affairs of the Empire in the future, to the end that those men might learn not to disturb peace nor to vex the Empire with arms.

Here I would break off my pen; for we have come to factions, to deceptions, and to crimes, of which to write true things is a danger, to write false, a crime. "Here the wolf threatens, there the hound."[26] What, therefore, shall I do? "Shall I speak, or be silent?"[27] My hand begins and falters, writes and rejects, notes and erases, so much that I almost do not know what I will.[28] But it is foul to leave mutilated something begun and to have painted the head without the members. I shall persevere, therefore, as I began,[29] steadfast and secure in the fact that as your trustworthiness has been completely proven to me,[30] so you will reveal these writings to no one; or if perchance they go abroad, that you will not reveal the author.

2. When Emperor Henry whom we discuss here, still a boy, succeeded in the kingship his father, the most glorious Emperor Henry III (for while he was still a boy his father yielded to nature),[31] war did not disturb the peace; trumpet calls did not break the quiet;[32] rapine was not rampant; fidelity did not speak falsely—since the kingdom yet held to its former state. Justice was still full of its own vigor; power[33] was

[25] Cf. Jeremiah 17:8. [26] Horace, *Satires* II, 2, 64. [27] Cf. *Aeneid* III, 39.

[28] Ovid, *Metamorphoses* IX, 522 ff. [29] Sallust, *Jugurtha* 102, 9.

[30] Cf. Ovid, *Ex Ponto* II, 7, 82; Sallust, *Catiline* 20, 2; Sulpicius, *Life of St. Martin*, chap. 5.

[31] 1056. Sallust, *Jugurtha* 14, 15. [32] Cf. Lucan IV, 395.

[33] The Gelasian "potestas" of the regal office. See A. K. Ziegler, "Pope Gelasius I and His Teaching on the Relation of Church and State," *Catholic Historical Review*, XXVII (1942), 3–28.

still full of its own right. Agnes, the most serene Empress, a woman of manly disposition, sustained greatly this happy state of the kingdom, she who together with her son with equal right governed the common-wealth. But since immature age inspires too little fear, and while awe languishes, audacity increases, the boyish years of the King excited in many the spirit of crime. Therefore, everyone strove to become equal to the one greater than him, or even greater, and the might of many increased through crime;[34] nor was there any fear of the law, which had little authority under the young boy-king.

And so that they could do everything with more license, they first robbed of her child the mother[35] whose mature wisdom and grave habits they feared, pleading that it was dishonorable for the kingdom to be administered by a woman (although one may read of many queens who administered kingdoms with manly wisdom). But after the boy-king, once drawn away from the bosom of his mother, came into the hands of the princes to be raised,[36] whatever they prescribed for him to do, he did like the boy he was. Whomever they wished, he exalted; whomever they wished, he set down; so that they may rightly be said not to have ministered (*ministrasse*) to their king so much as to have given orders (*imperasse*) to him. When they dealt with the affairs of the kingdom, they took counsel not so much for the affairs of the kingdom as for their own; and in everything they did, it was their primary con-cern to put their own advantage above everything else.

This was certainly the greatest perfidy, that they left to his own devices in his boyish acts him who ought to have been kept, so to speak, under seal, in order thus to elicit from him what they strove to obtain.[37]

But when he passed into that measure of age and mind in which he could discern what was honorable, what shameful, what useful, and what was not,[38] he reconsidered what he had done while led by the suggestion of the princes and condemned many things which he had done. And, having become his own judge, he changed those of his acts which were to be changed. He also prohibited wars, violence, and rapine; he strove to recall peace and justice, which had been expelled, to restore neglected laws, and to check the license of crime. Those accustomed to crime whom he could not coerce by edict, he corrected, more mildly, indeed, than the wrong demanded by the stricture of the

[34] Sallust, *Jugurtha* 14, 7; Catiline 39, 1.
[35] 1062.   [36] Cf. *Aeneid* VII, 484.
[37] See Gregory VII, *Register* I, 29a.   [38] Horace, *Epp.* I, 2, 3.

law and the legal prerogative of the Curia. Those men called this not justice, but injury; and they who had cast law aside disdained to be bound by law, just as they who were racing through every impiety,[39] disdained to suffer the reins, and they gave their attention to plans by which they might either kill him or deprive him of his office, not remembering that they owed peace to their citizens, justice to the kingdom, fidelity to the King.

3. Therefore the Saxons, a hard people, harsh in wars, as rashly inclined to arms as bold, making for themselves a claim to pre-eminent acclamation by having undertaken the furious raid, suddenly rushed upon the King with arms.[40] The King considered it dangerous to engage in conflict with a few against innumerable armed men and escaped with difficulty;[41] he preferred life to praise, safety to the changes of fortune. When the Saxons thus saw that their undertaking had not answered to their desires—O inhuman mind, O shameful vengeance!— they disinterred the bones of the son of the King[42] (for he had not yet been made Emperor). The King, aroused by these two most heavy wrongs, led an army against that people, fought, and was victorious.[43] He was victorious, I say, over the armed host set up against him, not against the stubborn resistance which had been built up. For although he conquered those gathered in battle, put the conquered to flight, followed hard on the fugitives; although he laid waste their goods, destroyed their fortifications, and did everything which is to the victor's taste—for all that, they could not be forced to surrender. After he had departed thence and had, in a short time, restrengthened his army, he moved against them a second time. Since they mistrusted their own forces, most gravely shaken as they were in the earlier war, they decided on what was the next best thing to safety—to give themselves up. They hoped that the King would be content with surrender alone and would grant his pardon easily. But the outcome was far different from what they had hoped. For the King sent those who had been sentenced to exile into other lands where, under close confinement, they awaited the edict of release.

From this exile, some slipped away in flight; others were released

---

[39] Cf. Lucan V, 312.   [40] 1073.   [41] From the Harzburg, 1073.

[42] At the Harzburg, 1074. The body of Henry's brother, Conrad, also buried at the Harzburg, was likewise disinterred.

[43] The Battle of the Unstrut, 1075. See Letter 6, p. 143.

by their guards through bribery. When they had returned to their country and their homes, they bound themselves together in a new conspiracy [pledged] that they were ready to die before being cast down again in surrender. But their conspiracy became even stronger, for some Lombards, Franks, Bavarians, and Swabians adhered to them after exchanging the faithful assurance[44] that they would batter the King with wars on every hand.

They saw, however, that the King would be touched by wars, not cast down; vexed, not conquered; indeed, his strength until that time was unassailable. In order to extenuate his resources, they fabricated and wrote up criminal charges against him mixing true things with false—the worst and most foul which hate and spiteful malice could devise and which, if I were to put them down, would make me ill in writing and you, in reading them. Thus they accused him before the Roman pontiff, Gregory, saying that it was not seemly that so profligate a man, known more by crime than by title, should rule, most of all since Rome had not conferred the regal dignity upon him;[45] that it was necessary that her right in setting up kings be returned to Rome; and that the Pope and Rome, according to the counsel of the princes, should provide a king whose life and wisdom would be congruent with so great an honor.

The Pope, deluded by this act of stealth and, at the same time, urged on by the honor of creating a king, which they had thrust upon him in a spirit of deception, bound the King with the ban and commanded the bishops and the other princes of the kingdom to withdraw themselves from communion with the excommunicated King: [He announced] that he would go very soon into the German regions, where one might deal with ecclesiastical affairs, and most especially with the problems of the kingship. Nay, he even added this: he absolved all who had vowed fealty to the King of their oath, so that this absolution might force against him those whom the obligation of fealty held.[46] This deed displeased many—if one may be displeased with what the Pope does—and they asserted that what had been done was done as ineffectually as illicitly. But I should not dare to present their assertions, lest I seem to rebut with them the act of the Pope.

Soon most of the bishops, those whom love as much as those whom

[44] In 1076, after Henry‚s excommunication. Sallust, *Catiline* 44, 3.

[45] See Letters 12, 13, pp. 150–154.

[46] This did not occur until 1080.

fear had drawn to the side of the King, fearing for their office, withdrew their assistance from him. This also the greater part of the great nobles did. Then, indeed, seeing that his cause was set in the narrows,[47] the King conceived a plan as secret as astute and seized upon a sudden and unexpected journey to meet the Pope. And with one deed he did two—namely, he both received the loosing of the ban and cut off at mid-point a conference of the Pope with his adversaries which he had suspected. As for the criminal charges placed upon him, he answered little, since he averred that it was not for him to answer the accusation of his enemies, even though it were true.[48]

What did it profit you to have done this, to the end that he might be bound with the ban, when loosed from the ban he is free to use mightily his might? What did it profit you to have accused him with fabricated crimes, when he should have scattered your accusation with easy response, as the wind [scatters] the dust? Nay more, what madness armed you against your king and the ruler of the world? Your conspiratorial malignity profited nothing, accomplished nothing.

Whom the hand of God had established in kingship, yours could not cast down. Where was the fidelity which you vowed to him?[49] Wherefore were you forgetful of the benefices which he conferred upon you with regal liberality? Use sane counsel, not rage, to the purpose that you repent you of the undertaking, lest perchance coming upon you more strongly, he may conquer you[50] and crush you with his feet, and lest that vengeance rage which may show to future ages what the royal hand can do. At least, you, O bishops, see "lest ye perish from the just way";[51] see lest you transgress your promises of fidelity. Otherwise, you yourselves know what will overtake you.

4. When the King returned from the Pope, having received a benediction in place of a malediction, he found Duke Rudolf created king over him. After the news of his return had been heard, he [Rudolf] fled into Saxony, prepared for flight rather than for battle, pushed aside rather than conquered. It is easy to receive a kingdom, difficult to guard it. But let no one be amazed that a man trained and vigorous in martial affairs now had fled, since the more just and the victorious cause[52] often sends brave men into fear and flight. O avarice, that worst of plagues, which turns athwart good habits and often drags the

[47] Livy XXVI, 17, 5.   [48] Canossa, 1077.   [49] Ovid, *Heroides* II, 31.
[50] Cf. Luke 11:22.   [51] Psalm 2:12.   [52] Lucan I, 1, 8.

very virtues into vices![53] This Rudolf, an excellent duke, a man of great authority and praise through the whole kingdom, tenacious of the true and the right, brave in arms,[54] and, finally, proven in every kind of virtue—he, I say, conquered by avarice which conquers all else, and become the supplanter of his lord, gave fidelity second place to an uncertain honor. There were those, indeed, who said that he had been spurred on by the Pope[55] and that a man of such great virtue had never yielded to avarice more than to counsel. As their proof, they mentioned the following fact: when, after the absolution of the King, Rudolf usurped the royal office, the Pope kept silent, in accord with the sentence of the comic poet: "Who keeps silent gives acclaim enough."[56]

And so, after Rudolf had withdrawn—whose head, if he had been apprehended, the avenging sword would, with good reason, have turned around[57]—the king invaded Bavaria and Swabia and inflicted devastation upon those who had banded together in the conspiracy against him; he shattered their fortification. And yet, he did not avenge himself in measure of the substance of the wrong done to him, but knowing how to use the bridle in vengeance, he held the reins of revenge far below the measure of the wrong.

But Rudolf, to compensate for the shame of flight with a deed of valor, besieged the city of Würzburg, where the fight was waged, however, with deceit more than with valor. For after the King had called together an army to cast forth the enemy,[58] and a battle line of the two sides had been drawn up, and the foremost men in the ranks were joining battle among themselves, certain horsemen of the royal side who placed themselves beside the King, like dependents [acting] in good faith, suddenly turned their weapons upon him, having been bribed for this purpose. But since his body was protected by bronze [armor], they inflicted a bruise, not a wound. Woe, most wretched men, for whom a price was the cause both of crime and of destruction, whom both crime and vengeance enveloped on one and the same spot; for so many avenging right hands fell upon them in frenzy that they preserved not even the form of human corpses. There is a tumult; a clamor is raised;[59] word is spread that the King has been killed; the army, terrified at this word, flees, the enemy follows. And since,

[53] Sallust, *Catiline* 10, 4; 11, 1.   [54] See Letter 17, p. 164. Lucan V, 345.
[55] Cf. Sallust, *Catiline* 48, 8.   [56] Terence, *Eunuchus* III, 2, 23.
[57] The figure is that of the falling head. Cf. Lucan VIII, 673.   [58] 1086.
[59] *Aeneid* II, 313.

except for a few, the horsemen found safety in their horses, a pitiable fate befell the foot soldiers alone.[60] Thus, the more criminal the nature of the victory, the less its glory.[61]

So the enemy returned into Saxony after the city [Würzburg] had been taken and a garrison stationed there.[62] What profit, O reprobate [Rudolf], did you get, either from the random slaughter of a fleeing mob or from the lucky capture of a city, when you were not master of the city long and of the kingdom never? For the King, after a short time, returned with an army and retook the city which had been snatched away; for those to whom the province of guarding the city had been handed over had fled from the city.[63] Afterwards, he entered Saxony on several occasions with an army[64] and retired either as victor or with things at a standstill.[65] But on his last return, he was victorious in a victory as noteworthy as happy, and a great proof was given to the world that no one might rise up against his lord. For Rudolf, with his right hand cut off, provided an example of the most worthy vindication of treachery, he who did not fear to violate the fealty sworn to his king. And as though other wounds were not sufficient for death, a penalty was inflicted upon that member [with which the vow was made], that the guilt might be known through the penalty.[66]

But something else noteworthy happened in this victory—namely, that the victorious army, as well as the conquered, fled. Indeed, divine clemency ordained this from above, so that after the ruin of the head [Rudolf] the impiety of slaughter on both sides might be prevented through flight on both sides.

But the harsh people was not warned by the loss suffered or by the sign shown; but rather, to conquer through obstinacy which it could not conquer through fighting, it constituted Herman[67] its new king.

He likewise perished in a strange way. For when the Saxons drove him away from their land (whatever it was in him that displeased them)[68] he returned into his native land[69] bearing the empty name of

---

[60] Cf. Lucan IV, 769 f.　　[61] Cf. Ovid, *Metamorphoses* VII, 333.

[62] The author seems to have confused the battle with Rudolf at Mellrichstadt (1077–1078) with the Battle of Bleichfeld (1086). Rudolf besieged Würzburg in 1077; Herman of Salm, in 1086.

[63] Sallust, *Catiline* 46, 4.　　[64] 1079, 1080, and 1087–1089 on frequent occasions.

[65] Cf. Sallust, *Catiline* 39, 4.　　[66] 1080, in a battle on the Elster River.　　[67] 1081.

[68] They had turned to Ekbert, margrave of Meissen.　　[69] Lorraine.

king.[70] Then, he betook himself to Herman, the bishop of Trier,[71] whom, too, the inexpugnable strength of his fortifications had driven to the rash venture of declaring against the king. How great was the power of the king, who had to be fed not from his own resources, but from those of others! One day, when he was on a journey, he thought that, as a prank, they should rush as seeming enemies upon the castle to which they were going and test how much boldness, how much valor, lay in the spirits of the defenders. How amazing was the way, how unlooked-for, in which he discovered how what was going to happen [that is, death, the inevitable] might be! When they tore into the gate, which was found without bars and without a guard, some who were within seized arms against the attackers in a manly way, whereas others weakly sought shelters. But a woman who had gone into the tower, woman in sex, not in spirit, cast a millstone down upon the King's head. And so he died at a womanly hand, that his death might be the more ignominious. But to whitewash this dishonor, they transferred by agreement the deed of the woman to the person of a man.[72]

5. After the two kings had met this fate, there was long hesitation in the creation of kings, and the fear [produced by] the past disaster stretched into the future as well.[73] Finally cupidity was victorious and drove Ekbert the margrave with a bold hand to strive for the kingship.[74] In death, indeed, he learned too late what one can be taught from the losses of another.

There was a city in Saxony which turned to his [Henry's] side, since it saw the fortune of the King going in a favorable course, taking for granted its security both because of the strength of its position and because of the royal succor. The Saxon nobles bore this with poor grace and invested the city with a siege.[75] But Margrave Ekbert, who had become swollen with the hope of becoming master of the royal power, went with greater zeal than anyone else to that siege in order to adapt himself to the end which he strove to attain. After he had

---

[70] 1088. Cf. Lucan V, 389.

[71] Egilbert was then archbishop of Trier. Herman of Metz, who seems to be meant here, was subsequently expelled from his see.

[72] 1088.   [73] Cf. Lucan II, 333.

[74] Actually, Ekbert was elected while Herman was still alive.

[75] No other source tells of this siege, though in 1088 Ekbert besieged Quedlinburg, which was held by the Abbess Adelheid, half-sister of Henry IV. The chronicler Bernold says that Ekbert was slain in ambushes through the craft of Adelheid (*MGH SS.*, V, 450).

sent a multitude of men ahead, he himself followed with a few.[76]

A hidden path led him through a certain grove after he had turned off from the public road not perchance to fall among enemies—for who is so powerful he lacks an enemy or who does not fear hostile ambushes? How hidden are your judgments, O God, and with what wondrous order do you hide what you are going to do and reveal what you have hidden.[77] Already the noonday heat of the sun burned the horses and those seated on the horses, and, as it happened, the heat of the day kindled thirst. So heavy a sleep, moreover, stole upon the weary men that they hung their necks drooping in sleep, and the horses, not turned with their bits, took free rein. Not very far in the recess of the forest, they saw a solitary mill,[78] where they turned aside and gave themselves to sleep. Meanwhile, the miller was sent to bring drink from the village for those athirst.

While he was hastening with a goatskin bag set on his shoulders, he met on his way some shield-bearers going to the afore-mentioned siege who were secretly vassals of the King although they belonged to the opposing side. He was questioned by them, whence he came, whither he went, why he hurried so out of breath; and, not knowing how to conceal what he knew, he revealed the identity of his guest and the reason for his trip.

These men, stunned with fear, or rather with joy, discussed among themselves what they should do—what danger, on the other hand, what reward, what valor, what praise, what mark of fidelity would be in it if they should smite so great an enemy of the King. [They argued] that this opportunity had not been brought before them for nothing, that very great valor was proved through very great hazards. Thus they stirred up the spirits of each other and hurried with horses spurred to the mill; they arrived there in desire before they had with horses.

The fight, once begun, was long and doubtful of outcome, since the combatants were equals in valor and number. The one side [the partisans of Henry] fought for praise; the other, for life.[79] The fortune of the King finally was victorious, and the fiercest enemy, slain not in the battle line, but in a mill, fell ignominiously.[80] You are happy, indeed,

[76] 1090.   [77] Cf. Romans 11:33.   [78] Apparently near the Selke River.
[79] Cf. Sallust, *Jugurtha* 94, 5.
[80] Cf. *De unitate ecclesiae conservanda* II, 35: "Afterwards he was slain in a wretched manner, discovered in some hut, not to say what is truer, in a mill."

and have always a great name, O mill,[81] to which men are attracted not so much by the turning which is your purpose as by your fame, you who tell about this battle while grinding and grind while telling.

Thus this assembly of nobles [at the siege] was put into confusion; it cleared the battlefield; and so withdrew from the siege without having achieved their aim.[82]

And so the affairs of the King were advanced daily into a higher and happier state. Those of his adversaries, however, turned downward, and all of their undertakings ended with a shameful outcome.

6. When, therefore, they saw that they had no success, either in arms or in the election of kings, they armed themselves again with calumnies and accused him before the Pope, besides other things, of many and impious deeds.[83] They asserted that often he had been exiled from the royal office because of his crime; that he had slain the most Christian kings whom they themselves had created, not without the authority of the Pope; that he had usurped the royal office through bloodshed; that he had laid everything waste with fire, pillage, and the sword; and that he had exercised his tyranny against the Church and the kingdom in every way.

On their accusation, the Pope again bound him with the ban, as they proposed. But this ban was not considered to be of great weight, in that it was seen to be not an act of reason, but of whim; not of love, but of hate.[84]

The King, however, perceiving that the Pope was inclined to strip him of the kingship, and that he would not be content with any [act of] obedience from him other than his renunciation of the kingship, was forced to relapse from obedience into rebellion, from humility into swollen pride, and readied himself to do to the Pope what the Pope intended to be done to him. Cease, I pray, O glorious King, cease from this attempt to cast down the ecclesiastical head from his summit, to make yourself a criminal by recompensing injury. To suffer injury is the part of felicity; to render it, that of crime.

And so the King sought reasons and opportunities to cast him out. And it was found that he had occupied the Roman See, which he had rejected once before and which, therefore, he should have rejected [at the time of his election], since he had willfully aspired to it while

---

[81] Lucan VII, 139; Horace, *Carmina* III, 9, 7.   [82] Sallust, *Jugurtha* 58, 7.   [83] 1080.
[84] See Letter 34, p. 181.

he was archdeacon and his lord was still living.[85] Whether these things are true or false can be discovered with too little accuracy. Some averred it; others said that it was a fabrication. For each party, Rome entered into the argument: the one argued that Rome, the mistress of the world, would never countenance such an impiety; the others, that this handmaid of cupidity [Rome] would easily let any impiety pass, for a price. As for me, however, the matter must be left unsettled, since I cannot defend, nor do I dare to affirm, uncertain things.

Therefore, the King went to Rome with an army, crushing whatever stood in his way.[86] He subdued the cities: those which were proud, he pressed hard; the lofty, he bent low; he scattered factions.

At his approach, Rome, who ought to have prepared honors for him, was persuaded to ready arms, as though the Punic Hannibal had crossed the Alps;[87] and she shut her gates to her king as though to an enemy. Whence, the King, stirred by just indignation, cut off the city by a siege, as the state of affairs demanded.[88] Men were sent out all about to destroy castles, to devastate villages, to pillage goods; and he caused harm to the province without, since Rome had shut herself within. Without, there was war; within, fear.[89] On every side, war machines lept forth; here, the battering ram struck the wall; there, a soldier prepared to climb a ladder. On the other side, those who were in the city hurled shafts, stones, stakes burned on the end [hardened in fire],[90] and fire; sometimes they came out and entered close combat.[91] On each side, the fight was carried on bravely; their good cause made these [the Henricans] bold; their peril made the others so.

One day,[92] when each army, weary from the fighting and the summer heat,[93] had given themselves up to sleep about midday, and, as fortune wished, no look-out kept watch, one of the shield-bearers went alone to the wall to gather stakes. He saw that the wall and ramparts were unoccupied, and with his pricked and attentive ears he also discovered that no one was near within the walls. Assisted by confidence of mind and lightness of body, he worked his way up with

---

[85] These charges had already been presented by Henry and his bishops at Worms in 1076. See Renunciation of Gregory VII by the German Bishops, p. 147.

[86] 1081. See Letter 18, p. 165.   [87] Cf. Lucan I, 304 f.

[88] 1081–1084. Sallust, *Jugurtha* 35, 5.   [89] II Corinthians 7:5.   [90] *Aeneid* VII, 524.

[91] Cf. Sallust, *Jugurtha*, chaps. 57, 60.   [92] June 3, 1083.

[93] Cf. Sulpicius Severus, *Life of St. Martin*, chap. 3.

hands and feet, until finally he touched the summit of the wall.[94] Then, indeed, when he cast his eyes around and saw no one, set between hope and fear,[95] he signaled to his comrades by every movement of his body, and scarcely did he keep himself from shouting when they gave attention too slowly to his signals. Hastening with arms and ladders which they had snatched up, and going over the wall more swiftly, as they say, than can be told, they slew, captured, put to flight those who had come too late to the defense of the captured city.[96]

The King disdained to enter by way of the gate which now had been thrown open, for at that point every man in the ranks to the rear would have been slowed by the ones marching in front of him and every man to the fore would have been shoved on by the pressure of those behind. But to avenge the rash shutting [of the gates], he ordered that the wall be broken and that they lay open an entrance for him so wide that the whole army drawn up side by side and shoulder to shoulder could sweep in at the same time.

Then, certainly, death was everywhere; everywhere, mourning.[97] Rome trembled while the height of her towers was battered and fell.[98] The Pope fled,[99] and he who had pushed everyone into peril deserted all in peril. At last, Rome contritely repented her of her presumption, and she who could have deserved earlier to be honored by the King with gifts now, in the presence of the King, obtained with difficulty, and with a great deal of money, the privilege not to be wholly destroyed.

Shortly, when everything had been quieted, the King presented in public the reason why he had come; he reported what criminal treatment he had received at the hands of the Pope; and after many had

---

[94] Cf. Sallust, *Jugurtha*, chaps. 93, 94.   [95] *Aeneid* I, 218.

[96] In Gregory's November Synod, 1083, the following report was made: "But the persecution of this same Henry precluded three Lenten Synods. Once he approached St. Paul [St. Paul's without the Walls]; twice, St. Peter's; and finally, after much blood was shed, he took the walls of Porticus [the Leonine City] not so much through the bravery of his men, as through the negligence of the citizens. Indeed, the Roman mob (that is, the more copious part of the city), wearied by the two-year's war, was laboring under keen hunger, since they were not allowed to go out to neighboring towns or camps, nor did Henry's sworn men wish to go to the city for trade. Many also had left the city, driven away by hunger. And at length as their interest in the war declined, the others prosecuted it with increasingly less zeal, and without any qualms, they neglected their guard posts as much as they pleased."

[97] *Aeneid* II, 369.   [98] The destruction of the walls of the Leonine city.

[99] Actually Gregory VII took refuge in the Castel Sant' Angelo until the Norman forces under Robert Guiscard forced Henry's retreat from Rome (1084).

confessed that this had indeed happened so, he designated Pope Clement for the election of all.[100] After he had been consecrated Emperor with the common approval of all and made patrician by him [Clement], he confined himself in Rome for some time,[101] to remold everything into solid concord.

7. We must not pass by a story which the account of reliable persons spread into the German regions and which Rome herself averred.

The Emperor was accustomed to frequent a certain oratory to pray, and he let no day pass without going there. He had chosen for himself, however, a familiar place in that same oratory for prayer, a place where he might spend his time the more intently, the more secretly, in prayer.[102]

A certain man of impious mind observed this habit of his. And, whether urged on by his own or by the wickedness of another, he placed a great stone on a beam in position to strike from above the head of the Emperor; and, by removing from the paneled ceiling a tablet which looked directly down on the head of the Emperor, he opened a hole to send the weight through. He tested this arrangement very often, using a slackened rope so that the stone would not go awry in falling. After everything had been tested sufficiently, this servant of guile scaled up one night and watched from above until the Emperor stood to pray in his customary place. Then, that men, greedy for the destruction of another, but ignorant of his own, hurled the weight against the head of the Emperor.[103] The unhappy man, himself a weight, fell together with his weight, but the Emperor was not harmed, for he had moved slightly from his place. The affair became known swiftly through all of Rome,[104] and the common mob (*plebs*), which cannot be quieted easily once it has been aroused, in a frenzy, and against the will of the Emperor, pulled the half-living body[105] over rocks and stones and rent it asunder.[106] But everyone, attributing the affair to a miraculous sign, not to an accident, became the more devotedly subject to the Emperor in the bonds of fidelity and of their feelings. And the hostile plot not only confirmed in loyalty those already faithful to

[100] Wibert of Ravenna had already been elected as Clement III in 1080 at Brixen. The election was repeated in 1084, and Wibert was consecrated. See Letter 18, p. 166.

[101] For one month.   [102] Cf. Sulpicius Severus, *Life of St. Martin*, chap. 10.

[103] Cf. Sulpicius Severus, *Life of St. Martin*, chap. 5.

[104] Cf. I Maccabees 7:3.   [105] Cf. Ovid, *Fasti* II, 838.   [106] Cf. Jude 14:6.

him, but also made many loyal who had been his enemies; and so, he [the would-be assassin] who strove to do harm actually did good.

Finally, when everything in Rome was set in order and a garrison had been established in the City,[107] lest she alter her state of fidelity, the Emperor, functioning in the height of his new dignity, went back into the German kingdom. But no fortune lasts long; for those whom the Emperor had established as a garrison in Rome were seized with sickness which both the place and the season produced—for it was summer—and died without even one survivor.[108] Then, when the yoke of the garrison had been removed, Rome, made mistress of her own decisions, reverted to type;[109] and, after she had taken up arms again against the Emperor and had expelled the Pope [Clement],[110] she constituted another; for that earlier Gregory had departed from life. When this was revealed to the Emperor, he set out again with an army against Rome. But when he came into Italy, he was met by envoys from Rome who bore a pact of peace, and [at the same time] a report reached him of a hostile enterprise at his back. Thus he returned to Germany[111] and left behind in Italy his son Conrad, who at that time was already the heir-designate of the kingdom,[112] assigning to him the task of working against Mathilda—that grasping woman who was laying claim to almost all of Italy—and taking out of the hand of a woman that kingdom which would be his in the future.

What may enemies do when children themselves rise up against their parents? Or whence may one assure himself of security when he is not safe from him whom he begat? Let marriages now cease; let no one hope for an heir: your heir will be your enemy, for not only does he rob you of your house and lands, but he also makes haste to rob you of your life.

The son of the Emperor, who as we have said, was left by his father in Italy, and left for a definite reason, as we have also told, was won over by the persuasions of Mathilda—for whom may not womanly

[107] The garrison consisted of 300 German knights under the command of Udalrich of Godesheim (1083).

[108] One account says that "scarcely thirty" survived. (*MGH SS.*, V, 438.)

[109] Terence, *Adelphi* I, 1, 46.

[110] Wibert was expelled during the summer of 1085, but returned shortly after. He was expelled again in 1089 and returned again in 1091.

[111] He remained in Italy until 1097; when Conrad rebelled in 1093, he stayed in northern Italy.

[112] Conrad was consecrated as king in 1087.

guile corrupt or deceive?—and joined his father's enemies. He set the crown upon his own head,[113] usurped the royal office, profaned right, confounded order, fought against nature, and sought the blood of his father, since he would not have been able to reign save by the blood of his father.

When a running report brought this news to the enemies of the Emperor, they were exultant, they applauded, they sang, they praised the deed of the son, [and they praised] especially the woman who was the chief mover of the deed.[114] They sent envoys straightway to thrust a spur into the spirit of the new king and to add oil to the fire,[115] to vow perpetual fidelity and material assistance for their own interests (but actually against them), although long ago they had covenanted never to obey the son or the father.

The Emperor, on the other hand, however much he grieved inwardly at this report, outwardly maintained himself, nonetheless, in his grave demeanor and lamented, not his own, but his son's fortune. When, however, he could not recall him from his undertaking, he sought not so much to avenge his own injury as through vengeance to remove a model of wrongdoing. And so he turned his thoughts toward disinheriting his son and to advancing his [Conrad's] brother Henry, still a boy, into the royal office.[116] Therefore, after the Emperor had held many assemblies with the great nobles, he stated his complaints against his son Conrad: namely, that he had joined the enemies of the royal office and usurped the royal office and that he strove to deprive his father not only of the royal office, but also of life. He said that the wrong done to him ought to be considered a wrong done to the state, or if this were not to cause concern to anyone, at least they should serve the cause of the state so as to avoid the danger that anyone would become king through force and crime;[117] or rather, that they should transfer the election which the elder son had rightly lost to his younger son. Many raised objections against this, relying more on ingenuity than on the just and the true; many, however, were in favor of the public good and were in accord with the decision and the desire of the Emperor. Finally, all came together on one decision and gave their approval with harmonious good will.

First, the invader [Conrad] was adjudged by decree of the Curia, and

[113] He was crowned king of Italy by Anselm, archbishop of Milan, in 1093 at Monza.
[114] Cf. *Aeneid* I, 364.   [115] Horace, *Satires* II, 3, 321.   [116] 1097.
[117] Sallust, *Jugurtha* 14, 7. See Letters 34 and 37, pp. 181–184.

then the Emperor constituted his younger son heir to the kingdom.[118] Lest he also go into the path of his brother,[119] he [Henry IV] received from him a solemn vow,[120] specifically that he would never intrude himself either into the royal power or into the lands of his father while he [the father] was living, except, perchance, by his consent. Already then, there was muttering and fear that there would be intestine war in the future between the two brothers and that a great disaster was in store for the kingdom. But He who dispenses all removed this fear with the death of the elder son[121] and gave an opportunity for the kingdom to return into single harmony.

When these things had been transacted thus, the enemies of the Emperor who had found themselves so often deprived of a head, not having anyone else to whom they might adhere, were rendered more agreeable by treaty and converted, which was the very best thing, wars into peace and castles into [bastions of] domestic security.

8. Therefore, so that there might be peace and tranquillity everywhere, when the magnates had been called together to the Curia,[122] he [Henry IV] had the peace strengthened throughout the whole kingdom under an oath, and, to bridle the evils which came into being before that time, he decreed grave punishments against transgressors [of the decree]. Indeed, the decree of peace profited the miserable and the poor as much as it harmed the perverse and the powerful, for to those [the poor] it brought resources; to these [the powerful] want and hunger.[123] For as regards those who had squandered their goods on soldiers so that encompassed by a large force of knights they might advance in the world and might far outstrip others with their force of armed men—when the license to do robbery was taken from them (so it may be said of them in time of peace), they toiled in poverty; hunger possessed their storehouses. He who lately was borne on a frothing steed now began to be content even with a rustic draft horse. He who lately sought no robe other than one which glowed, tinted with reddish purple, said that he had done well if now he had a robe which nature had tinted with her own color. Gold rejoiced that it was no longer trampled in the mire, when want forced the use of iron spurs. Finally, whatever vanity, whatever superfluity corrupt fashions had

---

[118] 1098, at Mainz.   [119] Cf. Matthew 10: 5.

[120] Repeated in 1099 during the coronation of Henry V at Aachen.   [121] 1101.

[122] Mainz, 1103.   [123] Sallust, *Historia* II, 96, 6.

brought in, Mistress Penury destroyed it all. Securely, the sailor passed hamlets situated on river banks, for which the loot of captured ships used to afford sustenance, while now the chief of the hamlet hungered. A wondrous fact and no less amusing: while others avenged their injuries with injuries, the Emperor avenged his with peace.

When, however, the lords with their followers had been restrained. for some years by this law, distressed because they were not allowed to practice their wickedness with freedom, they set in motion again muttering against the Emperor; they sowed again a dark rumor[124] about his deeds.

Of what, I ask, has he been guilty? Without doubt, it was this: that he forbade crimes, that he recalled peace and justice, that the highwayman did not beset the road, that the forest did not conceal his ambushes, that the merchant and boatmen might go their way freely, that the robber hungered since robbery was forbidden.

Why, I pray, does it please you to live in no way other than from robbery? Return to the fields those whom you have assigned from the field to arms; balance the number of your followers with the amount of property you have to protect; reassemble your lands which you scattered foolishly in order to have more men-at-arms; and then your barns and storehouses will abound with all good things. And no longer will it be necessary to take things not one's own, when everyone can subsist abundantly on his own.

Under such conditions the Emperor would not be charged with a crime, nor war be promoted in the kingdom; under such conditions you would have [the wherewithal] to satisfy the body, and you would save your souls as well, which is most felicitous. But I waste my time; I ask the ass to play the lyre:[125] bad customs grown usual are never removed or, if so, with difficulty.

9. Therefore, those accustomed to rapine turned their minds again to the promotion of wars in order to find occasion for recovering their habitual way of life. They sought again to find a rival for the Emperor; to this end they thought his son most suitable.[126]

And so to find a place for the suggestion—these were the first allure-

---

[124] Cf. Lucan VII, 2.   [125] Cf. St. Jerome to Marcellus 27, 1.

[126] See Letter 34, p. 181. The leaders in this conspiracy as named by the chronicler Ekkehard of Aura were Diotpald, margrave of the Nordgau; Bernger, count of Sulzbach; and Otto, count of Hapsburg.

ments of deception—they frequently took him along with them on hunts.[127] They baited him with lures of feasts; with jests they launched into the sundering of his spirit and dragged him along with them to the doing of many things which youth inspires. Finally, as is the case among youths, they were bound together with a certain bond of comradeship, so that they even plighted their fidelity and gave the right hand in common secrets. When, therefore, they thought that he, ensnared as he was with much craft, could be caught, one day among other things, as though in an aside, they brought his father into mention. They were amazed [they said] that he could suffer so harsh a father, that he was no different from a slave. His father was an old man and incapable of managing the reins of the kingdom; and if he put off the assumption of the kingship until his [father's] death, beyond all doubt another would snatch it from him ahead of time. Because of the envy and hatred which existed toward his father, he would have many supporters; indeed, he would transfer the good wishes of all to himself if he made no delay in taking over the government of the kingdom which he had received, most of all since long ago both the Church had cast away his father, excommunicate, and the great nobles of the kingdom had rejected him. And finally, they said that that which he had imprudently vowed should not be observed, but rather that he would at last have sanctified himself if he made void the vow vowed to an excommunicate.

Since the father, on his side, suspected no evil from his son, he approved his familiarity with the greater men of the kingdom, hoping that just as they had become united in affection in the present so they would afterwards bear him assistance the more faithfully and efficaciously in obtaining the kingship.

What more? Suddenly enticed and drawn away by lust, as youth is always seducible, he was lacking neither in desire nor in action for [the fulfillment] of the malignant proposal. Therefore, the son of the Emperor watched for the time when his defection from his father would be of the greatest inconvenience to his father. And when the Emperor was marching with an army against certain rebels among the Saxons, at the very time when the Saxons, through envoys, were pressing for negotiations, his son suddenly deserted him, taking many men away from him.[128] Without doubt he [Henry V] will be deserted by those who had persuaded him to become a deserter.

[127] 1104.   [128] December, 1104, from the Imperial camp at Fritzlar.

The Emperor sent envoys[129] after him and recalled him as much with tears as with commands, entreating him not to cause grief to his old father; rather, not to offend the Father of all, not to expose himself to the scorn of men, not to make himself a subject of idle talk for the world. [He urged him], moreover, to be mindful of the bond with which he had obligated himself to him. Those who had suggested such things to him, [he said], were enemies, not friends; waylayers, not advisers in good faith.

He [Henry V] cast all this completely aside and averred that he would have no further dealing with him since he was excommunicate. Thus he pursued his own cause under the guise of the cause of God. Instantly, he rushed through Bavaria, Swabia, and Saxony; he convened the great nobles; he attracted all, as they were "characters desirous of revolution"; and he crept into the regal power as though he had entombed his father. Soon he besieged threateningly the castle of Nürenberg. The disaster sustained there by each side is evidence of how great the valor was with which the battle was joined. But the less hope those besieged had, the greater their spirit; and unless the Emperor, forbearing to punish crime, had ordered the surrender of the castle,[130] he [Henry V] would still labor there with a useless siege if only hunger, which overcomes everything, did not subdue it. Lo, how great the father's pious sense of duty! In return for the deed of his son, he showed the spirit of paternal affection; he paid no heed to the wrong, but to nature; he preferred that the town be given over rather than that it be freed by bringing peril to his son; he preferred to endure his wrongs rather than to avenge them. The townsfolk, therefore, after they had been offered the sort of settlement they wanted, surrendered the town; and after the army was disbanded, the King betook himself to Regensburg, to make it stable for himself and immovable in solidly established good faith, since until that time it had been ambivalently disposed.

As soon as the Emperor learned this—he resided at that moment in the city of Würzburg—he thought that his son could be apprehended either on his journey or in the city; and with so swift and so silent a course did he follow his footsteps that no one had foreknowledge of his journey before a rather considerable band of his men crossed the Danube and rushed up to the city with swiftly driven horses. His son,

---

[129] 1105. The Archbishops of Cologne and Trier, Frederick, duke of Swabia, and Erlung of Würzburg. See Letter 34, p. 181

[130] Not supported by other accounts.

dumbfounded at so sudden and unexpected a thing, fled from the city.

Why do you flee him whom you ought not to flee; why do you flee your father?[131] He follows you, he does not pursue you; he follows, I say, not as an enemy, but as a father, not to destroy, but to save; he follows to restore to a quiet state the commonwealth thrown into turmoil by you, and to provide for your affairs in the future.

After sending out messengers immediately through Bavaria and Swabia, the King recollected his scattered army, a fact which forced the Emperor to summon an army for himself. Thus the two armies came against each other on the Regen River; here the father, there the son; here devotion, there madness settled down together.

And when the more powerful of each side convened as mediators in such great dissension, those who were from the side of the Emperor were enticed by persuasive words and attracted by many and great promises and thus grew cold in their loyalty toward the Emperor; and unless he had sensed this deceitfulness of his intimates, he would have been left in danger alone, with only a few men.

Therefore, he thought that he had to yield to crime and fortune, and after the fashion of David, he fled lest his son become a parricide.

How wondrously works the grace of God! With how plain a sign[132] does it teach us, if we would be taught, if we would not have a blind heart.

Since the Emperor assumed that his enemies would pursue him in the direction in which he had gone, he turned aside to the Duke of Bohemia, who received him with great honor, although of late in no good way he had abandoned him in the narrows, and he conducted him into Saxony. Although he had dangerous and brave enemies there, he was nevertheless honorably conducted through their midst and by them to the Rhine.

Whence this unless "the hand of the Lord was with him,"[133] and he had an invisible leader who led him safe through shafts, through enemies?[134] You had been warned by this miracle, O son of the Emperor, if you could have been warned, to learn to revere your father, not to harry him whom even his enemies revered when he had come into their hands. But you will be warned more harshly, since you are not corrected by this very mild admonition.

When, however, the flight of the Emperor had become known, that

---

[131] Cf. Eusebius-Rufinus, *Historia ecclesiastica* III, 23.   [132] II Maccabees 14:15.
[133] Luke 1:66.   [134] *Aeneid* II, 527.

event took many men away from him and caused much to be added to the affairs of his son, but to be subtracted from his own affairs.

10. In order to spur on the fortune which favored him, the King straightway scheduled a Curia at Mainz on the birth of the Lord. He invited the great nobles and summoned many so that he could announce to all that he wished to be the master of things. Even the Emperor, when he had summoned those men needful to him [his intimate advisers], was disposed to go to this Curia, for he wished to place in question whether what had been done to him had been done rightly or otherwise. When his adversaries had learned this, they feared both for themselves and for their case if his armed retinue should prove as mighty as his legal grounds.

Thus they suggested this act of deception to the King. [They proposed] that he confess his wrong before his father, having assumed an expression of deepest repentance, and earnestly entreat him for pardon. [He was to say] that he was sorry to have agreed to malignant proposals and that he was ready [to render] full satisfaction if only he found his pardon. And if he could thus find an opportunity for deception, he should use it; if not, however, fraud itself should be held for fidelity, pretense for truth.

When he came to his father,[135] instructed in this artifice, the father believed the words and the tears of his son and fell upon his neck, weeping and kissing him, joyful after the example of that father in the Gospel [who learned] that the son who had been dead had revived and that he who had been lost was found.[136] What more? He acquitted his son of punishment as of crime; and to reproach his son with fatherly gentleness was to him to avenge the wrongdoing of his son, as in that comment of the comic poet: "For a great sin of the son, slight punishment is enough for the father."[137]

After these dealings, just as he had deceived his father with feigned repentance, so also he did with counsel. For he suggested to his father, as it had been suggested to him himself, that they both should dismiss so great a host and then go to the Curia with moderate forces, that there was nothing which would offer resistance to him since they had come together in concord, and that everything would be destroyed if they went on with this great force.

[135] At Coblenz.   [136] Luke 15:24.   [137] Terence, *Andria* V, 3, 32.

This advice (good, indeed, had it not been deceptive) pleased his father, and after the great host had been dismissed, he went with not more than three hundred men to the Curia, accompanied by his son. He turned off for the night to a resting place,[138] and there the father amused himself with his son in a wondrous way through that whole night; he conversed and joked, he embraced and kissed him, eager to make up for what he had lost through the long interruption of this enjoyment, but not knowing that that night of amusement was the last.

It is amazing that fraud ever had so well-ordered a fortune. For on the next day, when they were drawing near to Mainz, there came a man under the guise of a messenger whose task was to say that the Bavarians and the Swabians had come to Mainz with a monstrous host. Then his son suggested to the Emperor that it would not be safe to go into the midst of enemies, unless their dispositions had been fathomed beforehand, and [added] that the audacity of men is unbridled. [He advised] that he should rather turn aside to a castle[139] which was near-by, while he himself convened them, sought out the resolve of their undertaking, and conducted them to him to seek his favor.

The Emperor did as his son suggested; he turned aside to the castle, not discerning the snare of craft which the lovely appearance of lying faith had woven. When, however, the Emperor had entered with a few men, the gate was closed and entrance was denied to his vassals. Then the fraud was revealed: he who had been received as lord was held as captive.

And so after he had posted guards to watch over his father, he return-ed with this triumph of deceit to the Curia at Mainz and related with great boasting, as though he had done a deed of valor, how ingeniously he had caught his father. Then, indeed, the Curia resounded with applause and gladness, and they ascribed impiety to justice and deceit to virtue. At once he sent an envoy[140] to his father, ordering him, if he wished to save his life, to transmit without delay the cross, the crown, the lance, and the other regalia to him and to transfer into his hand the strongest fortifications he held. Neither did the father delay to do everything which he had been ordered, nor did he consider the Empire more valuable than himself. But it was thought that he had not rendered satisfaction enough in this [matter] unless he himself came also in person and, in the sight of all, renounced the Empire. He came,[141]

---

[138] Bingen.   [139] Böckelheim.   [140] Wibert of Groitsch.   [141] To Ingelheim.

therefore, not of his own power, but brought forth under arrest. Alone he stood before those who once had stood before him, and not having the liberty of arguing his case in debate, he spoke as the fortune of a captive demands. Asked whether his renunciation of the Empire were voluntary, he answered not what his desire would have, but what necessity constrained [him to say]. He said that, indeed, he renounced the Empire not constrained by force, but induced by his own will. Already, [he said], his powers to manage the reins of the royal power had failed him, and he was no longer possessed by fierce desire for it [the power], since from long practice he had learned that it held more trouble than glory. It was time, [he added], for him to set off the honor together with the burden and to provide for his soul. Only, [he warned], his son should be wary lest he do something against him which would be unworthy both for him [Henry V] to do and for him [Henry IV] to suffer.

Both the speech of the Emperor and his fortune moved many to laments and tears;[142] not even nature herself, however, could move his son to pity. And when he fell at the feet of his son, praying that he acknowledge in him at any rate the rights he held through nature [that is, the father–son relationship], he turned neither countenance nor mind to his father,[143] although it was rather he who ought to have fallen prostrate at his father's feet in that, impatient of delay,[144] he had seized ahead of time the kingdom from that very man by whom he had been designated its inheritor. Moreover, he prayed forgiveness from all whom he had ever unjustly injured. But he also prostrated himself at the feet of the apostolic legate,[145] praying and beseeching him to loose him from the ban and to restore him to the communion of the Church. Laymen, moved by compassion, gave their forgiveness; but the legate of the Apostolic Lord denied absolution, averring that this was not of his power and that it was necessary for him to look for the grace of absolution from the Pope himself.

What more? After he had renounced the imperial dignity, he departed deprived and retired to a certain manor which his son had allowed him for sustenance. How impotent is the power of the world, how uncertain, how unstable! But that ought not to be called power which cannot bring to pass everything it wishes and which he who attains it can lose.

[142] Lucan IX, 146 f. Cf. Sulpicius Severus, Ep. 2.   [143] Cf. *Aeneid* II, 741.
[144] Lucan VI, 424.
[145] Richard, cardinal bishop of Albano. On his actions, see Letter 39, p. 194.

11. After things had been transacted in this fashion, and the Curia was ended,[146] the King passed through the upper regions and cities of the Rhine, and, as circumstances demanded, he subjected to himself some by grants of benefices, others by inflicting injuries upon them.

When, however, he had entered Alsace, his fortune came to a stand-still for some time,[147] as there he engaged in a battle the outcome of which was as unhappy as its inception unwise. For when his followers were loitering about arrogantly in the village of Ruffach, which was powerful by virtue of its large body of residents and its weapons, a numerous assembly of burghers stood in the way of wrongdoing; and yet, since wrongdoing exceeded measure, they could not endure it.

But when the King heard the tumult, he hastened not to prevent wrongdoing, but to help it on, not to quiet the battle, but to stir it up the more. This called out the whole village in a tumultuous throng; the irrevocable mob ran out,[148] the woman with the man, the servant with the master, the base with the brave; and, as is often the case, injury brought out the true feeling. The battle was begun, and flight was begun; for when those who were on the royal side saw the onslaught of the raging crowd and the matter set in the narrows, they thought that their ruin lay in valor, that safety lay in flight alone;[149] and those who could saved their lives through flight. O unhappy event, O shame of royal dignity: with the King in flight, the regal insignia were made the booty of the mob.

Come to your senses at last, good King, come to your senses, and recognize wrath from above in this which has fallen your lot. It is the judgment of the wrath of God that you should flee, who had put your father to flight, and that you should lose the insignia which you had stolen from your father.

But afterwards when they [the insignia] had been recovered through a pact of peace and a grant of pardon, the deep wound of the injury made the King change his attitude. And when he had gathered a rather large force,[150] he laid waste to the village with fire and looting and raged with indiscriminate slaughter against the men of this place.

But since he suspected that what fortune alone had dared against him[151] had resulted from a stratagem of his father, he began to plot new plots of injuries against him; and in order to obviate any source of

[146] 1106.   [147] Lucan VII, 547.   [148] Lucan I, 509.   [149] Cf. Sallust, *Catiline* 58, 16. [150] Lucan I, 466.   [151] Lucan IV, 402 f.

hindrance for himself, he directed his thoughts to a plan by which either to capture [Henry IV] or to expel him.

And so, he decided that, if it could come about, he would arrest him [Henry IV] at the Easter services which were to be celebrated for him at Liége (where he had heard that he [Henry IV] had found fidelity and a refuge for his fortune) and that he would demand satisfaction from the Bishop[152] who had wronged him by receiving the rival of his honor. And when the father saw that his son had decided to celebrate Easter at Liége, he directed a legation to him in this fashion:

"If I asked you, O sweetest son, whether the tradition of men or the mandate of God is to be held superior and greater, you would respond, unless you have been led away from truth, that he is like a dumb animal who does not prefer heavenly things to earthly, divine to human.

"Why, therefore, do you listen to those who suggest to you 'Harry your father' more than to the word of God Himself: 'Honor your father'?[153] These men deceive you; they do not instruct you; they do not provide for your honor, but they are envious of it;[154] they knit the snares of treacherous disloyalty under the appearance of fidelity. They cannot attain otherwise the destruction of your honor save through our destruction.

"It may very well have been because of the exigencies of my sins— this is the opinion of my adversaries—that God has cast me down so to rule no longer.[155] Nevertheless, it was not your part to have labored to cast me out and to have snatched away from me prematurely the kingdom which I had prepared for you. Barbarous kingdoms condemn and disavow such an inhuman deed; the very pagans abhor it, and those who do not know God recognize what they should owe to nature in loving men.

"But what wonder if malignant stealth succeeds in deception at the seducible and immature time of life [that is, youth] when evil counsels sometimes bend even old men and a fixed state of mind to evil? My fortune results from the crime of another rather than from yours; for you were in the hands of beguilers, not they in yours. If, however, you add injury [to this], you can no longer be excused, since you know that an injury is a crime once it has been done and that you cannot do one halfway.

"For I have heard that you have decided to celebrate Easter at Liége;

---

[152] Otbert of Liége. Cf. Terence, *Andria* IV, 1, 15.   [153] Exodus 20:12.
[154] Cf. Sallust, *Jugurtha* 85, 18.   [155] I Samuel 15:23.

there the Bishop received me with fidelity and devotion when there was no one who was mindful of our benefices or who shared our lot. Surely, it is fitting that you respond with royal liberality to the kindnesses he has shown me; and the more faithfully he is proven to have acted toward us, the more certain you will be able to be of his fidelity. Unless perchance he receive you here in his house, he has decided to keep me with him at the Easter festival. But you say that it is worthy and meet for this festival to join rather than to divide us and that you wish, that you strongly desire, me to pass the days of Easter gladness here with you.

"This, indeed, I also would desire altogether if there were not something which I should fear. For I am unable not to fear those who repent of having allowed me to live when my death and life was in their hands. All things are suspect to me; all things are to be feared, most of all in a crowd where it is the more difficult to guard against danger the greater the opportunity for criminal action. It is for this reason that I have retired far from the midst of those who hated me, and I have withdrawn myself into the outermost limits of your kingdom;[156] so that either I might be safe through remoteness of place or if my fortune should demand that I seek human company beyond [the borders] I could the more swiftly leave your kingdom.

"I pray, therefore, that, for the sake of your father, you set the Easter Curia for another place and that you let me abide (although this may not be permitted to an emperor, at least let it be allowed a guest) in the house of him who received me for the sake of humanity, lest it be told either to my ridicule or to your shame that on the feast of the Lord's resurrection it was my fate to be forced to seek uncertain lodgings. If you do what I ask, I shall be most thankful; but if not, I prefer to be a beggar in foreign realms rather than to be held for a laughing-stock[157] in the realms once my own."

The son heard this legation of his father with a deaf ear, nor could he be deflected from his resolve. For this reason, since Easter was now imminent, the father wanted to withdraw; but the Bishop and Duke Henry,[158] who himself had also been invited by the Bishop, kept him from departing. They said that they could not suffer that, cast from the houses of men on so great a festival, he should seek out the forests and

---

[156] Psalm 18:18–19.   [157] Terence, *Hecyra* I, 247.
[158] Henry of Limburg, duke of Lorraine.

the lairs of wild animals[159] and that he had, indeed, been stripped without cause of Empire, but not of the loving service of his friends. If they were permitted to enjoy peace, they added, they desired nothing more than peace; but if, on the other hand, the affair were to be carried on with weapons, weapons would not be far from their hands. Not to be a source of ruin to them, he averred that it would be more advantageous if he withdrew than if he stayed; but finally, he gave them his consent when they insisted more importunately and remained as they demanded.

12. And so a great cavalry force went far before the face of [that is, in advance of] the King and came to a bridge of the river which is called Meuse. [Walrabo], the son of the afore-mentioned Duke [Henry], occupied the bank on the opposite side of the river with a few men, for he had stationed the main body of his armed men in opportune places not far away for ambuscades. To provoke a battle, he now spurred on his horse in a straight course, and now he rode about in circles, asking if an equal number of them dared to engage in battle with him. With no delay, an equal number from the side of the King crossed over to them and joined battle; with varying moves, they now carried the battle forward, now turned to flight. Meanwhile, one man after another secretly crossed the bridge, increased the number of his comrades, and through this breach of the agreement on the terms of battle, changed the struggle from one between equals to one between unequals.

When the son of the Duke saw this, he turned his back with his men, not so much to flee as to deceive, not so much to avoid danger by fleeing as to lead those following them into danger. On the other side, when those on the opposite bank saw the flight, they crossed the bridge at full speed and pursued the one fleeing, ignorant of their future lot and of the deception which lay hidden.[160] But after they had come to the place where the ambushes were arranged, men dashed forth from the ambuscades and threw themselves with a great onslaught against the pursuers. The latter were terrified by the unexpected danger and turned back in flight, not being able to use their arms rationally[161] because of their confounding fear.

But of what advantage was it to have turned their breasts and to have lain open their backs to wounds? And so, many were taken, many

---

[159] Cf. Lucan II, 153; Ovid, *Metamorphoses* I, 592, and VI, 668.   [160] Cf. Joshua 8:14.
[161] *Aeneid* II, 314.

maimed, many killed; and the blood-stained victor[162] had no bounds to his enormities[162] save that dictated by his own aversion to the deed.

In fact, at the bridge where the fleeing mass was pressed together the impious hand[164] performed the more heinous deeds the less the tightly packed crowd could move. But the river engulfed more by far than the sword consumed;[165] for when the enemy pressed from the back, they cast themselves into the river impelled by fear, and thunder-struck and confused they dashed from death into death. One was yet to see another misfortune there, certainly the greatest one: for the bridge, heavily weighted by the multitude, suddenly collapsed, and the river enveloped men and horses alike. No one had an opportunity to escape; skill in swimming brought advantage to none; for hindered either by the weight of arms or by the press of clinging companions, everyone was drawn into the depths. This evil was the more heinous, as it occurred on the very Day of Preparation [Good Friday], and the magnitude of the heinous deed mounted through the religious awe of the season.

13. After things had passed in this way, the King changed his route and turned toward Cologne. But since it also had denied entrance to him in advance, after passing Easter Sunday in a village which is called Bonn, he returned quickly to Mainz, and, through legates whom he scattered everywhere, he directed a complaint to the nobles in this fashion:

"Even if I had seized the kingdom by usurpation, still I should beat back those resisting our power as much as I were able. Now, however, since I have obeyed your precepts in assuming the office of kingship, has anyone dared with impunity in abuse of the public weal to vex the kingdom and us with arms?

"For when we were on the way to Liége, where our Easter Curia was to be held, and had come to the river Meuse, the Bishop of Liége and Duke Henry, in both of whose faith and devotion to service we placed great confidence, secretly set ambuscades for us; and they slaughtered, captured, and put our men to flight, as ours were unprepared for battle. It is as much a cause of shame to tell that this disaster, as great as it was, should have happened there as it is to dismiss it unavenged. Therefore, constrained as I was both by the severity of the

---

[162] Lucan V, 758.   [163] Lucan I, 334.   [164] Sallust, *Jugurtha* 14, 14.
[165] Cf. II Samuel 18, 8; *Aeneid* II, 600.

outcome and by the pressure of time [that is, by the nearness of Easter],
I turned aside to Cologne. When she, quite proudly, refused to receive
me, I spent the holy day of Easter as I might in the village of Bonn. To
which royal person was such great and degrading abuse ever offered?

"This degrading abuse does not touch me alone; you have been cast
into contempt. These usurpers do not wish your decrees to have authority; they want only their own statutes to be firmly established; and
finally, they long to be regarded as those upon whom the whole weight
of kingship rests. They are ready to destroy the king whom you have
constituted in order that none of those things which you have decreed
may be given any thought. Therefore, this, my injury, is an injury done
to the kingdom rather than to me; for the casting down of one head,
even the highest one, is a loss to the kingdom which can be repaired;
but to crush the princes under foot is to effect the ruin of the kingdom.

"Will we bear these things with impunity, and will their pride become the more puffed up through our base forbearance? O may we
who are called dishonored not also be called unavenged. It is enough
to have said a few words; only idle spirits need the spur of prolix
exhortation. May the cause serve as incitement more than words.

"Since, therefore, the forces of the commonwealth must be used
against such proud enemies, in asking we command, and in commanding we ask of you a campaign [against the enemy] for the assembling
of which we ordain the time, the Kalends of July, and the place, the
city of Würzburg."

When, therefore, Duke Henry and the people of Cologne, together
with the people of Liége, had heard that the King wished to lead an
army against them, they readied arms, they assembled troops, they
strengthened their cities and girded themselves for resistance with
equal will and zeal. They also urged the Emperor with counsels and
entreaties to resume the imperial office which he had set aside, convicted not by regular order, but constrained by force and by a death-
directed sword.[166] [They said] that they would fail him neither in arms
nor in spirit and that, in a short time, he would have many supporters,
since many were much horrified at so unwonted and inhuman an out-
rage. He resisted their urgent solicitation, basing his position on the
following argument: that it was impossible to recover a lost Empire by
force of arms, an Empire which he had not been able to hold fast by

[166] Cf. *Aeneid* I, 91.

force of arms when it was in his possession; that he did not regard it so highly that he deemed it worthy to be regained with the destruction of many men; and that it would be happier and safer for him to live as one deprived, although he had been undeservedly deposed. In this way, one side presented its argument and the other gave its in turn; and since they did not cease to insist that he not cast off from himself the good will which surrounded him, he neither consented nor declined entirely, but looking to the future, he kept their headstrong spirits in suspense with indecisive hope.[167]

They therefore fortified first Cologne, which was to bear the first onslaught, with a ditch and towers; they collected military levies, stationed a garrison there, and then awaited their peril with brave spirits. So also they strengthened the other cities which they believed would be invaded, with fortifications, war machines, and the strength of soldiers. But a manifesto was also sped to people everywhere with a severe admonition to the effect that they should be prepared against the army which was about to come upon them in great pride and should defend their fatherland, freedom, and life,[168] nor should they allow either their wives to be given up to the wantonness of corruption or their fields to be distributed among other lords.

Already the King had crossed the Rhine with a strong army, and with a great onslaught he assailed first Cologne, which stood out among the other cities like their head; he thought thus to subject the members to himself more easily after he had trodden down so strong a head. But the results did not, by far, match the expectation; for his men were driven back in a bloody repulse, and with their camps situated at a distance they had to beset the city with a siege.

Rather, however, I should have said that the besiegers were besieged by the besieged; for when the ships which came down the Rhine carrying provisions to the army were intercepted, they labored under oppressive hunger as though fettered by a kind of siege.

Meanwhile, to free the city from the siege, the strength of the whole fatherland came together from all sides. But the Emperor, detesting such impious bloodshed, counseled resolutely against a battle.[169] Why, he asked, did they have so great an ardor for breaking the siege which

---

[167] Rather, he went to Cologne and supervised its fortification himself. See Letter 42, p. 197. Cf. Ovid, *Metamorphoses* VII, 307.

[168] Cf. Sallust, *Catiline* 58, 11.   [169] This is dubious.

could not be broken except with a great disaster to their own side? If they devoted their whole concern to seizing the city, which was quite safe by virtue both of the strength of the walls and of the brave soldiery, and very well furnished with every kind of sustenance (with even the Rhine River adding its beneficial services since through ships it would afford [the besieged] with whatever delicacies they desired, despite the besiegers), they would give aid to the hated besieger. Rather, he said, they should permit them [the besiegers] to rage forth to their own ruin and to assail the inexpugnable city, whence they would carry away only wounds and the fallen.[170] They should permit them to devastate [the land] far and wide, since, when the supplies of the countryside were used up, they would begin to hunger; they should permit them to move about pillaging, since horses and men would be worn out by their labor. And, [he concluded], perchance victory would be won for them at slight cost, if only they would be patient for a little while and bide their time, which was all to their advantage.

Thus recalled from open battle by the urging of the Emperor, they merely observed the sallies of the enemy and, by killing[171] here and there those ignorant of the terrain, struck such fear into the enemy that he no longer roamed afield.

Everything, indeed, which the Emperor had predicted came to pass. For as often as they attempted to break open the city gates, to tear through the walls with a battering ram, to cast down the towers with catapults, they bore only wounds and corpses back to the camps, their aim still unattained. Men and horses were exhausted as much by the lack of food as by the enormity of their labor, and they lost their strength; for with the fields all about laid waste, they found nothing, but they did not take it upon themselves to go farther because of the enemy lying hidden in ambushes. To these evils sickness also was added, which the stench of the camps, as is usually the case, spread abroad with diseased air. This disease either weakened or killed outright not only common men, but even the princes themselves. Wearied by this kind of adversity in their affairs, they were in doubt as to what they were to do, since though they wished to die, they found no occasion for battle; or if they were ready to retreat, they were certain that the enemy would press them from behind; and thus they feared that their army would be scattered in flight.

[170] *Aeneid* VII, 574.   [171] *Aeneid* II, 384.

While they tossed in this tempest of the mind, a report came suddenly and left only serenity where there had been the clouds of such great perturbation. For the report was that the Emperor had paid his debt of death.

At this news, they were first doubtful; but when a messenger[172] had come bearing with orders the last gift of the father to his son—namely, a ring and a sword—such great gladness arose that the voices of those rejoicing could scarcely be stilled.

But there was no less mourning[173] around the bier of the Emperor: the great nobles wailed; the common men lamented; everywhere moaning was heard, everywhere the agony of lament, everywhere the voice of those grieving. At these exequies widows, orphans and finally, the paupers of the whole fatherland came together;[174] they weep that they have been orphaned of their father; they shed tears on the body; they kiss his great hands. With difficulty they were drawn away from embracing the dead body; with difficulty it was made possible to bury it. But they did not desert the tomb;[175] they spent their time there with vigils, tears, and prayers, reciting with weeping, and weeping in reciting them, what works of mercy he had done toward them.[176]

And yet, his death was not to be lamented, since it had been preceded by a good life. He had held to the upright faith and the steadfast hope and also, in his last days, to a bitter contrition of the heart; he also was not ashamed to make public confession of the shameful things which he had committed and ate with all the eagerness of his heart the bread of the Lord's body.

You are happy, O Emperor Henry, who have procured for yourself such guardians, such intercessors, you who now receive in manifold abundance from the hand of the Lord that which you hid secretly in the hands of the poor. You have exchanged a turbulent kingdom for a tranquil; a defective, for an eternal; an earthly, for the celestial. Now

---

[172] There were two messengers, Erkenbald, the treasurer of Henry IV, and Burchard, bishop of Münster.

[173] *Aeneid* IX, 452.   [174] Cf. Sulpicius Severus, Ep. 3.

[175] According to Otto of Freising (*Deeds of the Emperor Frederick*, I, x), Henry's viscera were buried at Liége, and his body was carried to Speier, where it was buried "in the church of Mary, the Blessed Mother of God and Perpetual Virgin, in royal state beside the emperors, his father and grandfather." Actually this was delayed for some time until Henry V obtained release of his father's excommunication and moved the body from the unconsecrated chapel in Speier where he had first buried it.

[176] Cf. Psalm 74:21.

at last you reign; now you bear a diadem which neither your heir may snatch from you, nor an enemy envy. Therefore, tears must be contained, if they can be contained. To this, your felicity, is owed dancing, not lamenting; exultation, not wailing; the voices of rejoicing, not of lamentation.

After this outcome of affairs, those who had undertaken war against the royal majesty [Henry V], with their hope dead, lost in spirit and in strength. They did what had to be done in these straits, and whoever could do it, in whatever way, by surrender or by the payment of money, returned to the favor of the King.[177]

Lo, then, you have something about the deeds of the Emperor Henry, about his expenditures for the poor, about his fortune, and about his death. Just as all this could not be written by me without tears, so it cannot be read by you without tears.

[177] Among them, Otbert, the bishop of Liége, Henry's former protector, who received Henry V as a canon of his cathedral church in 1107.

THE LETTERS OF HENRI IV

The letters of Henry IV indicate explicitly and in detail the dominant part that the Emperor assumed in ecclesiastical as well as in temporal administration. He himself confessed to Gregory VII that he even usurped ecclesiastical property and sold churches. In three of his earliest letters, he recorded the exercise of his power over the monastery of Lorsch so as to force it to submit to Archbishop Adalbert of Bremen. From subsequent letters, one learns that throughout his reign he continued to claim great authority in the government of the Church. Those claims are most forcefully stated in the documents issued during the Investiture Controversy. There, Henry argues that Gregory VII, having wrongfully acceded to the Papacy, had rent asunder the divinely ordained government of the Church by king and bishop, usurping all power for himself; and he further maintains that, as emperor, consecrated to his office by divine election and sacred unction, he must of his own efforts restore order in the Church and in the Empire. As these letters show, the deposition of Gregory, the election of Wibert of Ravenna as the Imperial pope, and the effort to supply a successor to Wibert upon his death were all effluences of Henry's concept of the emperor's duty to guard and rule jointly over the Church. Other letters illustrate with considerable pathos and clarity the political distractions which plagued Henry throughout his reign.

    1 *Henry asks Bishop Adalbero of Bamberg for an order remitting a fine to N., one of Adalbero's vassals (1054–1056).*

Henry,[1] King by the grace of God, sends his grace and the due gift of

[1] The first element of medieval charters and letters was regularly what students of diplomatics call the "protocol," the classical form of which consists of five parts. The first of these is the *invocatio*, or the appeal to divine authority with the words "In the name of the Holy and Indivisible Trinity" or some similar expression. Occasionally, as in the nineteenth letter of Henry IV, the *invocatio* is represented by a monogram representing the name "Christ." The *invocatio* is followed by the *intitulatio* (the name and title of the sender) and a formula of devotion which states that the sender owed his

love to Adalbero, the reverend pontiff of the holy church of Bamberg, his own beloved cousin.[2]

If all your affairs are proceeding prosperously, we rejoice, as is just; and if any adversity has come upon you—may divine protection prevent this—we extend our sympathy, as is fitting; and we doubt not that you in turn will hold this same affection for us.

Wherefore we ask Your Affection for an order: Since a certain man named N.,[3] who belongs to your military retinue, has come seeking our mercy and assistance, we ask that for the sake of our love and our request, you remit to him the fine which he promised to you under oath, together with the security he offered. If you do this, I, for my part, shall make compensation to you and shall urge my father also to compensate you.

2 *Henry warns Abbot Ulric of Lorsch against rebellion and commands him to go to Goslar at the Feast of All Souls (1065).*[4]

Henry, King by the grace of God, sends grace provisionally to Abbot Ulric.

position to divine grace. Finally, there is the *inscriptio*, or the name and title of the recipient, and the *salutatio*, or the formula of greeting. For the sake of smoothness, the "salutatio" has been transposed in these translations between the *intitulatio*—formula of devotion—and the *inscriptio*. As an illustration, the components of the protocol in Letter 1 may be described as follows:

invocatio: omitted; *intitulatio*: Henry, King; *formula of devotion*: by the grace of God
salutatio: sends grace and the due gift of love
inscriptio: to Adalbero, the reverend pontiff of the holy Church at Bamberg, his own beloved cousin.

The tone of a letter is very frequently indicated by its protocol, and the omission or addition of titles and "salutationes" in a series of letters may reflect the policies being followed by the sender, as the protocols of Letters 2 and 3 and the letters to Gregory VII show very clearly. The inversion of *intitulatio* and *inscriptio*, as in Letter 5, is a mark of deference.

   [2] Adalbero's mother was the sister of Henry III's mother, Gisela.

   [3] Unknown. Occasionally in the protocol or in the body of a letter itself, an initial is used in place of a name in full. In most instances, as here, these initials represent specific names; but sometimes, they are used for "any name," as, for example, in the protocol of Letter 13, an encyclical letter to all royalist bishops. In these last cases, the function of the initial is that of the modern notations "X" or "so-and-so." See also Letters 1, 6, 9, 10, 39.

   [4] In 1064–1065 the monastery of Lorsch, together with Corvey, was given in fief to Adalbert of Bremen, then the guardian of Henry IV and regent of Germany. On Palm Sunday, 1065, Henry and Adalbert were cordially received at Lorsch, and Henry took

We are astonished that we find you disobedient, whom, before all others, obedience befits, and that we see you taking no thought for what you are and for what you cannot do with impunity. We have heard that, in fact, you wish to promote sedition; you do not reflect at all judiciously upon how this sedition may end. For this reason, we wish and firmly command, as a condition for the keeping of our favor, that if you wish to hold anything in our realm, you come to us at Goslar without delay on the festival of All Souls.[5]

3 *Henry commands Ulric of Lorsch to surrender his abbacy and to give the the abbatial staff to the royal envoy (1065).*

Henry, King by the grace of God, to the monk Ulric.

We are astonished that by some effrontery or through someone's abetment you should have wished to hold our abbacy in resistance to us. In this, you neither serve us nor do you manifest any obedience to our guardian, Adalbert,[6] to whom we have given this abbacy. Wherefore we wish and firmly command you, at the peril of your own welfare, neither to make any delay in relinquishing what is ours nor to presume to interfere further with any of these things. We also order you to hand over to our messenger the staff, which is to be brought to us.

4 *Henry forbids the monks of Lorsch to obey Ulric, their former abbot, any longer (1065).*

Henry, King by the grace of God, sends his grace to the brethren of Lorsch.

Just as we have always received obedience from you, so also now do

the opportunity to attempt to reconcile Abbot Ulric to the new state of affairs; at the same time, Adalbert professed his eagerness to foster the well-being of the monastery. The Archbishop's indiscreet choice of administrators for the monastery, however, precipitated strong armed resistance to his authority. On behalf of his guardian, and doubtless at his insistence, Henry issued Letters 2, 3, and 4. The next year, Adalbert was removed from the court by a coalition of powerful nobles, and Henry began his personal rule. During the next two years, he issued a guarantee of the liberties of Lorsch, confirmed in 1069 by Alexander II, and conferred many privileges upon the monastery, including the right to hold markets and the regalian right of coinage. See "Life of Henry IV," chap. 2, p. 105.

[5] November 1, 1065.   [6] Adalbert of Bremen.

we wish to put it to the test. We command that Ulric, once called your abbot, whom we have judged contumacious because of his disobedience and bad example, is to give you no orders, and we decree that you are not to obey him further. Therefore, you gratify our will if you obey him no longer.

5 Henry confesses to Pope Gregory that he has wronged the priesthood and sold churches to unworthy men. He asks Papal help, particularly in regard to the church of Milan, pledges his constancy, and promises to send another legation (1073).[7]

To the most watchful and zealous Lord Pope, Gregory, distinguished by heaven with the apostolic dignity, Henry, by the grace of God King of the Romans,[8] sends the most faithful expression of due subservience.

Since, in order to continue rightly administered in Christ, the kingship and the priesthood are always in need of the strength which He delegates, it is surely fitting for them, my lord and most loving father, not to disagree with one another, but rather to cleave to each other, inseparably joined with the bond of Christ. Thus and in no other way, the concord of Christian unity and the condition of the Church's religious life are preserved in the bond of perfect charity and peace.[9]

---

[7] Shortly before his death in 1073, Alexander II had excommunicated five of Henry's advisers and threatened Henry himself with the ban. Hard-pressed by a fresh rebellion in Saxony while his forces were deployed in Poland, Henry was in no position to enter a second conflict, and he chose to attempt a reconciliation with the Papacy. Therefore, although the tumultuous election of Gregory VII in 1073 violated both canon law and the Papal election decree of 1059, Henry declined to affirm those rights in Papal elections he subsequently claimed; to the contrary, he sent a personal envoy to Gregory's consecration, and he was also represented by his mother, the Empress-dowager Agnes, and his aunt, Beatrice of Tuscany. Letter 5 represents his attitude at the time of Gregory's accession. A new controversy began with Gregory's actions at the Lenten Synod of 1075: his edict against lay investiture and his excommunication of five of Henry's bishops for simony and contumacy are the first major documents of the Investiture Controversy. In an effort to avoid entering another conflict just as he was suppressing the Saxon rebellion, Henry made a futile effort at reconciliation, represented by Letter 7.

[8] The regal title adopted by kings of the Germans regularly from the days of Henry V. It is rarely met in the documents of Henry IV.

[9] Cf. Ephesians 4:3; Colossians 3:4.

With God's consent we have held the office of kingship for some time now, but we have not shown to the priesthood the proper justice and honor in all things. To be sure, we have not borne in vain the avenging sword of the power given us by God;[10] yet we have not always unsheathed it justly in judicial punishment against wrongdoers. Now, however, through divine mercy, we have been stung in some measure[11] by remorse, and having turned against ourself in self-accusation, we confess our former sins to you, Most Indulgent Father, placing our hopes in the Lord that absolved by your apostolic authority we may be worthy of forgiveness.

Alas, we are guilty and wretched! Partly through the inclination of youthful pleasure, partly through the license of our mighty and imperious power, partly also through the seductive deception of those whose counsels we have followed, all too easily misled, we have sinned against heaven and before you, and now we are not worthy to be called your son.[12] For not only have we usurped ecclesiastical properties, but we have also sold the churches themselves to unworthy men—men embittered with the gall of simony—who entered not by the door but by some other way;[13] nor have we defended the churches as we should have. And now, since alone, without your authority, we cannot reform the churches, we earnestly seek your counsel together with your help in these matters as well as in all our affairs. We stand ready to keep your commands most zealously in every respect. And now especially for the church of Milan, which has fallen into error through our fault,[14] we ask that it be corrected canonically by your apostolic stringency and that your authoritative judgment should then proceed to the correction of other churches.

Therefore, God willing, we will not fail you in anything, and we humbly beg you, O father, actively to stand beside us, showing mercy in all things. In a short time you will receive our letter with our most faithful men, from whom, God granting, you will hear more fully about those of our affairs which await further discussion.

---

[10] Romans 13:1, 4.   [11] Cf. Luke 15:17.   [12] Luke 15:18 f.   [13] John 10:1.

[14] This controversy began during the pontificate of Alexander II, when Atto, the candidate of the "popular" party (the *Patarini*) and of the reformers, led by Erlembald, was elected to the archiepiscopacy, in opposition to Godfrey who had been elected in haste by the royalists and invested with ring and staff by Henry. Godfrey was forced to withdraw to Brebbia, where he was steadfastly supported by Henry, while the Papacy continued to support Atto. In this state of schism Henry made his request for assistance.

6 Henry asks Abbot Theoderic and the monks of St. Maximin of Trier to retain in perpetuity the fief which his sergeant H. is returning to them, and he asks them to pray for him during his forthcoming Saxon expedition (1075).

Henry, king by the grace of God, sends loving greetings to Abbot Theodoric[15] and to all the brethren.

Others may delight in the vows of the righteous,[16] but the pious, just, and faithful man can fulfill his vows without their help, instructed as he is by the spirit of loving-kindness wherein all righteous men must abide.

Wherefore we have rejoiced in the petitions of our sergeant H. We know that in order to make good the loss of your prebend and to further his designs for his own salvation, he is returning to you a fief which he holds from you. Accept, therefore, what is returned, and never grant it to anyone in fief. Together with him, we ask this.

Remember, then, to pray for him; pray also for us. We have proclaimed our expedition against the Saxons, which, we have decreed, will begin on the eighth day before the ides of June.[17] Therefore, begin to pray then, and as long as the expedition continues, let your prayers follow us. But pray continually for him, and beseech God with prayers that he will not fail in his designs.

7 Henry affirms to Pope Gregory the secrecy of his legation and promises to send another legation after the conclusion of his Saxon expedition (1075).

Your Holiness should know, Father, that since I am aware that almost all of the princes of my realm rejoice more in our discord than in our mutual peace, I am sending these messengers secretly to you.[18] I know them to be quite noble and religious men, and I do not doubt at all that they are united in the desire for the blessing of peace between us. I wish no one to know the message I am sending, except you, the lady my mother,[19] my aunt Beatrice, and her daughter Matilda.[20]

[15] Of St. Maximin in Trier.

[16] Proverbs 15:8. The translation of this paragraph is, at best, approximate; the original Latin follows: "Vota iustorum placabilia: quaecumque autem spiritus benignitatis, in quo omnes iusti sunt quod sunt, vota vovere iustum quemlibet docuit, hec ut ipsa sibi solvat, pius iustus fidelis, potens erit [*Erdmann suppl.* efficere]."

[17] June 6. See "Life of Henry IV," chap. 3, p. 107.

[18] Radbod, Adelprecht, and Uodscalk, otherwise unknown.

[19] The Empress Agnes.   [20] The Countesses of Tuscany.

Upon my return, with the Lord's help, from the Saxon expedition, I shall send other envoys, the most trustworthy and faithful I have, through whom I shall signify to you all my wishes, and the reverence which I owe to Saint Peter and to you.

8 *Henry asks Bishop Hezilo of Hildesheim to release Lord William from excommunication and to restore the divine office to his church in Ölsburg (1065–1079).*

Henry, king by the grace of God, sends greetings and grace to Bishop Hezilo.[21]

A few words from a friend, with evidence of good will, are sufficient for a proven friend.

Therefore, we shall relate in a few words those things which we seek so zealously: namely, that you release the lord William[22] from excommunication and grant to his church in Ölsburg[23] permission to celebrate the divine office there.

9 *Henry asks Bishop Hezilo of Hildesheim to defer to the King's presence the disposition of the episcopal jurisdiction in Goslar (1075?)*

Henry, King by the grace of God, sends love, greetings, and everything good to bishop Hezilo.

Whatever is freely given is received with greater pleasure than a debt. It has sometimes been the case that a debt has been exacted without rigor, after something has been gratuitously and devotedly presented. We have wished you to act in this fashion—to discharge a debt imposed not by command but by love—as regards the following small petition; and we promise faithfully that if you satisfy our wishes in this, you will undoubtedly be pleased when we have the opportunity to repay you with an act of good will.

In fact, the sum of our request is that you should promise to no one your jurisdiction which the provost R.[24] held over the people of Goslar, and grant it to no one, but that you defer to our presence whatever you may be about to do in this matter (or rather, whatever you are

[21] Of Hildesheim.   [22] The lord of the proprietary church in question, not a priest.

[23] Ölsberg is west of Braunschweig, in the diocese of Hildesheim.

[24] Erdmann supposes that the reference is to Rupert, provost of SS. Simon and Jude, whom Henry named bishop of Bamberg in 1075.

about to do to satisfy us). See that you do not disregard us, therefore, if you love us at all, or if you ever intend to ask for anything.

10 *Henry declares to the Roman clergy and people that Hildebrand is his enemy. He sends them a copy of his decree of deposition (Letter 11) and exhorts them to take a new pope after forcing Hildebrand to step down (1076).*[25]

Henry, King by the grace of God, sends grace, greeting, and every good thing to the clergy and people of the entire holy Roman Church:

That fidelity is believed firm and unshaken which is always kept unchanged for one whether he is present or absent—fidelity altered neither by the extended absence of him to whom it is owed nor through the wearisome passage of a long time. We know that this is the sort of fidelity which you keep for us; we are thankful, and we ask that it continue unchanged. Specifically, we ask that just as you act now, so in the future you will steadfastly be friends of our friends and enemies of our enemies.

Noting particularly among the latter the monk Hildebrand, we urge you to enmity against him, since we have found him to be an assailant and an oppressor of the Church, as well as a waylayer of the Roman commonwealth, and of our kingdom, as may be known clearly from the following letter sent to him by us:

[In the original of Letter 10, the full text of Letter 11 is given here. Letter 10 continues:]

This is the text of our letter to the monk Hildebrand, which we have also written to you so that our will may be both yours and ours—nay rather, so that your love may bring satisfaction to God and to us. Rise up against him, therefore, O most faithful, and let the man who is first in the faith be first in his condemnation. We do not say, however, that you should shed his blood, since after his deposition life would

[25] In December, 1075, almost six months to the day after Henry's great victory on the Unstrut over the Saxons, Gregory, prosecuting the policy he had begun at his Lenten Synod earlier in 1075, threatened to excommunicate Henry should he not shun the company of the bishops excommunicated at the Synod, obey the synodal edict against lay investiture, and conform to Papal orders in regard to Imperial churches in Italy. Henry received Gregory's letters early in 1076 and vigorously accepted their implicit challenge, dispatching Letters 10, 11, 12, and 13 at once, and summoning the Synod of Worms, where the majority of German bishops joined him in pronouncing Gregory's deposition.

indeed be a greater penalty for him than death. We say rather that if he prove unwilling to descend, you should force him to do so and receive into the Apostolic See another, elected by us with the common counsel of all the bishops and of yourselves, one who will be willing and able to cure the wounds which that man has inflicted upon the Church.

11 *Henry charges Hildebrand with having stolen his hereditary privileges in Rome, striven to alienate Italy, abused the bishops, and threatened his office and his life. He reports the sentence of deposition issued by the Diet of Worms, and as patrician of the Romans, he commands him to descend from the throne of St. Peter (1076).*

Henry, King by the grace of God, to Hildebrand:

Although hitherto I hoped for those things from you which are expected of a father and obeyed you in all respects to the great indignation of our vassals,[26] I have obtained from you a requital suitable from one who was the most pernicious enemy of our life and kingly office. After you had first snatched away with arrogant boldness all the hereditary dignity owed me by that See, going still further you tried with the most evil arts to alienate the kingdom of Italy.[27] Not content with this, you have not feared to set your hand against the most reverend bishops,[28] who are united to us like most cherished members and have harassed them with most arrogant affronts and the bitterest abuses against divine and human laws. While I let all these things go unnoticed through patience, you thought it not patience but cowardice and dared to rise up against the head itself, announcing, as you know, that (to use your own words) you would either die or deprive me of my life and kingly office.

Judging that this unheard of defiance had to be confuted not with words, but with action, I held a general assembly of all the foremost men of the kingdom, at their supplication. When they had made public

[26] The Latin original is *fidelis*, a word which appears frequently throughout Henry IV's letters. At the risk of imprecision, the requirements of translation have forced a rendering as either "vassal" or "subject." The reader should not be misled, however, by the modern meanings of "vassal": *Fidelis* denoted no servile status, but, to the contrary, indicated a man who had taken an oath of "fealty" *(fidelitas)* to an overlord—and invariably, therefore, a *fidelis* was a person of high station within feudal political society.

[27] A reference to Gregory's denial of Henry's right to name Tedald archbishop of Milan and to fill the sees of Fermo and Spoleto.

[28] Cf. II Samuel 1 : 14.

through their true declaration (which you will hear from their own letter) those things which they had previously kept silent through fear and reverence, they took public action to the end that you could no longer continue in the Apostolic See. Since their sentence seemed just and righteous before God and men, I also give my assent, revoking from you every prerogative of the papacy which you have seemed to hold, and ordering you to descend from the throne of the city whose patriciate is due me through the bestowal of God and the sworn assent of the Romans.

Renunciation of Gregory VII by the German Bishops (Synod of Worms, 1076)[29]

Siegfried, archbishop of Mainz, Udo of Trier, William of Utrecht, Herman of Metz, Henry of Liége, Ricbert of Verden, Bido of Toul, Hozeman of Speier, Burchard of Halberstadt, Werner of Strassburg, Burchard of Basel, Otto of Constance, Adalbero of Würzburg, Rupert of Bamberg, Otto of Regensburg, Egilbert of Freising, Ulric of Eichstätt, Frederick of Münster, Eilbert of Minden, Hezilo of Hildesheim, Benno of Osnabrück, Eppo of Naumburg, Imadus of Paderborn, Tiedo of Brandenburg, Burchard of Lausanne, and Bruno of Verona, to Brother Hildebrand:

When you had first usurped the government of the Church, we knew well how, with your accustomed arrogance, you had presumed to enter so illicit and nefarious an undertaking against human and divine law. We thought, nevertheless, that the pernicious beginnings of your administration ought to be left unnoticed in prudent silence. We did this specifically in the hope that such criminal beginnings would be emended and wiped away somewhat by the probity and industry of your later rule. But now, just as the deplorable state of the universal Church cries out and laments, through the increasing wickedness of your actions and decrees, you are woefully and stubbornly in step with your evil beginnings.

Our Lord and Redeemer impressed the goodness of peace and love upon his Faithful as their distinctive character,[30] a fact to which there

---

[29] For the sake of completeness, this declaration, as well as the *Promissio Oppenheimensis* (pp. 154–155), the vow at Canossa (pp. 156), and the decree of the Synod of Brixen (pp. 157–160), though not properly letters of Henry IV, have been placed among them in chronological order.

[30] John 13:35; I John 2:5.

are more testimonies than can be included in the brevity of a letter. But by way of contrast, you have inflicted wounds with proud cruelty and cruel pride, you are eager for profane innovations,[31] you delight in a great name rather than in a good one, and with unheard-of self-exaltation, like a standard bearer of schism, you distend all the limbs of the Church which before your times led a quiet and tranquil life, according to the admonition of the Apostle.[32] Finally, the flame of discord, which you stirred up through terrible factions in the Roman church, you spread with raging madness through all the churches of Italy, Germany, Gaul, and Spain. For you have taken from the bishops, so far as you could, all that power which is known to have been divinely conferred upon them through the grace of the Holy Spirit, which works mightily in ordinations. Through you all administration of ecclesiastical affairs has been assigned to popular madness. Since some now consider no one a bishop or priest save the man who begs that office of Your Arrogance with a most unworthy servility, you have shaken into pitiable disorder the whole strength of the apostolic institution and that most comely distribution of the limbs of Christ, which the Doctor of the Gentiles so often commends and teaches.[33] And so through these boastful decrees of yours—and this cannot be said without tears— the name of Christ has all but perished. Who, however, is not struck dumb by the baseness of your arrogant usurpation of new power, power not due you, to the end that you may destroy the rights due the whole brotherhood?[34] For you assert that if any sin of one of our parishioners comes to your notice, even if only by rumor, none of us has any further power to bind or to loose the party involved, for you alone may do it, or one whom you delegate especially for this purpose. Can anyone schooled in sacred learning fail to see how this assertion exceeds all madness?

We have judged that it would be worse than any other evil for us to allow the Church of God to be so gravely jeopardized—nay rather, almost destroyed—any longer through these and other presumptuous airs of yours. Therefore, it has pleased us to make known to you by the common counsel of all of us something which we have left unsaid until now: that is, the reason why you cannot now be, nor could you ever have been, the head of the Apostolic See.

In the time of the Emperor Henry [III] of good memory, you bound

[31] I Timothy 6:20.   [32] I Timothy 2:2.   [33] Romans 12:5; I Corinthians 12:2.
[34] Cf. I Peter 2:17.

yourself with a solemn oath[35] that for the lifetime of that Emperor and for that of his son, our lord the glorious King who now presides at the summit of affairs, you would neither obtain the papacy yourself nor suffer another to obtain it, insofar as you were able, without the consent and approbation either of the father in his lifetime of or the son in his. And there are many bishops today who were witnesses of this solemn oath, who saw it then with their own eyes and heard it with their own ears. Remember also that in order to remove jealous rivalry when ambition for the papacy tickled some of the cardinals, you obligated yourself with a solemn oath never to assume the papacy both on the plea and on the condition that they did the same thing themselves. We have seen in what a holy way you observed each of these solemn vows. Again, when a synod was celebrated in the time of Pope Nicholas [II], in which one hundred twenty-five bishops sat together, it was decided and decreed under anathema that no one would ever become pope except by the election of the cardinals and the approbation of the people, and by the consent and authority of the king. And of this council and decree, you yourself were author, advocate, and subscriber.

In addition to this, you have filled the entire Church, as it were, with the stench of the gravest of scandals, rising from your intimacy and cohabitation with another's wife[36] who is more closely integrated into your household than is necessary. In this affair, our sense of decency is affected more than our legal case, although the general complaint is sounded everywhere that all judgments and all decrees are enacted by women in the Apostolic See, and ultimately that the whole orb of the Church is administered by this new senate of women. For no one can complain adequately of the wrongs and the abuse suffered by the bishops, whom you call most undeservedly sons of whores and other names of this sort.

Since your accession was tainted by such great perjuries, since the Church of God is imperiled by so great a tempest arising from abuse born of your innovations, and since you have degraded your life and conduct by such multifarious infamy, we declare that in the future we shall observe no longer the obedience which we have not promised to you. And since none of us, as you have publicly declared, has hitherto been a bishop to you, you also will now be pope to none of us.

---

[35] "Corporali sacramento": an oath (1) on the Blessed Host, or (2) on the Scriptures; (3) on a cross, or (4) on relics. See "Life of Henry IV," chap. 6, p. 114f.

[36] Mathilda of Tuscany.

12 *Henry charges Hildebrand with having thrown the whole Church into confusion and with having threatened his life and office. He declares that Hildebrand was not ordained of God, but is damned by the precept of St. Paul and by the judgment of all Henry's bishops; and he commands him to descend from the Apostolic See (1076).*

Henry, King not by usurpation, but by the pious ordination of God,[37] to Hildebrand, now not Pope, but false monk:

You have deserved such a salution as this because of the confusion you have wrought; for you left untouched no order of the Church which you could make a sharer of confusion instead of honor, of malediction instead of benediction.

For to discuss a few outstanding points among many: Not only have you dared to touch the rectors of the holy Church—the archbishops, the bishops, and the priests, anointed of the Lord as they are[38]—but you have trodden them under foot like slaves who know not what their lord may do.[39] In crushing them you have gained for yourself acclaim from the mouth of the rabble. You have judged that all these know nothing, while you alone know everything. In any case, you have sedulously used this knowledge not for edification, but for destruction,[40] so greatly that we may believe Saint Gregory, whose name you have arrogated to yourself, rightly made this prophesy of you when he said: "From the abundance of his subjects, the mind of the prelate is often exalted, and he thinks that he has more knowledge than anyone else, since he sees that he has more power than anyone else."[41]

And we, indeed, bore with all these abuses, since we were eager to preserve the honor of the Apostolic See. But you construed our humility as fear, and so you were emboldened to rise up even against the royal power itself, granted to us by God. You dared to threaten to take the kingship away from us—as though we had received the kingship from you, as though kingship and empire were in your hand and not in the hand of God.[42]

Our Lord, Jesus Christ, has called us to kingship, but has not called you to the priesthood. For you have risen by these steps: namely, by cunning, which the monastic profession abhors, to money; by money to favor; by favor to the sword. By the sword you have come to the

---

[37] Romans 13:2.   [38] Psalm 105:15; II Samuel 1:14.   [39] Cf. John 15:15.
[40] Cf. II Corinthians 10:8; 13:10.
[41] Gregory I, Pastoral Rule II, 6.   [42] See "Life of Henry IV," chap. 3, p. 108.

throne of peace, and from the throne of peace you have destroyed the peace. You have armed subjects against their prelates; you who have not been called by God have taught that our bishops who have been called by God are to be spurned; you have usurped for laymen the bishops' ministry over priests, with the result that these laymen depose and condemn the very men whom the laymen themselves received as teachers from the hand of God, through the imposition of the hands of bishops.

You have also touched me, one who, though unworthy, has been anointed to kingship among the anointed. This wrong you have done to me, although as the tradition of the holy Fathers has taught, I am to be judged by God alone and am not to be deposed for any crime unless—may it never happen—I should deviate from the Faith. For the prudence of the holy bishops entrusted the judgment and the deposition even of Julian the Apostate not to themselves, but to God alone. The true pope Saint Peter also exclaims, "Fear God, honor the king."[43] You, however, since you do not fear God, dishonor me, ordained of of Him.

Wherefore, when Saint Paul gave no quarter to an angel from heaven if the angel should preach heterodoxy, he did not except you who are now teaching heterodoxy throughout the earth. For he says, "If anyone, either I or an angel from heaven, preach any other gospel unto you than that which we have preached unto you, let him be accursed."[44] Descend, therefore, condemned by this anathema and by the common judgment of all our bishops and of ourself. Relinquish the Apostolic See which you have arrogated. Let another mount the throne of Saint Peter, another who will not cloak violence with religion but who will teach the pure doctrine of Saint Peter.

I, Henry, King by the grace of God, together with all our bishops, say to you: Descend! Descend!

13 *In this encyclical letter to his bishops, Henry admonishes them to help the beleaguered Church against Hildebrand, who has destroyed the peace between the kingship and the priesthood and has recently abused royal envoys. He invites them to participate in an assembly at Worms on Whitsun (1076).*

Henry, King by the grace of God, sends to A., the grace, greeting, and love which he sends not to all men, but only to a few:

43 I Peter 2 : 17.   44 Galatians 1 : 18.

In the greatest affairs there is need for the greatest counsels of the greatest men, who externally should have power and within should not be lacking in good will, so that they may be both willing and able to deliberate well about that matter for which they wish well. For in the advancement of any enterprise, neither power without good will nor good will without power is useful. O most faithful subject, you possess, we think, each of these in equal proportion. To tell the truth, although as one of the great, you possess great power, your good will for our advantage and for that of our kingdom grows even greater than this great power—if we know you well and have properly noted your fidelity. From past actions faithfully done, the hope grows that future actions will be done yet more faithfully. We trust to your love, however, that your fidelity may not fall short of our hope, since from the fidelity of none of the kingdom's princes do we hope for greater things than from yours. Thus until this very time, we have rejoiced not only in what past affairs reveal but also in your promise of things still to be hoped for.

Let your good will stand by us, therefore, together with your power at this opportune time, the good will for which not only our need is earnestly longing, but also that of all your fellow bishops and brethren, nay rather, that of the whole oppressed Church. Certainly, you are not ignorant of this oppression. Only see to it that you do not withdraw assistance from the oppressed Church, but rather that you give your sympathy to the kingship and to the priesthood. Just as hitherto the Church was exalted by each of these offices, so now, alas, it is laid low, bereft of each; since one man has arrogated both for himself, he has injured both, and he who has neither wanted nor was able to be of benefit in either has been useless in each.[45]

To keep you in suspense no longer as to the name of the man under discussion, learn of whom we speak: it is the monk Hildebrand (a monk indeed in habit), so-called pope who, as you yourself know clearly, presides in the Apostolic See not with the care of a pastor but with the violence of a usurper and from the throne of peace dissolves the bond of the one catholic peace. To cite to a few things among many:

[45] The following passage from *De unitate ecclesiae conservanda* (I, 10) is of interest as it shows that at this time even within the royalist camp the symbolism of the two swords was not firmly established: "Not only did he [Gregory VII] double the sword, according to what one reads in Ezechial [Ezechial 21:14], or treble it, but he multiplied it, and he divided not only the Christian people but also the priesthood." *MGH Ldl.*, II, 198.

without God's knowledge he has usurped for himself the kingship and the priesthood. In this deed he held in contempt the pious ordinance of God,[46] which especially commanded these two—namely, the kingship and the priesthood—should remain, not as one entity, but as two. In his Passion, the Savior Himself meant the figurative sufficiency of the two swords to be understood in this way: When it was said to him, "Lord, behold there are two swords here," He answered, "It is enough,"[47] signifying by this sufficient duality, that the spiritual and the carnal swords are to be used in the Church and that by them every hurtful thing is to be cut off. That is to say, He was teaching that every man is constrained by the priestly sword to obey the king as the representative of God but by the kingly sword both to repel enemies of Christ outside and to obey the priesthood within. So in charity the province of one extends into the other, as long as neither the kingship is deprived of honor by the priesthood not the priesthood is deprived of honor by the kingship. You yourself have found out, if you have wanted to discover it, how the Hildebrandine madness has confounded this ordinance of God; for in his judgment, no one may be a priest unless he begs that [honor] from his arrogance. He has also striven to deprive me of the kingship—me whom God has called to the kingship (God, however, has not called him to the priesthood)—since he saw that I wished to hold my royal power from God and not from him and since he himself had not constituted me as king.[48] And further, he threatened to deprive me of kingship and life, neither of which he had bestowed.

Although he often contrived these outrages against us, and others like them, as you yourself know, nonetheless he was not satisfied unless from day to day he cast new and coarse sorts of affliction upon us, as he recently showed in dealing with our envoys.[49] This paper is not sufficiently long to set forth how he handled those messengers of ours; how demeaningly he afflicted them; how cruelly he imprisoned them; and when they had been imprisoned, how he harmed them with nakedness, cold, hunger and thirst, and blows. Finally, he ordered them to be led about through the middle of the city to offer a spectacle to all,

[46] Cf. Romans 13:2.   [47] Luke 22:38.

[48] See "Life of Henry IV," chap. 3, p. 103, Otto of Freising relates that the crown Gregory sent to Rudolf of Rheinfelden bore the inscription, "Roma dedit Petro, Petrus diadema Rudolfo" (Rome gave the diadem to Peter; Peter, to Rudolf.") *Gesta Fredirici* I, vii.

[49] The cleric Roland of Parma, and a royal *ministerialis*.

after the example of the martyrs. So you may believe and say that in common with the tyrant Decius he rages and torments the saints.

Wherefore, be not ashamed, most cherished friend, be not ashamed to satisfy the petition we make in common with your fellow bishops: that you come to Worms at Pentecost[50] and hear many things there with the other princes, a few of which this letter mentions, and advise us what is to be done. For you are besought by the love of your fellow bishops, admonished through the advantage of the Church, and bound by the honor of our life and of the whole kingdom.

The Promise of Henry IV to Gregory VII (Promissio Oppenheimensis, 1076)[51]

Admonished by the counsel of our vassals, I promise to maintain a due obedience in all things to the Apostolic See and to you, Pope Gregory.[52] I shall take care to emend with dutiful reparation whatever diminution of the honor of that See or of your own honor is seen to have arisen through us.

Since certain rather serious schemes which I am supposed to have against that same See and Your Reverence are now at issue, at a fitting time, either I shall clear them away through the prayer of innocence or through the help of God or at that very time I shall gladly undertake suitable penance for them.

It is also altogether fitting, however, for Your Sanctity not to ignore those things which have been spread abroad about you and which bear

---

[50] May 15, 1076.   [51] See note 29, p. 147.

[52] In joining battle with Gregory, Henry severely miscalculated his strength. While most of the German bishops supported him against Gregory, a great number of temporal princes led by his old enemies Welf of Bavaria, Rudolf of Swabia, and Berthold of Carinthia took the opportunity to rebel against their excommunicate King. The threat of revolt in Saxony also revived immediately. In October, 1076, Henry's army gathered at Oppenheim, facing the rebel army at Tribur just opposite them across the Rhine. Fearing the results of open battle, Henry offered this promise to the Papal legates who were with his enemies; it was accepted and, with the understanding that points at issue between Henry and Gregory's partisans would be settled at a future meeting, both armies disbanded. In letter 14, Henry declared his altered policy to his supporters and urged them to conform themselves to it. For their part, the rebellious princes sent a legation to Gregory, asking him to go to Germany the next February to arbitrate the conflict between them and their King. Gregory accepted these proposals and was making his way toward Germany when Henry intercepted him at Canossa and, after making his submission, was released from excommunication.

scandal to the Church. But after this scruple has also been removed from the public conscience, it is fitting that the universal tranquillity of the Church as well as that of the kingdom be made firm through your wisdom.

14 *Henry declares to his princes that he wishes to obey and to render satisfaction to Pope Gregory; he exhorts them to follow his example and to obtain release from excommunication (1076).*

Henry, King by the grace of God, sends the glorious esteem of his good will to archbishops, bishops, dukes, margraves, counts, and to every order of dignity:

We have learned by the assertion of our vassals that on behalf of Our Mercy some men have detracted from the Apostolic See and its venerable pontiff, the Lord Pope Gregory. For this reason, it has pleased us, on beneficial counsel, to change our former position and after the fashion of our predecessors and ancestors to reserve in all respects due obedience to that same sacrosanct See and to the Lord Pope Gregory, who is known to serve as its head. It has also pleased us to make amends with fitting reparation if anything serious has been done against him.

We wish that you also admonished by the example of Our Serenity, like us, will not refuse to show solemn [obedience][53] to Saint Peter and to his vicar. And may whosoever know that they are bound by his ban strive to be absolved formally by this same Lord Pope Gregory.

15 *Henry informs his mother, the Empress-dowager Agnes, that at a recent Diet he was persuaded to allow the case of the bishops who had deserted him to be discussed at another assembly in the near future. He grants her petition (1074–1076).*

To the mother of blessing and well-being, Henry, King by the grace of God, sends love from his whole heart and whatever is better and beyond:

Since it is right for you to know well how we progress, we want to send you word, inasmuch as you are our dearest mother, of what this Curia and assembly has ordered and ratified. After much consideration

[53] A lacuna, supplied by Erdmann; the Codex Udalrici has, less probably, "satisfaction."

of our case, we were finally overcome by the apostolic legation and by the counsel and persuasion of all our vassals, many of whom were present, and we granted and permitted the restitution of the deserter-bishops.[54] Nonetheless, we did this in such a fashion that in whatever manner we wish, we may continue warily to watch these men in the interests of our side until the day we have set to consider their case. Know that those same legates[55] of the pope are awaiting that day and time here.

But for the sake of that good faith which we have in you, ask earnestly of God that our cause may receive its long-expected outcome. As for that, however, which you have asked of us, most certainly you will receive it on that condition which you wish and of which you have notified us. In addition [you will receive] whatever we can grant to your love.

The Vow of Henry IV to Gregory VII at Canossa (1077).[56]

Oath of Henry, King of the Germans.

Before the date the Lord Pope Gregory is to set, I, King Henry, shall bring about justice according to his judgment or harmony according to his counsel with regard to the complaint and objection now being made against me by archibishops, bishops, dukes, counts, the other princes in the realm of the Germans, and those who follow them by reason of the same objection. If a concrete obstacle hinder me or him, I shall be ready to do the same when that hindrance has been overcome. Also, if the same Lord Pope Gregory should wish to go beyond the mountains to other lands, he, those who are among his retainers or guards, and those who are sent by him or come to him from any region, will be safe in coming, staying, and going thence, from any harm to life and limb and from capture by me and by those whom I can control. Moreover, no other difficulty prejudicial to his honor will occur with my assent; and should any person create one for him, I shall help him [Gregory] in good faith, according to my ability.

Done at Canossa, 28 January, the fifteenth Indiction.

---

[54] Most prominently, Adalbert of Worms, and perhaps also Burchard of Halberstadt.

[55] Gerald of Ostia and Hubert of Palestrina, if the letter were written in 1074; Sigehard of Aquileia and Altmann of Passau, if in 1076.

[56] Gregory VII, *Registrum*, IV, 12a. See above, notes 29. 52.

Decree of the Synod of Brixen (1080)[57]

In the year of the incarnation of the Lord 1080, with the most serene King Henry IV as moderator, in the twenty-sixth year of his reign, on the seventh day before the Kalends of July, on the fifth day of the week, in the third indiction, when an assembly of thirty bishops and of the leaders of the army, not only of Italy but also of Germany, was gathered at Brixen in Bavaria by royal order, of one accord a voice came forth as though from the mouth of all complaining terribly[58] against the cruel madness of one false monk, Hildebrand, also called Pope Gregory VII. It complained that the ever-unconquered King suffered this madness to rage untouched for so long, when Paul, the vessel of election, witnesses that the prince does not carry a sword without cause[59] and Peter, the first of the Apostles, cries out that the king not only is supreme but that governors[60] are to be sent by him specifically for the punishment of evildoers and for the praise of the good.[61] In fulfillment of these sayings it seemed just to this most glorious King and to his princes that the judgment of the bishops with the sentence of divine censure ought to issue against this Hildebrand before the material sword went forth against him, with the consequence that the royal power might resolve to prosecute him with greater freedom after the prelates of the Church had first deposed him from his proud prelacy.

Which of the Faithful knowing him would fear to let fly the shaft of damnation against him? From the time he entered the world, this man strove to procure position for himself[62] over men through vain glory,[63] without the support of any merits; to set dreams and divinations, his own and those of others, ahead of divine dispensation;[64] to appear a monk in habit and not to be one by profession; to judge himself exempt from ecclesiastical discipline, subject to no master; to devote himself more than laymen to obscene theatrical shows; publicly for the sake of filthy lucre,[65] to attend to the tables of the money changers[66] on the

---

[57] See note 29, p. 147.   [58] Cf. Acts 19:34.

[59] Acts 9:15. Romans 13:4.

[60] "Duces," or "dukes," to the medieval reader.   [61] I Peter 2:13 f.

[62] "Se commendare," in the feudal sense of commending oneself to a lord in order to gain lands and position.

[63] Cf. Philippians 2:3.   [64] Cf. II Corinthians 10:18 f.   [65] Titus 1:11.

[66] Matthew 21:12.

porch of those who do business?[67] And so from these pursuits, he garnered his money and, supplanting the abbot, usurped the abbacy of Saint Paul.

Thereafter, seizing the archdiaconate, he led a certain man named Mancius astray by guile so that man sold him his own office. And against the will of Pope Nicholas, a popular tumult attending his action, he forced his advancement to the stewardship of Saint Peter's. Finally, he is convicted of having murdered four Roman pontiffs with violent deaths. His instrument was poison administered at the hands of one of his intimates, namely, John Braciutus.[68] Although he repented too late, while others still kept silent this ministrant of death himself bore witness to these deeds with dire cries, pressed by the nearness of his own death. And then, on the same night in which the funeral rites of Pope Alexander were lovingly performed in the basilica of the Savior,[69] this oft-mentioned plague-bearer fortified the gates of the Roman city and the bridges, the towers and the triumphal arches, with detachments of armed men. When a military force had been brought together, like an enemy he occupied the Lateran Palace. And lest the clergy should dare oppose him, since no one wished to elect him, he terrified them by threatening them with death upon the unsheathed swords of his followers. He sprang upon the long-occupied throne before the body of the dead man reached its tomb. But when certain of the clergy wanted to remind him of the decree of Pope Nicholas (which was promulgated with the threat of anathema by one hundred twenty-five bishops and with the approval of this same Hildebrand and which stated that if anyone presumed to be pope without the assent of the Roman prince, he should be considered by all not pope, but an apostate), he

---

[67] Cf. II Chronicles 8:12, 15:8. Possibly the bishops refer to the fact that, in his capacity as custodian of the altar of St. Peter's, Gregory was associated with Leo di Benedetto, a Pierleone. See P. Brezzi, *Roma e l'impero medioevale (774–1252)* (Bologna, 1947), p. 253.

[68] Probably Victor II, Stephan IX, Nicholas II, and Alexander II are meant. Mr. C. B. Fisher, to whom I owe the reference in note 12 to Gregory's association with the Pierleoni, has also shown me interesting collateral evidence on this point in the *Annales Romani* (Stephan IX, in Duchesne, *Liber Pontificalis*, II, 334): After the Romans had despoiled him of his treasure, Stephan left their city in anger. "Tunc post eum Braczutum Transtiberinum nomine ...qui in dicto itinere ut fertur venenum dedisse, et mortuus est." John Braciutus was, in addition, an associate of the Pierleoni. See Brazzi, *Rome e l'impero medioevale*, p. 238, and F. Gregorovius, *Geschichte der Stadt Rom im Mittelalter*, IV, 4th ed. (Stuttgart, 1890), 120, 124.

[69] April 22, 1073.

denied that he knew there was a king anywhere, and he asserted that he could adjudge the decrees of his predecessors void.

What more? Not only Rome, indeed, but the Roman world itself, bears witness that he has not been elected by God but that he has most impudently thrust himself upward through force, fraud, and money. His fruits reveal his root; his words show his intent. He it was who subverted ecclesiastical order, who threw the rule of the Christian empire into turmoil, who plotted death of body and soul for the catholic and pacific King, who defended a king who was a breaker of vows[70] and a traitor, who sowed discord among those in concord, strife among the peaceful,[71] scandals among brothers, divorce among the married, and who shook whatever was seen to stand in quiet amidst those who lived piously.

Wherefore, as was said before, we who have been gathered together through the agency of God, supported by the legates and letters of the nineteen bishops who assembled at Mainz on the holy day of last Pentecost,[72] pass judgment against that same most insolent Hildebrand: for he preaches acts of sacrilege and arson; he defends perjuries and murders; long a disciple of the heretic Beringer, he places in question the catholic and apostolic Faith in regard to the Body and Blood of the Lord; he is an open devotée of divinations and dreams, and a necromancer working with an oracular spirit;[73] and therefore he wanders beyond the limits of the true Faith. We judge that canonically he must be deposed and expelled and that, unless he descends from this See after hearing these words, he is forever damned.

I, Hugh Candidus,[74] cardinal priest of the holy Roman Church, from the Title of Saint Clement in the third district of the city, have assented

[70] Rudolf of Rheinfelden.   [71] Proverbs 6:19.   [72] May 31, 1080.

[73] Probably a reference to the prophecy Gregory made at the Lenten Synod of 1080, after he had excommunicated Henry for the second time: "Be it known to all of you, that if he does not repent before the feast of St. Peter, he will be killed or deposed. If it does not happen thus, no one need believe me ever again." Bonizo, *Liber ad Amicum*, chap. 9, MGH Ldl., I, 616. Sigebert of Gembloux (*Chronicon*, MGH SS., VI, 369) reports, "Pope Hildebrand predicted, as though it had been divinely revealed to him, that the false king was to die in this year. Indeed, he predicted the truth; but the conjecture about the false king deceived him, since, according to his construction, the prediction referred to King Henry." Sigebert refers to the death of Rudolf of Rheinfelden.

[74] At first a supporter of Gregory, he turned to the royalists within a year of Gregory's election, charging that it was uncanonical, and became a leader of the Synod of Worms (1076).

to this decree promulgated by us, and I have subscribed it in the name of all the Roman cardinals.

I, Diepold, archbishop of Milan, have subscribed.
I, Kuono, bishop of Brescia, have subscribed.
I, Otto, bishop-elect of Tortona, have subscribed.
I, William, bishop of Pavia, have subscribed.
I, Reginald, bishop of Belluno, have subscribed.
I, Sigebod, bishop of Verona, have subscribed.
I, Dionysius, bishop of Piacenza, have subscribed.
Udo, bishop of Asti. I have subscribed.
I, Hugh, bishop-elect of Firmo, have subscribed.
Milo of Padua has subscribed.
I, Conrad, bishop of Utrecht, have subscribed.
Henry, the patriarch [of Aquileia], has subscribed.
Didald, bishop of Vicenza, has subscribed.
Regenger, bishop of Vercelli, has subscribed.
Rupert, bishop of Bamberg, has subscribed.
Norbert, bishop of Chur, has subscribed.
Eberhard, bishop of Parma, has subscribed.
Roland, by the grace of God, bishop of Treviso, most willingly has subscribed.
Arnold, bishop of Cremona, has subscribed.
Arnold, bishop of Bergamo, has subscribed.
I, Diedo, bishop of Brandenburg, have subscribed.
Leomar, archbishop of the holy church of Hamburg.
I, Werner, by the grace of God, bishop of Bobbio, have subscribed.
I, Altwin, bishop of Brixen, have subscribed.
I, Meginward, bishop of Freising, have subscribed.
I, Burchard, bishop of Lausanne, have subscribed.
I, Conrad, bishop of Genoa, have subscribed.
Henry, King by the grace of God. I have subscribed.

16 *Henry praises the constancy of the clergy and people of Rome and announces his imminent arrival at Rome to assume his hereditary dignity (the Imperial office), to remove the conflict of kingship and priesthood and to restore all things to peace and unity (1081).*[75]

Henry, King by the grace of God, sends to the clergy and the Roman

[75] Between Canossa and Gregory's Lenten Synod of 1080, the Papacy took no major part in German affairs. Toward the end of this period, however, Gregory gave his support openly to the antiking Rudolf of Rheinfelden, whom Henry defeated and killed

people, to the greater and lesser [feudatories], his affection in the most sincere expression of his favor and best wishes:

From many accounts of the elder nobles of our empire we have learned with what great fidelity and benevolence you honored our father of sacrosanct memory and with what great acts of honor he advanced publicly and privately both the dignity of your church and the universal grandeur of the Roman name. Nor, indeed, after his death did you cherish us in our infancy with less love and reverence. On all counts you stood beside us with faithful constancy as far as was possible in the face of the wickedness of certain pestilential and proud men. The helplessness of our youth was at first our plea for not responding to your enduring love with due requital by granting you our favor. And after we put on the man,[76] so great a madness of tyrannical perfidy swelled up against us that supreme necessity forced us to direct the entire concern of our effort toward crushing it.

But now since we have cut off with the sword both the life and the pride of those most bitter enemies, not by our power but by that of God, and in large part have set in order the members of the disrupted and sundered Empire, we intend to come to you. Our specific aim is to receive from you, by the common assent and favor of you all, our due and hereditary dignity and to bestow with every kind of honor the thanks which you deserve. We are surprised, however, that when our approach became known, no legation from you came to us in the customary manner. For that reason we have refrained from sending our envoys to you. You yourselves know with what infamous abuse

in battle in January, 1080. This defeat and Henry's steadfast refusal to obey Gregory's edicts against lay investiture led to Gregory's second excommnnication of the King at his Lenten Synod two months after Rudolf's death. Henry's position in Germany was then quite strong, and, in addition, the greater part of the German and Lombard bishops declared for him in this new crisis, rejecting Gregory as pope at the Synods of Bamberg and Mainz and electing Archbishop Wibert of Ravenna as his successor at the Synod of Brixen. With ample forces, Henry entered Italy early in 1080 to execute the judgments of his bishops; he then sent this letter to the people of Rome. Armed resistance to his march through the lands of his cousin, Mathilda of Tuscany, a stanch supporter of the reformed Papacy, kept him from Rome almost a year. Late in 1082 he withdrew from Tuscany, and in 1083 he began his brief and victorious siege of Rome. Letter 17 belongs to the period between his departure from Tuscany and his arrival at Rome, and Letter 18, written after his departure from Rome under Norman pressure in 1084, reflects his satisfaction with the progress of the campaign.

[76] Cf. Ephesians 4:24; Colossians 3:10.

our envoys,[77] honored and venerable men, were afflicted in the last year by him from whom such conduct was least fitting, in a manner exceeding the inhumanity of all barbarians.

This is the very thing with which those disturbers of peace and concord charge us. They scatter word among you that we come meaning to diminish the honor of Saint Peter, the prince of the apostles, and through our own power to overturn the commonwealth of you all. Indeed, these tactics accord with their usual conduct. But we tell the truth to you in good faith, for it is altogether our will and resolve to visit you peacefully, as far as is within us, and then, having considered the advice of all of you especially, and of our other vassals, to remove from our midst the long-lasting discord of the kingship and the priesthood, and to recall all things to peace and unity in the name of Christ.

17 Henry pardons the Roman cardinals, clergy, and laymen for their former opposition instigated by Gregory VII, proposes an assembly to determine whether Hildebrand can continue as pope, and after referring to him as an oppressor of the Church, he assures Hildebrand of his safety, even in the event of his deposition, and promises the Romans rewards if they render him "justice" (1082).

Henry, King by the grace of God, sends grace, love, and every good thing to all the Roman cardinals, clerics, and laymen, to his greater and lesser vassals, whether already his vassals or about to become his vassals:

The Roman authority ought always to be strong in justice, especially for the sake of all nations, since its sin is the destruction and its merit the increase of right living for those subject to it. Now, you can see the proof of this everywhere; indeed, you could have seen [this earlier] if you had not been hindered by a certain man. Because of that hindrance even if you have been less than diligent in some regard, the charge against you is lightened, since he who ought to have been a mirror of right living has become an obstacle not only to you but also to all who venerate Rome's headship of the catholic Faith, to so great an extent that now the Church virtually threatens to fall, not into error, but into irreparable ruin.

Seeing this unhappy state and being unwilling to tolerate it longer,

[77] Archbishop Liemar of Bremen, Bishop Rupert of Bamberg, and the Archdeacon Burchard, who met these difficulties at the Lenten Synod of 1080.

we are coming to Rome,[78] where we hoped to find you all faithful. And we even had such hopes of your justice and steadfastness in the filial fidelity you have shown us, that [we expected] to be able to treat with you of all matters of right appertaining to the kingship and the priesthood even if we should come alone with very few soldiers. But we found you far different from what we had hoped, since those whom we had thought friends we perceived to be enemies. They were our enemies, although we came to you for mere justice, and by your counsel and by canonical authority to establish peace between the kingship and the priesthood.

Assuredly we know and freely believe that you are friends of justice and that you would not have denied us the justice which you deny to no man, had you not heard that we are coming to bring injustice and disorder to you. Certainly, we are not ignorant of the machinations of this Lord Hildebrand. It is not surprising that he could deceive those living in the same city with him; for he was the same man who seduced the world far and wide and stained the Church with the blood of her sons, when he made sons to rise up against their parents and parents against their sons and armed brother against brother.[79] Certainly, if you wish to consider the matter, this persecution is more cruel than the persecution of Decius, since Christ crowned in heaven the ones whom Decius slew for Christ, but this persecution deprives of present life and condemns those deprived to hell.

To set this trouble aright, the Church has summoned Hildebrand very often to purge himself of the crime charged to him and to free the Church of scandal. But when summoned, he disdained to come; neither did he hear our envoys nor did he allow you to hear them, fearing to lose you as his supporters once the just cause had been heard. But we beseech the common justice of all that through your actions even now he may come before us, that even now he may hear the Church lamenting. If the Church has been committed to him, why does he suffer her to perish? No true shepherd, but a hireling who has obtained the position of shepherd, withdraws his help from the sheep while the wolf is tearing them to pieces.[80] Tell him to come, to give satisfaction to the Church, to fear no one save God; let him accept oaths, let him accept hostages from us, assured of safe conduct to us and safe return to you, whether he is to be retained in the Apostolic See or deposed.

[78] 1081.   [79] Cf. Matthew 10:21; Mark 13:12.   [80] John 10:12.

Behold, with the favor of God we shall come to Rome on the set date. If he should wish, let everything be done there. If it is more agreeable to come with our messengers to meet us, we approve that plan also. Come with him yourselves, as many of you as wish; come, hear, judge. If he can and ought to be pope, we shall obey him; but if the opposite is true in your judgment and ours, let another, one whom the Church requires, be provided for the Church.

You ought not to reject this proposal. If it is righteous to heed a priest, it is righteous also to obey a king. Why does Hildebrand strive to destroy the dispensation of God? And if he attempts this, why do you not oppose him? God has said not that one, but that two swords are sufficient.[81] But Hildebrand intends that there be only one, since he struggles to ruin us, whom (though unworthy) God ordained king from our very cradle. God has shown daily that He had so ordained us; as anyone can see who considers well how He guarded us from the ambushes of Hildebrand and his partisans. For we still reign, though against his will; it was the Lord who destroyed our knight, the perjurer whom Hildebrand ordained king over us.[82]

In the name of the faith which you kept for the emperors, our grandfather and our father Henry [III], and which you ought to keep for us and indeed did keep well until the time of Hildebrand, we ask that you not deny us our patrimonial honor bestowed by you upon us through the hand of our father.[83] On the other hand, if you wish to deny it to us, we ask that you say why you deny it, since we are prepared to do all justice to you,[84] to reserve all honor to Saint Peter, and to reward all who are deserving, whoever they may be. We have come to assail not you, but those who are assailing you.

Do not oppress the Church any longer through Hildebrand; do not fight with him against justice. Let there be a trial in the sight of the Church. If it is just that you should consider him pope, defend him as pope. Do not defend him as a thief seeking his lair.

What does he gain by sacrificing justice for power? Does he; therefore, wish to be more unjust, because more exalted? These are his

---

[81] Luke 22:38.

[82] Rudolf of Rheinfelden, elected king by the princes at Forchheim in 1077, and mortally wounded in battle in October, 1080, after receiving the full support of Gregory at his Lenten Synod in the same year.

[83] Probably a reference to the assurances given Henry III by the Romans in 1055.

[84] Cf. Matthew 3:15. See "Life of Henry IV," chap. 4, p. 109ff.

very words, "That he ought to be judged by no one."[85] And his meaning is the same as if he had said: "He may do as he pleases."[86] But this is not the rule of Christ, where it is said, "He who is greater among you will be your servant."[87] And so it is unjust for him who names himself servant of the servants of God to oppress the servants of God through his power.[88] It ought not to shame him to be reduced to a low estate in order to remove a scandal common to all the faithful by whose common obedience he ought to be exalted. "For whoso," said the Lord, "shall offend one of these little ones which believe in me, it were better for him that a millstone were hanged about his neck."[89] Lo, little ones and great ones cry out against the scandal he presents and ask that it be removed from their midst.

Let him, therefore, come bravely. If his conscience is pure, assuredly he will rejoice in that all are present, since when these things have been refuted together, the glory will be his. Let him be certain that his life will not be in danger, even if by your judgment and the authority of the canons it be decided that he ought to be deprived of his unjustly held dignity. We are ready to do nothing without you but all things with you, if only we do not find you resisting our good acts.

Finally, we ask nothing except that justice abide in that place where it is most fitting for justice to be. We wish to find justice among you; and, with the favor of God, we are resolved to reward it when found. Farewell.

1 8 *Henry assures Bishop Theodoric of Verdun of his continued confidence in him, reports his success in the Roman campaign, accepts Theodoric's proposal on the terms to be extended to formerly rebellious subjects, requests his presence at Augsburg, and, with his antipope, orders the immediate consecration of Egilbert of Trier (1084).*

King Henry, by the grace of God Emperor of the Romans and Augustus, sends to Bishop Theodoric[90] love second to none:

Since we trust no one more than you, we particularly want you to know that we have not sent the bishop of Utrecht[91] to you as a proctor of the Faith, but as a colleague working with you for the honor of the kingdom. And now, as for the specific problems which you have re-

---

[85] *Dictatus Papae XIX*, Gregory VII, *Register* II, 55a. Cf. I Corinthians 2:15.
[86] Proverbial.   [87] Matthew 20:26 ff.   [88] Cf. Leviticus 25:46.   [89] Matthew 18:6.
[90] Of Verdun.   [91] Conrad.

ferred to us, we give specific replies, but very brief ones, since we are reserving a vast number of things to say to you face to face.

Especially, indeed, we speak to you about what you communicated to us in the margin of your letter on the Roman problem. We entered Rome on St. Benedict's day.[92] We believe you have heard from many others, however, how we were received by the Romans, how we stayed with the Romans, and how we withdrew from the Romans, as we ourself also indicated to you in our letter. You have not, we think, seen that letter yet, but at any rate we should prefer that you learn from a mouth other than ours how the Lord has dealt with us; for that seems incredible which has proved absolutely true. What we did in Rome with ten men, so to say, the Lord wrought through us;[93] if our predecessors had done it with tens of thousands, to all it would have been a miracle. When we were thinking of returning to German territory, already despairing of gaining Rome, behold, the Romans sent envoys, asked us to enter Rome, and promised to obey us in all respects. And so they did: for when we entered, they received us with the greatest joy; while we remained with them, they assisted us with the greatest zeal; when we departed from them, they followed us with the greatest triumph and fidelity. In sum, we may say, trusting in the Lord, that all Rome is in our hands, with the exception of that castle where Hildebrand was shut up—namely, in the house of Crescentius.[94] Know that this Hildebrand has been cast down by the legal judgment of all the cardinals and of the whole Roman people and that Clement has been elected our pope and exalted to the Apostolic See by the acclamation of all the Romans. Know, too, that we have been ordained by Pope Clement and, by the consent of all the Romans, were consecrated as emperor on the Holy Day of Easter,[95] with the exultation of the whole Roman people. When this had been done with the blessing of God and of Saint Peter, we withdrew from Rome admidst the rejoicing of all. And as quickly as we were able, we hastened to these parts; on the return route your messenger found us. Let those who wish rejoice; let those who wish grieve; we are here through the favor of God!

We are not taking pains to learn what that lord[96] to whom you referred may be doing; but readily we shall watch out for what you have mentioned, lest he do us harm.

[92] March 21, 1084. See "Life of Henry IV," chap. 6, p. 116.
[93] Cf. Psalm 68:29.   [94] Castel' Sant' Angelo.   [95] March 31, 1084.
[96] Perhaps the antiking, Herman of Salm.

But as for the Saxons, as for the Archbishop of Salzburg,[97] as for Count Adalbert,[98] and as for those others who wish to return to our side, we give you this answer: so that there may only be true peace in our times, we gladly accept your advice that they may once again be our vassals when they return to us.

If you do not find it burdensome to do what we wish, we ask you to come to us at Augsburg after the feast of the apostles Peter and Paul,[99] since, with the favor of God, we shall be at Regensburg on the day of their festival. Make an effort, therefore, to come to us, as you can gladden us by your coming.

Moreover, Pope Clement and Emperor Henry order you, as surely as you love us, to hasten quickly to consecrate the archbishop of Trier.[100] Farewell.

19 Henry orders his Westphalian vassals to pay annually the tithes due the cathedral church of Osnabrück and promises them his support (1084).

✠ Henry, by the grace of God Emperor Augustus of the Romans, sends grace, love, and every good thing to all his vassals in Westphalia, to the greater and the lesser:

We know that you have been quite forward at all our assemblies. Therefore, the more avid we think you are for justice, the more confidently we expect that you will be more forward yet in those things which we decide to be just.

Wherefore we wish our decrees about the tithes and rights of justice of the church at Osnabrück to be the more firmly established the more rightful we judge them. Because it is just, we command, and because we love you, we ask that you pay annually all tithes in the whole diocese of Osnabrück, as canonical law requires. Fear no one in doing this, for we who enjoin justice [upon you] will help you to do justice. Farewell.

---

[97] Gebhard, a supporter of Gregory VII.

[98] Possibly Adalbert of Kalw, a supporter of Rudolf of Rheinfelden.

[99] June 29, 1084.

[100] Egilbert of Trier, who had been invested with ring and staff by Henry in 1079, but was not able to receive the consent of clergy and people at that time. Theodoric consecrated him in October, 1084.

20 Henry summons Bishop Rupert of Bamberg to an assembly at Mainz to take counsel on affairs in Saxony, Metz, and other parts of the kingdom (1084?-1097?).

Henry, by the grace of God Emperor Augustus of the Romans, sends grace and every good thing to Rupert, bishop of the church at Bamberg:

You know in what immense peril the whole Church is adrift, how vast is the dissension which surges forth in all Saxony and with what great desolation that noble church at Metz is utterly ravished. And you also know that the Church of our Empire is divided, not only there, but also in divers other regions.

Therefore, we have decreed with the counsel of our vassals that an assembly is to take place at Mainz on the Lord's Day preceding the next feast of St. Andrew.[101] All the faithful princes of our realm will participate in this assembly and besides them all those whose good faith or provident counsel is shown advantageous to us. We ask you very cordially to come to it, since never could such difficult affairs of state and the problem of the divided Church be dispatched without your consummate wisdom, excellent counsel, and good faith. For frequently hitherto in our necessities and when the realm was divided by controversies of this sort, this faith has served us as far as we have wished and the affair demanded.

All our Saxon vassals will come to this assembly, asking us above all to go into Saxony and to settle these new dissensions. The people of Metz, for their part, cry out for us to cross over to Metz so peace and security may by restored at last to the church there. Also, by the invitation of the Archbishop,[102] we are going to celebrate the nativity of the Lord at Cologne. And for this reason, we have decreed that this assembly take place before [we go], so that we may settle dissensions of this sort in the kingdom before we cross over into more distant places. Consequently, we have delayed the expedition which has been announced so that the things which we must do may be considered with the common counsel of all our men.

Therefore, we ask you by that love in which you became our Godfather that no infirmity of body or any other matter stand in your way but that you come at the stated time to the aforesaid assembly and there

[101] November 24, 1084, or November 29, 1097.
[102] Sigewin (1078–1089) or Herman III (1089–1099).

arrange with us things essential to our welfare and to that of the kingdom, according to your great wisdom and your accustomed good faith.

21 *Henry praises the spiritual and temporal officials of the March of Fermo-Ancona, his vassals, for their constancy, promises them a reward, and commends his envoy to them (1084–1105).*

Henry, by the grace of God Emperor Augustus of the Romans, sends grace and good will to all bishops, counts, military leaders, burghers, and post commanders of the whole March[103]—to his greater and lesser vassals:

We render you the greatest thanks for the unbroken fidelity which, as the best vassals, you keep toward us and for the labor which you undertook in resisting our enemies manfully for our honor. For this—know in all certainty—we intend to make you worthy remuneration.

We would have written much about these matters, which pertain to the maintenance of the kingdom and our welfare, had we not sent you so dear and so reliable a messenger, one of our vassals and an intimate member of our household. For through him we make known to Your Fidelity a great many things which pertain to our honor and to the stability of the kingdom, since we trust him as we do ourselves, knowing that he wishes and does nothing except what his unsullied fidelity owes to our honor.

Therefore, we send to you and we command and earnestly ask, as we trust you, that you receive his words as though from our mouth and that through love of us, under sure hope of remuneration worthy of your effort and with joyous acquiescence, you accomplish whatever he asks of you on our behalf or orders as regards our honor.

22 *Henry thanks Bishop Hartwig of Magdeburg for his efforts on behalf of the royal honor, exhorts him to continue them, and particularly urges him to watch over the benefice of the provost N. (1088 - 1089).*

Henry, by the grace of God Emperor Augustus of the Romans, sends grace and every good thing to Hartwig, Archbishop of Magdeburg:

We have heard of your immense labor and zeal on behalf of our

[103] Of Fermo-Ancona.

honor, and we render worthy thanks to you for it, as is just. Now, indeed, we thank you with a few words; but when, by God's assent, we come to you, we shall do so with many deeds. Meanwhile, only remain solicitous, as you have been from the beginning, to gain the honor of the kingship for us in these regions. Trusting your fidelity above that of all others, we committed all our interests to your good faith when last we parted from you.[104] As you have faithfully observed this [trust] toward us until the present, we believe in truth that you will continue to preserve it inviolate. Act, therefore, as a good and discreet man and in all things continue until the end in that fidelity which we believe firmly fixed in you. We consider you an intimate friend, and we are confident that you will do for us whatever perfect fidelity requires. As evidence of this trust, we commit ourselves and all our interests to you again, to the end that you may act in all things in accordance with the good trust we place in you.

We commit to you again the benefice of the provost N. our vassal, which we also committed to you earlier, so that you may preserve it to his advantage. We also wish that, on our behalf, you deny it to him who is holding it unjustly; for the lord of the man who now has illicitly usurped this same benefice for himself gave it up to us when contention arose because of it.

23 *Henry thanks Duke Almus for his support and promises him a reward. He confirms an alliance made earlier with Almus's father, urges Almus to exhort his brother, Coloman of Hungary, to greater fidelity toward Henry, and asks him to release those vassals of his vassals who are held captive (1096).*[105]

Henry, by the grace of God Emperor Augustus, sends to Almus, glo-

---

[104] In the summer of 1088, Henry was in Saxony concluding arrangements for his marriage to the widow of Margrave Henry of the Nordmark, the Kievan princess, Praxedis (or Adelheid).

[105] In 1095, King Ladislas of Hungary died and was succeeded by] his son Coloman. Through the intercession of Almus, a second son of Ladislas, Henry, ever careful for his eastern lands, sought to win the support of the new king and particularly to persuade him to harass the deposed Welf IV of Bavaria, who had joined Henry's eldest son Conrad in rebellion two years earlier. The references in the last part of the letter to Coloman's victories are not clear, but they may pertain to his suppression of marauding bands returning from the first Crusade. The reference to the captive vassals in the last paragraph may relate to the same incident. In 1096, Welf reconciled himself with Henry and was reinvested with his duchy.

rious duke and friendly vassal, whatever affection a faithful friend can send:

It is firm friendship when someone disregards his own private good and toils in services useful to a friend.[106] We rejoice that you have meted out to us this friendly benevolence, and we mean to make remuneration worthy of the best vassal and of an intimate friend. Though you wish to go against the Greeks and although the Duke of Poland,[107] your friend and relative, sought your aid against his enemies, you remained on our account, like a very faithful friend, to give assistance in advancing our cause solely, resisting our enemies and reckoning your own good for naught. What remains except that with all prayerful desire we should return the greatest thanks to you as our best vassal? We earnestly hope that an opportunity may be given us to repay you, most loving [friend], with the requital you deserve.

As you have made a good beginning toward us, we ask the Sweetness of Your Love so to persevere and to wipe out and shatter our adversaries. Give them no quarter until they are completely crushed. Likewise, as we embrace your friends, we will be the most unrelenting enemies toward your enemies. And the alliance into which we once entered with your father,[108] we wish to preserve unimpaired for your benefit from this day forward through all our life.

We ask you, most cherished friend, that through your intervention your brother[109] may amend his actions in the future, although he has hitherto neglected our interests because of his own necessities. Since he has gotten out of his straits with a victorious right hand, [we ask] that, as a loving vassal, he may be mindful of our injuries. Having gone with an escort into those regions where our enemies stand waiting and where their goods are situated, he has found the place and the opportunity both to inflict harm on our enemies and to make us disposed toward him in the most friendly way. Therefore, in every way you can, dearly beloved, persuade your brother to pursue N.,[110] no longer duke but one condemned by judicial process, and in every way to oppose him as our most unrelenting enemy.

We ask, however, that, for the sake of our love, you have any members of the household of the Archbishop of Salzburg[111] given back together with any others of our vassals who have been led captive.

---

[106] Cf. Sallust, *Catiline* 20, 4.   [107] Boleslas III.   [108] Ladislas of Hungary.
[109] Coloman of Hungary.   [110] Welf IV.   [111] Berchtold.

24 Henry thanks Bishop Rupert of Bamberg for his constancy and promises him a reward. He asks that Rupert make no disposition of the benefice held by O. the Wealthy before he knows Henry's wishes about it (1099).

Henry, by the grace of God Emperor Augustus of the Romans, sends grace and every good thing to Rupert, bishop of Bamberg:

Since you have always been faithful to us as was your duty, and have sedulously upheld our honor like a wise man and an excellent vassal, we give you our greatest thanks. And for this constancy—know without doubt—we mean to give you worthy remuneration.

In confident trust, therefore, we ask your fidelity not to promise or grant to anyone the benefice which once belonged to O. the Wealthy,[112] until you speak to us or know our will about it through trustworthy letters. If you attend to this in consideration of your love, we shall do what you have asked of us in your letters. Strive, as we trust you will, to provide for our honor.

25 Henry asks Bishop Rupert of Bamberg to enfeoff the son of G. with G.'s benefice (1084-1102).

Henry, by the grace of God Emperor Augustus of the Romans, sends grace and every good thing to Rupert, bishop of the people of Bamberg:

You know very well for how long a time and with what splendid fidelity we were served by O. and by his son G., who recently departed from the world in a death to be pitied by all good men because it was premature. So the compassion of humanity as well as the necessity of justice urges us to remember on behalf of the children of this same G. the service of their grandfather and father and to ameliorate their orphanhood with properly pious support. Wherefore we admonish you solicitously, and we beseech you with the greatest prayers to grant kindly to the son his father's benefice, out of respect for God and for our intervention. Delay this cession on no pretext; neither make any excuses nor reject this petition for any reason. We ask, however, if you care for us, that you delay the investiture of the boy until it can take place in our presence.

---

[112] Perhaps Count Ulric "the Very Rich" of Passau (died 1099).

26 Henry asks Bishop Rupert of Bamberg, pending further orders, to retain the money he has collected for Henry's use; commands his presence at a royal assembly and commissions him his agent among the princes should they hold a rival assembly; promises royal support in the difficulty with O.; exhorts him to shun association with C.; and with a final promise of reward, asks him to send him whatever information touches Henry's affairs (1084–1102).

Henry, by the grace of God Emperor Augustus of the Romans, sends grace and every good thing to Rupert, bishop of Bamberg:

Since we have found by experience that you remain steadfastly faithful to us through all events, just as you should, and since we have found you commendably to be a friend to our friends and an enemy to our enemies and to those unfaithful to us, we tender the greatest possible thanks to you as to an excellent vassal. We praise and view with affection your willingness, for the sake of our honor, to divide among those who ought to have come to our assistance the money you have collected. We wish the money to be kept with you, however, if you have not divided it yet, until we send you our will in regard to it by our messenger and written order.

Since we have summoned you and our other princes by our messengers, we wish you to some and in every way to entreat others to come to our assembly, where we desire to consider the honor of our kingly office with you and with them. If, however, you can in no way persuade them to come, and they, being unwilling to come to our assembly, schedule their own, we ask your fidelity to participate in their assembly and there by comforting our friends and manfully gainsaying our enemies to negotiate diligently in behalf of our honor.

We are moved very much by the fact that O. has offended you, as you have informed us. But we are sending our messengers to him about this matter, and we shall do whatever we can to your honor.

What you have told us about C.[113] pleases us very much. Wherefore, we ask you most of all, as we trust in you, in all ways to put him to the chase and to abhor him, like Judas and a most vicious liar.

Now then, have the greatest care and solicitude to send back to us through a faithful messenger whatever good or evil you can discover about the next assembly or about other things which pertain to us.

Finally, receive our thanks since you have spared our men; for this we shall act to your abiding honor.

[113] Perhaps Conrad, the son of Henry IV (1093) or Conrad of Hohenburg (1098).

27 Henry exhorts Bishop Rupert of Bamberg to obey his orders in regard to the wardency of Bamberg cathedral and to refer all action about the benefice of the late Count U. to their common presence (1094–1102).

Henry, by the grace of God Emperor Augustus of the Romans, sends to Rupert, his most reverend and beloved sponsor[114] in Christ, his grace and best greeting in Christ:

Since I trust you more than anyone else, I am surprised that I have so often asked you for one and the same thing and that you have given me no answer corresponding to my hope. And I am especially amazed since I should never have thought anything so difficult that you would deny it to me. But still, in reiterating again and again these prayers already repeated, I wish the Sweetness of Your Love, moved by entreaty, to offer your ear more indulgently to me in the matter of the wardency of your church and to transfer that to me through the present messenger.

Besides, since Count U. is reported to be dead, I ask only that you recall whether I have done anything for the sake of your love and good will. This done, may I discover clearly in this petition how much you love me. I ask you only such things as are to your honor and profit. I ask, I say, that you promise the benefices which he held of you to no one and that you do nothing in regard to them, but that you delay all action in this affair until we are both present.

28 Henry thanks Bishop Rupert of Bamberg for obeying his orders in regard to the wardency of Bamberg and urges him to see that the warden sustain no loss of his goods and to restore to the wardency lands illegally alienated from it (1084-1092).

Henry, by the grace of God Emperor Augustus, sends the best good will of his grace to the venerable bishop Rupert, his beloved godfather:

Since you have fulfilled our will in regard to wardency of Bamberg, we render you great thanks worthy of our best vassal. Consequently, it only remains for us to ask and firmly to order you to keep the warden of this same church from suffering...[115] or abuse from anyone about his goods.

Fetter by the episcopal authority those who assert that they hold as benefices portions of that wardency. Smite the benefices from their

[114] In baptism.   [115] Lacuna.

hands and restore them; for by the decision of our princes, it has been granted, conceded, and confirmed that no provost or warden of a church has the power to grant anyone as a benefice any of the goods of the church. If such a grant is made, it is to be considered void.

29 Henry commends his envoy N. to Bishop Rupert of Bamberg, requests the Bishop's presence at an assembly in Worms, and requires him to surrender money due the king (1097–1101).

Henry, by the grace of God Emperor Augustus of the Romans, sends to Rupert, the venerable bishop of the church at Bamberg, the bond of his grace, now old, and every good thing:

We have earnestly commissioned our man N. to execute diligently on your behalf certain of our inmost wishes. We request only that you render yourself exorable to him and grant him what he asks in our name. But if you do not do so, refer the issue to our presence, taking no action yourself about it.

We definitely wish and most directly ask you to set aside all business and, offering no excuse, to come to us at Worms, since we are very much in need of your most prudent counsel and aid. In addition to our own business, we are going to consider there the problem of Duke Welf[116] and of his sons.[117] Besides we will have many Saxons and their envoys there.

It has been told us very recently that you have not yet surrendered that money for which we have asked. Wherefore, I ask you, if you have not fulfilled our petition in this matter, to hasten as quickly as possible to surrender the money, since it is a great hindrance and detriment to us that these men delay so long.

30 Henry summons Abbot Udalschalk of Tegernsee to a Diet at Mainz the following Christmastide to take counsel about the Roman See and the unity of the Church (1100).

Henry, by the grace of God Emperor Augustus, sends grace and every good thing to the Abbot of Tegernsee:[118]

Recently, when the death of the Lord Pope Clement[119] became known at our court, the princes who were with us advised that we

[116] Welf IV of Bavaria.
[117] Welf V and Henry the Black.   [118] Udalschalk.   [119] September 8, 1100.

summon all the princes to a general Curia in Mainz at Christmastide,[120] so that by their common counsel the Roman See might be set in order and a method adopted for remolding ecclesiastical unity, now long pitiably rent asunder. Wherefore by admonishing, by asking, and by commanding, we garner most diligently the fidelity you owe us that, as you care for God, for Christian peace, and likewise for our love and grace, so you will not neglect attendance at the aforesaid Curia under any pretext or omit it because of any other business. You should know for certain that we excuse none of the princes from this work and in this we will suffer the negligence of none with equanimity.

> 31 *Henry declares to Abbot Hugh of Cluny that he wishes to restore order to the Church and to heal the schism he himself has caused, and he proposes, upon the restoration of peace to go to the Holy Land as a pilgrim. He asks the prayers of Hugh and of the brethren of Cluny (1102).*[121]

Henry, by the grace of God Emperor Augustus of the Romans, sends what a son [owes] his father to the Reverend Abbot Hugh:

Lord and father, for a long time you have not visited your sick son as you used to nor have you ministered to your contrite son with the palliatives of exhortation and consolation. But then we think this is not to the dishonor of Your Piety but is all to be imputed to our iniquities, since the spirit of the Lord probably prohibited Your Sanctity from exhausting yourself on behalf of a barren tree. It is true that to everything there is a season under the heaven,[122] and just as there is a time for the wrath of the Lord, so also there is a time for His mercy. This alternation we can observe very often in the people of Israel, who

---

[120] On this occasion, Henry and his princes announced their desire for reconciliation with Rome.

[121] In 1101, a year after the death of his antipope, Clement III, Henry declared to an assembly of princes at Mainz that he hoped to restore peace between himself and the new reformer-pope, Paschal II, and that he would even go to Rome if that were requisite for a successful reconciliation. His envoys, however, failed to win Paschal's favor; and the Pope, angered by Henry's refusal to abandon lay investiture, issued a new bull of excommunication against him in April, 1102. Henry continued to hope for a reconciliation, and, at another assembly in January, 1103, he announced his intention to attempt to reestablish harmony between the kingship and the priesthood and, for his own salvation, to make a pilgrimage to the Holy Land. Letter 31 belongs to the period just before the 1103 assembly.

[122] Ecclesiastes 3:1.

were punished by the Lord when they sinned but were judged worthy of pardon when they repented. Clearly, it was so when the walls of Jerusalem were destroyed by Nebuchadnezzar, the temple of the Lord ruined, and the people led away captive; it was so when the daughter of Zion sat for seventy years without king, without priest, and without sacrifice. But again, when the heavens rained down the mercy of God[123] under Cyrus the king of the Persians, the captivity was loosed; the people returned; Jerusalem was rebuilt; the temple was repaired; and liturgical rites were restored in their entirety. If, therefore, as the Apostle says, "All these things happened unto them for ensamples,"[124] why may not we, who have long sustained similar wrath of the Lord in the destruction of the religion held by the Church, hope for similar mercy in the reparation of that religion?

Inspired by this example, we declare to Your Serenity that as far as God may give us the power, we desire to work in every way for the reparation of ecclesiastical affairs which (alas) have gone to ruin in our time through our sins. Now, we also wish to labor and to acquiesce in the sound counsels of all good men, if we can in this way gather the things which have been scattered and bring together in the bond of union the opening made by the wedge of schism. Thus, we wish to recompense with a renewal of peace and justice the ruin of the Church, which we have brought about.

Besides we declare to you that if we shall, with the favor of God, be able to reconcile the kingship and the priesthood, we are determined to go to Jerusalem after the establishment of peace.[125] And we earnestly

[123] Cf. Exodus 16:14 ff., Psalm 68:9, Isaiah 45:8.

[124] I Corinthians 10:11.

[125] Henry expressed this desire during the divine service on Epiphany, 1103. Several notable events preceded this plan of Henry's and may have prompted it. The earliest and one of the most important of them was the German Pilgrimage of 1064–1065, led by Bishop Gunther of Bamberg and Archbishop Siegfried of Mainz. Otto of Regensburg and William of Utrecht, later close advisers of Henry (see the decree of the Synod of Worms), also participated, as did Herman, Gunther's successor. See E. Joranson, "The Great German Pilgrimage of 1064–1065," in *The Crusades: Essays Presented to Dana C. Munro* (New York, 1928), pp. 9 f. Subsequently, Gregory VII issued in 1074 a general summons to a crusade which he intended to lead personally to relieve the Christians in the East (U. Schwerin, *Die Aufrufe der Päpste zur Befreiung des Heiligen Landes* [Berlin, 1937], p. 70; S. Runciman, *The Eastern Schism* [Oxford, 1955], p. 59; C. Erdmann, "Die Aufrufe Gerberts und Sergius IV für das Heilige Land," *Quellen und Forschungen aus italienischen Archiven und Bibliotheken*, XXIII [1932], 2), and threatened forcibly to subject the Iberian peninsula, or that part of it under Alfonso VI of Leon and Castile, to

desire with His favor to see the Holy Land, in which our Lord appeared in the flesh and had concourse with men, in order more directly to adore Him there where we know He suffered for our sake blows, spittle, lashes, the cross, death, and entombment.

We make known all these things, however, to Your Sanctity so that you may pray for us the more earnestly and with the sacred college of your brethren may commend us the more carefully to God to the end that He, whose mercy surpasses our good will, may deign to direct our works to a fruitful conclusion.

32 Henry congratulates Bishop Otto of Bamberg on the auspicious beginning of his episcopacy and urges him to continued prudence, justice, and constancy. He promises Otto royal support in any future difficulties (1103).

Henry, by the grace of God Emperor Augustus of the Romans, sends grace, love, and every good thing to Otto,[126] bishop of the see of Bamberg:

Since perfect love assuredly makes its abode in the heart, it is of value not to the eye alone, nor does it concern the eye or depend upon the times. Through it persons absent one from another are bound together ever more closely through their common solicitude for each other the longer they are separated. Certainly, we, in the same spirit in which we have elevated you, take greater care for you when you are absent than when you are present; for we wish all things to be prosperous for you and fear adversities, although they may not happen, because they can happen.

For this reason, we are very pleased to learn, as we had hitherto

the rule of the Roman See (1080). (Gregory, *Register*, Epp. VIII, 2, p. 518.) C. Erdmann, *Die Entstehung des Kreuzzugsgedankens* [Stuttgart, 1035; reprinted, 1955], p. 160.) In 1080, Benzo of Alba urged Henry IV to go to the Holy Land to gain a crown of glory at the Holy Sepulchre (II, chap. 12, *MGH SS.*, XI, 617). A decade later, under the urging of Urban II, the crusading zeal swept Europe, and in 1099 it culminated in the capture of Jerusalem. Henry's proposal belongs to this climate of opinion. One must remark also that Henry may have been appealing specifically to the lively interest of Hugh, who as abbot of Cluny offered great material and spiritual support to Spanish rulers in the Reconquista. (See S. Runciman, *A History of the Crusades* [Cambridge, 1951], I, 90.) For the history of the idea of the Crusades, one should consult the works in the comprehensive bibliography by H. E. Mayer, *Bibliographie zur Geschichte der Kreuzzüge* (Hanover, 1960).

[126] Otto, long a servant of Henry IV, was named bishop of Bamberg at Christmastide, 1102, and installed in February, 1103.

hoped, that you have been received honorably by your Church, that you have found favor through a temperance of responses, habit, and actions pleasing to all, and that you have laudably shown the necessary caution in retaining your benefices.

We counsel and ask you to do what you do in such a way as not to lose the first fruits of good repute by relaxing your control, since a good beginning without a [good] end is like a handsome body without a head. Let no one divert you through terror from a just love for the advantage of the Church; let no one bend you with bribery; let no one seduce you with the galled honey of suasion, since if, tempted by all these things, you are proven, you will cast all before you with ease.

If, however, you think something too burdensome for your powers, refer it to us, making use of the opportunity afforded by our orders, and do not doubt that we shall come to succor you.

33 *Henry recalls the constancy of the church at Bamberg and praises it, at the same time warning against credulity and requiring loyalty toward Bishop Otto. He writes at the insistence of the church at Mainz (1103–1105).*

Henry, by the grace of God Emperor Augustus of the Romans, sends grace and every good thing to the church at Bamberg:

Mindful of the fidelity and devotion[127] of your predecessors towards us and towards our men, we trust you beyond all others, since we see that you have not yet strayed in any way from the path of such great virtue. We embrace with all affection such great constancy in you, being eager always and in every place to renew the favor of our predecessors toward you.

But, lo, the enemy of human salvation, as you know, strives with the zeal of [his] ancient malice to obstruct the attainment of so great a salvation. You, however, who have been illuminated by the Spirit of God, know his snares and ambuscades; consider well how the authority of the Doctor of the Gentiles warned you beforetime. For how did he who saw even the secrets of God when he was taken up to the third heaven[128] not foresee truly the danger to the Church committed to him? He said: "In the last days perilous times shall come, and men will go astray, loving themselves,[129] thinking piety a cause for complaint,"[130] and other things. We do not admonish Your Love with these citations

127 Cf. I Thessalonians 1 : 3.   128 Cf. II Corinthians 12 : 2, 4.
129 Cf. II Timothy 3 : 1–2.   130 Cf. I Timothy 6 : 5.

to shame you, knowing as we do your perfection in these things as in others. But we push you on with the pious hand of exhortation so that you will watch with care and discretion, lest, according to the voice of the Apostle, you believe every spirit[131] which, having, to be sure, a kind of piety,[132] practices works of impiety and toiling in various and vain labors involves itself in many woes. Since you see these things better than we, consider well what you owe to justice and to truth.

We order, in ordering we admonish, and yet in admonishing we ask, that you receive no legation [directed] against your bishop, since you can hear no just accusation against him. For I call to witness God and the conscience of each of us, that he has come legitimately and canonically to the administration of this government.

The mother church at Mainz[133] has persuaded us to write these things to you, very solicitous as she is for the salvation of her children, so that, just as she embraces you before others with fidelity and love, so she may rejoice in your perseverance with her in the Faith which is Christ's and ours.

34 *Henry reminds Pope Paschal of the amity between his predecessors and Paschal's and of that between himself and both Nicholas II and Alexander II. He deplores the subsequent destruction of good relations through Papal instigation to rebellion among his subjects. Hoping that Paschal will see fit to restore good relations, Henry sends an envoy to him and promises, on the successful outcome of these preliminary negotiations, to send another legation (1105).[134]*

Henry, the Emperor, to the Roman pontiff, Paschal:

If there had been between us that peace and harmony which once existed between our predecessors and yours and which flourished

---

[131] I John 4:1.   [132] II Timothy 3:5 f.

[133] That is, the cathedral chapter, as Archbishop Ruthard had been expelled from his see.

[134] Early in December, 1104, Henry V withdrew from his father's court and began the rebellion which lasted until the death of the elder Henry in 1106. In an attempt to win back his son, Henry IV dispatched legations to him headed by the Archbishops of Cologne and Trier and Duke Frederick of Swabia, his son-in law. Their efforts and those of Ulric, patriarch of Aquileia, failed to reconcile father and son. Following a second course, Ulric had also pressed Henry IV to reconcile himself with Rome. At his urging, the King wrote Letter 34 to Paschal II seeking to return to the good favor of the Roman pontiff and thereby to remove the grounds of Henry V's claim that his

with full love and unimpared devotion between us and Nicholas [II] and Alexander [II], catholic men and reverent Roman pontiffs, we would send you "whatever a son owes to his father."[135] But we have delayed doing this, waiting and desiring to discover if it is in God's good pleasure for us to be able to come together in love and friendship, and by our work, and with His assistance, in our time to restore His Church to the state of its pristine unity.

With God as our witness, we earnestly desired such a reconciliation even in former days, but when the extreme harshness of those who were in the Roman church[136] became known, it did not seem to us useful or fitting to come together with them for this purpose. Indeed, they seemed to persecute us with hatred and indignation more than with zeal for justice. It seemed that they wished to persecute us rather than with the sweetness of love to embrace us for the advancement of the Church. The events themselves prove this: When these men strove to stir up and to arm the kingdom against us (the kingdom conferred upon us by hereditary right and long held in peace by us during the days of those religious men, the Roman pontiffs) great destruction befell the people as a result—a destruction of bodies and also, which is even more to be bewailed, of souls.

Now also our son, whom we loved with such great affection that we exalted him to the throne of our kingdom, has been infected by this same poison and is rebelling against us on the advice of certain most perfidious perjurers who adhere to him.[137] He has set aside all the solemn oaths with which he bound himself to us. He has cast aside all fidelity and justice so completely that he and his minions are able freely to ruin, to ravish, and to divide among themselves the goods of churches and of the kingdom.

Many tried to persuade us that we should without delay exact vengeance from them by force of arms. Yet, until now, we preferred with

rebellion was just because it was against an excommunicate king. The conciliatory character of the letter is clearly indicated by Henry's omission of any reference to Paschal's rejection of his legation in 1102 or to the bull of excommunication issued against him later in the same year. This attempt to gain the good offices of the Papacy also failed, and Paschal gave his support to Henry V.

135 It is unclear whether the omission of Henry's usual formula, "by the grace of God," and of a greeting for Paschal is due to the carelessness of a copyist or to imperial coolness toward the Papacy. See note 1, p. 138.

136 Gregory VII and Urban II. See "Life of Henry IV," chap. 6, p. 114.

137 See "Life of Henry IV," chaps. 7, 9, pp. 118ff, 121f.

forbearance to delay, so that it might be manifestly known clearly in the Italian realm as well as in the German that it was neither our will nor our fault if at last, unwilling and under constraint, we should rise up against them, and if evil or ill-starred events, or even the destruction of the people, should result.

We have heard that you are a discreet, God-fearing man, toiling for love and not thirsting for human blood or rejoicing in rapine and arson but loving the unity of the Church above all. We send you this messenger, therefore, with our legation on the advice and suggestion of our princes, those religious men who love us. Through him we wish to discover if you desire to join yourself to us and us to you in love and friendship saving the honor of the kingship, of the empire, and of our entire dignity, as both our grandfather and our father and other predecessors of ours have had it, and with the honor of the apostolic dignity reserved to you by us, as our predecessors reserved it to your predecessors and as we reserved it to the aforesaid pontiffs.

But if it shall please you to deal as a father with us and to establish fully with us, and through the assurance of God, that peace which the world can not give,[138] and this in its fullness, send us a trusted envoy with private letters and a secret legation along with this envoy of ours, so that in this way we can know without doubt the full certainty of your will in this matter. When we learn this, we shall send you some of our greater princes, men such as would be fitting both for us to send to you and for you to receive from us for the purpose of settling so great a matter. Through these men, with all cause for doubt removed, you can know clearly that we truly wish to fulfill those secret proposals which we are sending you.

Besides those things which have been written here, we have committed certain things to this, our most faithful envoy, to be said to you. You may believe them as truly as the things which have been written.

35 Henry urges Bishop Otto of Bamberg to show his fidelity to him by bringing him troops at the siege of Würzburg and by complying with his request for the enfeoffment of A. (1105).

Henry, by the grace of God Emperor Augustus of the Romans, sends grace and every good thing to Otto, bishop of Bamberg, his beloved and sure vassal:

[138] John 14:27.

Now, when necessity is pressing us, those who are faithful to us ought to show themselves and reveal clearly in this situation how much they love us and our honor.

Know, therefore, that we have come to Würzburg with many soldiers and are waiting there for still more, desiring to come upon our enemies with the strength of God and to free our fortress of Nüremberg, which they are besieging.[139] Wherefore we send to you as to our best vassal, asking as we trust you that you come hurriedly to us with all the men you have under your control.

Moreover, we earnestly ask you to consider our present need and to grant A., a man needful to us, the benefice which he asks of you, considering the fact that now the current danger compels us to make supplication to many men and by doing their will to confirm them in fidelity to us. Thus we, whose actions are restricted for this reason, must petition you in these matters and in many others, for things which we would not wish in other circumstances. But, God willing, if prosperity come, we shall turn our attention to you and your church, in a worthy fashion. Act in this matter according to what N. tells you on our behalf.

36 *Henry assures Bishop Otto of Bamberg of his continued confidence and support and exhorts him to resist Henry V steadfastly by prayers and arms (1105).*

Henry, by the grace of God Emperor Augustus of the Romans, sends grace and every good thing to Otto, bishop of Bamberg:

We know that you are frequently wearied by legations from our son, as you have informed us by your messenger. We trust, however, in the faithful assurance of Your Goodness, that you will never ally with our enemies against us because of supplications, threats, suasions, or blandishments, but that you will always remain faithfully with us. However great the persecutions you may sustain at the hands of our enemies, never be afraid. Be certain that we shall not desert you either in peace or in peril, and trust in the omnipotent Lord that you will be freed with us quickly from the present peril.

Do not fail to come to us at the date and place we have set, as we trusted you would when we sent you word by your messenger.

Therefore, by the fidelity which you owe us, be not so frightened by

[139] See "Life of Henry IV," chap. 9, p. 123.

prayers or threats as to be carried over to our son. And have prayers said to God for us without intermission by every church and by all the congregations committed to you.

Also have your castle so diligently guarded that none of the guards may leave it.

And send your messenger to encourage the people of Nüremberg.

37 Henry narrates to Abbot Hugh and the brethren of Cluny the treacherous actions of his own son, the reconciliation at Coblenz, the betrayal at Bingen, his own imprisonment, the enforced abdication at Ingelheim, and his flight to Cologne. He asks Hugh for counsel and, saving only the royal honor, promises to do whatever Hugh thinks necessary for a reconciliation with the Pope (1106).[140]

Henry, by the grace of God Emperor Augustus of the Romans, sends to his most illustrious and beloved father Hugh and to all the holy brothers of the monastery of Cluny the tender affection of a son and the devoted affection of a brother, nay rather the lowly obedience of a servant:

In the spirit of loving-kindness, we have always experienced your pious devotion and paternal solicitude toward us, often under such conditions that we may believe we have been freed by your holy prayers from many of the perils which threatened us. We resort therefore,

[140] Abandoned by a large part of his army before Regensburg in October, 1105, Henry IV fled through hostile territory to Cologne, which remained steadfastly loyal to him throughout the rebellion of Henry V. Subsequently, he and his son agreed that the crisis should be settled in the presence of the papal legate, Richard of Albano, at an assembly of German nobles which Henry V had scheduled to be held at Mainz during Christmastide that year. The elder Henry was to appear in person before the whole assembly and to present his defense against the charges of his adversaries; but in order to prevent his father from appealing directly to the whole body of the princes, from which he might have expected some support, Henry V arraigned him before a smaller body of nobles, as is described in this letter and in Letters 39, 40, and 41. After his deposition and release, Henry IV fled to Liége. There, receiving vigorous support from the Lotharingians, particularly from the people of Liége and Cologne, he rallied his forces and prepared to renew the conflict. In March, Henry V's plan to disperse his father's troops by attacking Liége failed when a bridge near Visé collapsed under the weight of his army and many of his men were drowned. In July, he adopted a new strategem and besieged Cologne (Letter 42; Cf. "Life of Henry IV," chap. 13); but the resistance of that city proved stronger than he had anticipated, and he had begun to negotiate for a truce when Henry IV fell ill and died at Liége on August 7, 1106.

dearest father, to you after God, as though to the only refuge in our necessity, and we humbly ask that with you, at least, we may find solace for our miseries. O that we could see your angelic face in the flesh, so that falling familiarly at your knees we might rest our head, which you took [at our baptism] from the font of salvation, in the lap of Your Sanctity, and there while bewailing our sins might narrate[141] one after another the multitude of our tribulations.

Not only the vast lands which separate us but also the amazing hatreds of raging enemies begrudge us such consolation. We beseech Your Paternity, therefore, with all devotion not to disdain to receive letters from Our Humility which contain, with God as our witness, no false-hood or pretense and to give heed attentively and with mercy to the monstrous act of our unheard-of betrayal. This betrayal, indeed, is the more astonishing since it was not achieved by the hand of a domestic or an enemy. If someone who hated me had spoken great things against me,[142] I should have quickly eluded him. But even the son of our loins, signally beloved of us, impiously, inhumanly, and unworthily effected this against us in such a way that we can cry out to God, not without grief or immense wonderment, in the very voice of the Psalmist-King, fleeing from the face of a son not unlike ours, "Lord, how are they increased that trouble me!"[143]

For we believe that you know (since we do not doubt that you have heard) with what great affection and profound and heartfelt love we exalted that same son of ours to the throne of the kingdom against the will of many. At his very election, he vowed to us at Mainz that he would in no way, while I lived or against our will and precept, set his hand against our life and our personal welfare. At the same time he also vowed to respect the kingship and our every honor and all things which we had or which we were to have.[144] He took this oath to us in the presence of all the princes and on the Lord's nail with the Lance when he was enthroned at Aachen.[145] But all these oaths were cast aside and handed over to oblivion on the advice of treacherous perjurers and of our mortal enemies. So he was separated from us so completely that, wishing in every way to attack us in our holdings as well as in our person, he made it his constant goal from that hour to deprive us of kingship and life. He began to besiege our castles and to usurp our lands as well. Through a solemn oath, he bound to himself and against

[141] In baptism, at Cologne in 1051.   [142] Psalm 55:13.   [143] Psalm 3:1, 2.
[144] May, 1098. See "Life of Henry IV," chap. 7, p. 122.   [145] January 6, 1099.

us as many men of our household as he could and others also. For shame! Although we waited from day to day for him to look back, touched by grief of heart[146] and inwardly humbled, he burned more and more with the madness of perfidy, counting for naught fear of God and reverence for his father. And he did not hesitate to pursue us from city to city and to usurp all our holdings as far as he was able.

So we came to Cologne. At length, since he had scheduled an assembly at Mainz for the next Christmas, we began to go there, after our vassals had been gathered together. When he had heard this, he came to meet us at a place called Coblenz. Since he could do nothing against us there by force, he began to work with subtlety, craft, and all artifice. He sent his messengers to us asking that we talk with him; we, for our part, having accepted the advice of our vassals, consented to this. When we met there, we at once fell[147] prostrate at his feet and began to ask most affectionately for the sake of God alone and for the sake of his soul that he be willing to cease finally from the inhuman persecution of his father. He, on the other hand, threw himself down at our feet under the guise and veil of peace and agreement. Weeping, he asked and besought us to commit ourselves to his fidelity and to his inmost feelings, since he was our bone and flesh,[148] and he urged us not to hesitate to go with him to the aforesaid assembly at Mainz. He himself was to conduct us there with every guarantee of security and to take counsel solicitously with the princes about our honor as faithfully as possible. And at the end of the negotiations, whether they had been successful or not, he was to conduct us back thence with the utmost security from that to whatever place we should wish. After we had heard and had understood all this and our men had given their consent, we committed ourselves to his fidelity and to his inmost feelings, saying, "We commit ourselves to your inmost feelings under that fidelity with which God has wished a son to love his father". He gave his right hand with that same assurance of our well-being and honor and rendered us secure. In no way did we mistrust this assurance, therefore, and we sent our men back to the aforesaid assembly, ordering also the rest of our vassals to meet us there; and so we set out with him.[149]

When we were under way, however, it was announced to us privately that we were betrayed. When he knew that we had been told this, he

---

[146] Genesis 6:6. [147] Matthew 23:34. See "Life of Henry IV," chap. 10, p. 126.
[148] Genesis 29:14. [149] December 21, 1105.

began to make vows[150] and to deny that it was in any way true; and he received us again under the same assurances. Finally, about nightfall on the following day[151] we came to a place called Bingen. At dawn he surrounded us with a band of armed men and with every kind of terror, saying that he meant to conduct us to a certain castle rather than to Mainz.[152] Then when we fell to his feet and to those of others, in the hope that according to the safe-conduct which had been given, he would conduct us to Mainz or dismiss us, free to go but bound to return at the time which he should set, with every guarantee of security. He answered us that we would be allowed to do nothing other than to go to that castle.

What more? They led us away captive against our every desire. There, shoved into the most narrow confinement, we were handed over to our mortal enemies, and all our men, with the exception of three laymen, were shut out. At a time when we despaired of our life, we were not even left a priest from whom we could receive the body and blood of the Lord as a *viaticum* and to whom we could make confession of our sins. Then we were afflicted with hunger and thirst and every kind of abuse and terror, even to the very point of death, so that it was certain to us that, so far as lay within his power, we should live no longer unless we complied with his wishes. Meanwhile, we were sent word that there would be no discussion of our liberation, if the cross and the lance and the other regal insignia were not given to him straightway. When we understood beyond all doubt that we could be freed in no other way, we sent word to those who were in the castle[153] where the regalia were kept at all events to redeem [our] life for us in this way. These men, knowing the peril to our life, although they were unwilling to do so, surrendered the aforesaid cross and lance with the other insignia.

These things done in this inhuman way, with God and all right and justice set aside, they led us out the horrible prison to a place near Mainz, which is called Ingelheim. Our son came to this place with a multitude of our mortal enemies. Almost all our vassals were left at Mainz, hoping that he would be obliged to conduct us to them there. While all these men were deceived by this hope, we were brought

---

[150] Cf. Matthew 26:74. See "Life of Henry IV," chap. 10, p. 126.

[151] December 22, 1105.   [152] Böckelheim.

[153] Hammerstein, below Andernach, on the right bank of the Rhine. See "Life of Henry IV," chap. 10, p. 126.

forth again in that place to the most cruel questionings and to iniquitous exactions in the presence of the legate of the Pope.[154] There, we were charged with many unsuitable things by our enemies, not so much through zeal for righteousness as through eagerness for our ruin. In fact, they simply presented whatever points could be contrary to our welfare and honor. But, indeed, when we asked to be allowed to answer and with a worthy explanation to give satisfaction for all these charges, they refused the request imperiously. Even the barbarians would not do this to any slave. Seeing that violence and prejudgment were in store for us, we prostrated ourselves at their feet. We began to implore them humbly, as much for the sake of God as for that of their own honor, to refer questionings and charges of this kind to the Apostolic See, granting to us the dignity of personal liberty in the meantime so that we might go to Rome. We asked that there, with the Roman clergy and people present, with hatred and envy and the other things contrary to justice set aside, we would be allowed either worthily to exculpate ourself or humbly to give satisfaction for those things with which we were charged. But when this also was inhumanly denied to us, we finally asked in our wretched state if we had any hope for life or salvation or if there were ultimately a means for our release. We were then answered that we could be saved from grave captivity if we wished to comply with those propositions made to us, although they were against our right and honor: namely, that we should render up according to their will the crown of the Empire.

What more? After they had extorted everything from us according to their will and command, they departed from Mainz and left us there without honor. Behold, then we were ordered, unless we wished to suffer eternal captivity, to leave as quickly as possible. Wherefore, cursing that place, we boarded a ship; we went quickly to Cologne, and so by the gratuitous mercy of Divine Majesty, we were freed with difficulty from the cruel hands of our enemies.

But now it is time to set an end to this overly long tragedy of our miseries. We have taken care to weep forth this tragic story to Your Piety, most loving father, since we have great and singular hope in God and in you, hope for counsel and aid, for our salvation and release. Though hitherto we have delayed doing it, with full affection and with yearning of spirit we now entrust to Your Fidelity our whole plan of

---

[154] Richard, Cardinal Bishop of Albano (and Bishop Gebhard of Constance).

action. Whatever you may decide is to be done as regards our reconciliation with the pope, and whatever you may decide must be done
(saving violation of our honor) as regards the peace and unity of the
holy Roman Church, we promise to God and to you, in full certainty,
that we will do it all. Hasten, therefore, dearest father, to advise us.
We ask that you be not displeased to heed us; although your labor is
not for the liberation of a son, since we have sinned against heaven and
before you,[155] at least it is for the salvation of your hireling.

Finally, we complain to Your Piety that by his letters our son pro-
claims everywhere that we have given up all the regalia voluntarily.
Your Sanctity should know that this is absolutely untrue.[156]

*38 Henry asks Abbot Hugh of Cluny for help in his extreme necessity and
declares that he is ready, saving only his honor, to do for the Pope whatever
Hugh thinks requisite. He asks the prayers of Hugh and of the brethren of
Cluny (1106).*

Henry, by the grace of God Emperor Augustus of the Romans, to
Hugh, venerable abbot of Cluny, whatever a spiritual son, though he
be a sinner, owes with full devotion and humility to his most loving
and beloved spiritual father:

We have arranged to describe in our own letter and to impart to
you through the agency of familiar monks, your brethren, the whole
sequence of events surrounding our tribulation and horrible betrayal,
unheard-of to all ages. Yet, through these messengers we also wished
to supplicate you, holy Father, with the most earnest devotion, as a
publican seeks refuge for his sins[157] and a shipwreck a port of safety.[158]
This is our plea, venerable Father, to the memorable uprightness of
Your Sanctity: When you have heard and come to understand the
detestable misfortune of our monstrous betrayal, may the love of God

---

[155] Luke 15:18 f.

[156] In the year of Henry's death, Hugh wrote to Philip of France urging him to enter
a monastery, and so to gain the true, imperishable crown of the spirit. "May the woeful
downfall and the lamentable ruin of your contemporaries and neighbors, of William
[Rufus], I say, the king of the Angles, and of the Emperor Henry, move you and smite
you with terror; of them, the first perished by the thrust of a single arrow, not in
battle, but suddenly, in a forest. The other, as we believe you have already heard, died
recently amidst the many torments and grave afflictions which he had long sustained."
Migne PL, CLIX, 950, Letter 8.

[157] Cf. Luke 18:13.   [158] Cf. Augustine, Ep. 25, 3.

which is in you[159] so burn for the sake of God alone that it come to the defense of our execrable injury. May it be manifestly apparent, holy Father, that you are concerned with our unheard-of tribulations solely through the love of God.

We wished before with the counsel of religious men to open a full legal process in the presence of the Roman legate[160] about the case between us and the Pope. But since those men had already decided that in this life we were irrevocably lost, they would in no way receive us. And yet, however we may have been treated, we subject ourself to the judgment of you, our father, and of other religious men whom you wish to have for that purpose, so that, saving our honor, I may do everything for the Pope which you prescribe.

As for the rest, I commit myself to your prayers, venerable Father; and we ask to be presented by you to your holy congregation and to be commended most devoutly to their prayers.

39 Henry complains (to King Philip I of France) of his persecution by the Papacy and narrates the treacherous actions of his own son, the reconciliation at Coblenz, the seizure at Bingen and the subsequent captivity, the enforced abdication at Ingelheim, the denial of absolution by the Papal legate, and the flight to Cologne and Liége. He asks that this pattern for betrayal be eradicated from the earth (1106).

(Henry, Emperor of the Romans, sends to N., king of the Franks, the crown of fidelity and the inviolable constancy of kinship):[161]

O most illustrious prince and most faithful of all our friends, in whom, after God, we place our hope! It is you whom I have chosen first and foremost among all men; to you I have thought it necessary to lament my calamities and all my woes and to mourn them. And I should even have fallen to your knees, were that possible without prejudice to the majesty of the Empire.

First, indeed, there is something which we think most grave and unbearable not only to us but also to all men who profess the Christian religion. It is that now the full punishment of persecution, of excommunication, and of perdition is sent forth against us from that Apostolic See, whence arose, until within living memory, the salubrious fruit of

[159] I John 4: 12.   [160] Richard of Albano.

[161] The protocol is lacking in most manuscripts and survives only in the Wolfenbüttel Collection and in the Codex Udalrici.

consolation, of sweetness, and of the salvation of souls. They set no measure to their designs, save only the satisfaction of their rash will. Without regard for God or for what or how much evil might result from their actions, they have so abused me with the intemperance of this willfulness of theirs that they have assailed me in every fashion themselves and through their minions. All this, although on many occasions I should have shown obedience and all due subjection to the Apostolic See, had only due reverence and honor been shown also to me by the Apostolic See as it was shown to my predecessors.

Under more favorable circumstances I myself shall make known to you what they mean to do, should God give us the opportunity for the meeting we have hoped for.

When they saw that they succeeded but slightly in this inflamatory outbreak of their persecution and hatred, they worked against the very law of nature—and this I can not say without the greatest grief of heart and without many tears; now that it is said, I tremble violently—and they not only turned the mind of my son against me, I say the mind of my most beloved Absolom,[163] but they also armed him with great fury. So great was his rage most particularly against the fidelity and the solemn oath which he had vowed as a knight to his lord that he usurped my kingly office, deposed my bishops and abbots, and substituted my enemies and persecutors. Finally—and this I should wish most of all to be kept silent, or, if it can not be kept silent, I should wish it not to be believed—casting away all natural feeling, he turned his thoughts against my welfare and life, nor did he consider what importance it might have, that in any way whatsoever, by force or deceit, he should aspire to this height of his own peril and dishonor.

Since I was in peace and in security of my welfare, he, to prosecute this evil design, called me forth to a meeting on those most holy days of the Lord's Advent at a place called Coblenz, like a son who was going to treat with his father of [their] common welfare and honor. When I saw him, I at once fell prostrate at his feet, touched within by paternal affection and by the grief of my heart.[163] By God, by fidelity, and by the salvation of his soul I admonished and exhorted him that, were I to be scourged by God for my sins, he should himself seek no stain for his soul, honor, and name on my account, since no sanction of divine law ever established a son as avenger of his father's wrongdoing.

[162] II Samuel 18:33. [163] Genesis 6:6. See "Life of Henry IV," chap. 10, p. 127.

But excellently, nay execrably, instructed in malice,[164] he began to make denials as though he were abjuring an abominable and fearful crime. Falling prostrate at our feet, he began to beg pardon for his past actions and tearfully to promise on a relic that he would heed me with fidelity and truth in all respects, as a knight heeds his lord, as a son his father, if only I were disposed to be reconciled to the Apostolic See.

When I had eagerly agreed and promised that in this affair I would yield myself completely to his considered opinion and to the counsel of the princes, he promised that during the Christmas season then present he would conduct me all the way to Mainz and take action there as faithfully as he could in regard to my honor and my reconciliation [with the Papacy]. And he added that he would conduct me thence back into peace and security. This he promised in that attitude of truth and fidelity with which God orders a father to be honored by his son and a son to be loved by his father.[165]

Secure in an engagement of this kind which is binding even on a heathen, I set out toward Mainz with my son preceding me a little. Behold, certain of my vassals met me then and affirmed that in truth I had been deceived and betrayed under a false contract of peace and fidelity. I called my son back and admonished him again most earnestly; but with a protestation of the same fidelity and solemn oath, he promised that he would lay down his life for my life, if an opportunity for doing so should present itself.

When, therefore, we had come to a place called Bingen, it being then the day of Venus[166] before Christmas, the number of his armed men was appreciably increased; already this fraud was seen to uncover itself. And my son said to me, "Father, you must withdraw into a nearby castle,[167] since the bishop of Mainz[168] will not admit you into his city as long as you are under the ban; and I dare not carry you among your enemies, when are not at peace with them and are unreconciled to them. Spend Christmas there with all honor and peace; you may have with you whomever you please. Meanwhile, as earnestly and as faithfully as I can, I shall work for us both, since I consider your cause to be mine." And I said, "My son, may God be present as the witness and judge[169] today of the words and assurances between us, God who alone

---

[164] Cf. Terence, *Hecyra* 203.   [165] Exodus 20:12.
[166] Friday, December 22, 1105. See "Life of Henry IV," chap. 10, p. 126.
[167] Döckelheim.   [168] Ruthard. See "Life of Henry IV," chap. 10, p. 126.
[169] Cf. Jeremiah 29:23.

knows how I advanced you as a man and my heir, with what great tribulations on my part I labored in the service of your honor, how many and how great were the enmities I have borne and yet bear on your behalf." Then again for the third time,[170] he, with the protestation of the same assurances and of a solemn oath, promised that if a moment of peril broke upon us, he would lay down his life for mine.

The outcome of the affair—namely, the way in which he afterwards shut me in the same castle—clearly showed that he had spoken everything with a double heart.[171] I was shut away with three out of all of my men, and no one else could be admitted. And guards were appointed who were fierce enemies of my life. Blessed on all accounts is God, the most powerful King, who can exalt and humble whomever he wishes![172]

Although on this most holy day of His nativity, that Boy, the Saint of Saints, was born for all His redeemed, to me alone this Son was not given.[173] I shall not mention disgraces, injuries, threats, swords thrust against my neck if I did not do everything which had been ordered, hunger also, and thirst, which I endured at the hands of men whom it was wrongdoing to see and to hear.[174] Nor shall I mention that I was once quite happy,[175] for that would be too burdensome. May I never forget nor may I never cease lamenting to all Christians that I was in that prison during those most holy days without any Christian communion.

In those days of my penitence and tribulation, one of the princes, Wibert,[176] an envoy of my son, came to me, saying that according to the will and command of the princes, there was no prospect for me to continue living unless I gave up all the insignia of kingship without an argument. Although my realm comprised the whole inhabited earth, I was unwilling to lose my life for it. And since I understood that, whether I wished it or not, I had to do what they specified, I sent the crown, the scepter, the cross, the lance, and the sword to Mainz.

Then, after taking counsel with my enemies, my son went away [from Mainz], having left there our vassals and friends as though he were going to take me there. And after I had been led out to a village called Ingelheim under the surveillance of a great throng and guard of armed men, he had me conducted into his presence. There I found a

---

[170] Cf. the denials of Peter, Matthew 26:69 ff.
[171] Psalm 12:2.   [172] Psalm 75:8.   [173] Henry refers to Holy Communion.
[174] The reference is either to excommunicates or to outlaws.
[175] Cf. Boethius, *De Consolatione Philosophiae* II pros. 4, 2.
[176] Wiprecht of Groitsch. See "Life of Henry IV," chap. 10, p. 126.

very great multitude of my enemies assembled and I did not find my son better disposed toward me than any of the others. Since it seemed to them that their position would be more firm and stable if they forced me to lay aside the kingship and all the regalia with my own hand, all these men in a similar manner threatened that unless I did all the things which had been ordered I could not hope for life, Then I said, "Since only my life is at stake and I hold nothing more precious than my life[177] —for at least while I live I may offer penance to God—whatever you order, behold, I do it."

And when I asked if I could in this way be certain and secure at least in regard to my life, the legate of the Apostolic See[178] who was present there—I do not say that he had ordained all these things—answered that I could be delivered in no way unless I confessed publicly that I had persecuted Hildebrand unjustly, that I had imposed Wibert[179] above him unjustly, and that I had practiced until that time an unjust persecution against the Apostolic See and all the Church.

Then, prostrate on the ground, I began with the greatest contrition of spirit to pray in the name of God, in the name of justice itself, that a place and time be given me for a hearing in the presence of all the princes, where I should be harmless.[180] There, I said, I would exonerate myself in the judgment of all. There, in whatever regard I acknowledged my fault, I would seek from the counsel of all men of sound purpose, penance and amends of whatever kind they might order. There, I would give to the princes of the realm whatever hostages from among our vassals they should wish. But this same legate refused to set a day and a place for me, saying that unless everything was determined there I had no hope of leaving.

When I asked in that moment of extreme tribulation whether, should I confess everything they ordered, my confession would obtain my pardon and absolution, as was just, that same legate answered that it was not within his right to absolve me. And when I replied to his remarks, "Whoever dares to receive one in confession ought to absolve him when he has confessed," he said that if I wished to be absolved, I should go to Rome to give satisfaction to the Apostolic See.

Thus despoiled and desolate—for by their accustomed force and craft

---

[177] See "Life of Henry IV," chap. 10, p. 127. Cf. Boethius, *De Consolatione Philosophiae* II pros. 4, 23.

[178] Richard of Albano.   [179] Wibert of Ravenna, the antipope Clement III.

[180] See "Life of Henry IV," chap. 10, p. 127.

they had extorted from me castles, and patrimony, and whatever I had gained in the kingdom—they left me in that village.

When I was tarrying there for some time, my son, with his usual deceptive counsel, demanded that I await him there. Then a legation of some of my vassals came up and warned that, if I should remain there even for a moment, either I should be taken off into perpetual captivity or I should be beheaded on the spot. Wholly despairing of our life at this news, we fled at once; and in flight I came to Cologne. Tarrying there for some days, I came afterward to Liége. In these places I always found men who were faithful and constant in good faith toward the kingly office.

On the counsel of these and of other vassals of the kingdom, I now have to lament to you faithfully and honestly all these misfortunes of mine: faithfully, indeed, because of what is owed through common relationship and old friendship and honestly, on the other hand, because of the glorious name which so great a kingly office bears. Therefore, invited by fidelity and by friendship, counsel me, your kinsman and friend, in my very great tribulations, as though they were your own. Even if these bonds of fidelity and friendship did not exist between us, it would still be your task and that of all the kings of the earth to avenge our injury and the scorn which has been shown us and to uproot this pattern for such nefarious betrayal and violence from the face of the earth.[181]

40 Henry complains to his son, Henry V, of his treachery, declares himself ready to give satisfaction to the Pope, and asks that justice be done him and his vassals. Should this petition fail, he appeals to the Pope and to the Roman Church (1106).

Henry, by the grace of God Emperor Augustus of the Romans, to Henry, his son:

If you had dealt with us in that affection due a father, as you ought to have done, we would speak most cheerfully with you as a father and we would send you the things which are to be expected of a father. But since your attitude toward us has been far different from that which is marked by affection and decency toward a father, and is so still, we cannot speak to you in any way or send you any word other than what the actual situation quite patently demands.

[181] Cf. Genesis 7:4.

You yourself know, just as (even by public knowledge) you are conscious of your own action, how after you had given assurances and guaranteed the security of our person and honor, you promised in full affection and devotion to conduct us to Mainz into the presence of the princes and thence to conduct us back most securely wherever we should wish. When we went with you in this assurance with love and without question, you seized us at Bingen contrary to the assurances you had given. There neither paternal tears nor the grief and sadness of a father, with which we prostrated ourselves at your feet and at those of others, so moved you to compassion that you would not seize us and hand us over to be mocked and guarded by mortal enemies. There, afflicted with every kind of abuse and terror, we were driven almost to the very point of death. Even before this captivity you had taken the bishoprics from us and whatever of the honor of the kingdom you could take, both our allods and our dependents themselves. But in our captivity, you extorted from us by force and fear of death whatever was left, even the lance and the cross and all the regal insignia—as you yourself know well and as is now known to almost all of Christendom—and you scarcely left us life itself. Since you were not satisfied with what you had done to us, ever afterward, wherever we were, you did not cease persecuting us in every way you could, trying either to destroy us or to expel us from the kingdom.

We greatly wonder with what reason or pretext you do this so stubbornly, since you can no longer have a justification from the Lord Pope and the Roman Church.[182] For in your presence we have shown that we stood ready to render our obedience to the legate of the Lord Pope[183] and of the Roman church; and we are ready both now in his very presence and for all time to show all due obedience and reverence to him. And we are ready most gladly to do whatever the princes, our spiritual father Hugh, the abbot of Cluny, and other religious men counsel for the state of the Church and the honor of the kingdom.

Considering the honor of the kingdom, your own honor, and the devotion you owe to your father, we ask you, by the authority of the Roman pontiff and the Roman Church, to do justice for the wrongs inflicted upon us and for those things which you have taken away from us forcibly and unjustly. We also ask you to cease molesting us and our vassals—since you have no reason for persecuting us in any way—

---

[182] Cf. "Life of Henry IV," chap. 9, p. 123.   [183] Richard of Albano.

but rather to permit us to live in peace and quiet so that we can fully accomplish in tranquillity all the things mentioned above.[184] Acknowledge also and think within yourself that God is the just judge, to whom we have committed our cause,[185] and vengeance is His, whose judgments also are hidden like a great abyss.[186] However much you pride yourself on our affliction and misfortune and exalt yourself above our humility, perhaps by His gratuitous mercy and at the intercession of Justice, He has already decided between me and you from His holy seat,[187] in a way other than you yourself may think or plan.

But if no other cause, neither reverence nor intercession, avails us before you to the end that we may follow justice and that the onslaught of your persecution may cease, then to this same end we appeal to the Roman pontiff, to the holy and universal Roman See and Church.

41 *Henry protests (1) to the princes of the realm (2) to the princes and the people of Saxony against the injustice of his enforced deposition in their presence. He declares himself ready to obey the Pope, on the counsel of Hugh of Cluny and other religious men, and he asks that they who once looked on as he was deprived of office now intercede for him before his son. Failing in this request, he appeals to the Pope and to the Roman Church (1106).*

Henry, by the grace of God Emperor Augustus of the Romans, sends (a) to the bishops, dukes, margraves, counts, and the other princes of the realm, (b) to the archbishops, and other princes, and also even to the rest of the people of Saxony, grace and love to those who are worthy to receive it:

We lament to Omnipotent God, to my lady Saint Mary,[188] to Blessed Peter, the prince of the apostles, our guardian, and to all you princes, that we have been dealt with unjustly, inhumanly, and cruelly, having trusted in that fidelity which we ought not to have had to doubt. Against divine and human law and to the shame and abuse of the kingdom, we have been so despoiled of the honor of kingship, of our lands, and of everything else we had, that on the whole nothing but life alone has been left us. When almost all of you were there [where this was done], many of you seemed to grieve and to be saddened.[189] But alas!

---

[184] Psalm 7:12.   [185] Cf. I Samuel 24:15.   [186] Cf. Psalm 36:7.   [187] Cf. Psalm 45:6

[188] Henry was especially devoted to the cult of the Blessed Virgin, the patroness of the Speier Cathedral. See "Life of Henry IV," chap. 1.

[189] See "Life of Henry IV," chap. 10, p. 127.

Your sadness brought us nothing but the gratification at our expence of the hateful will of our enemies.

Upon the counsel and at the request of our son, we first received from him an assurance and a guarantee of the security of our life and honor and then set off confidently and eagerly to the presence of the Roman legate[190] and the princes at Mainz. This we did so as to comply with their dispositions in regard to the state of the Church, the honor of the kingdom, and the salvation of our soul. Then, amidst this good will and obedience, our son did not fear to seize us contrary to the assurances which had been given and to lead us almost to the point of death. Thus, we have not dared to trust him again so that he could use us at will with injuries and abuse as he did before.

Wherefore, we do earnestly ask you and heartily pray that you may see fit zealously to work for the fear of God and the honor of the kingdom and your own integrity, so that through you we can regain justice from the act of injustice inflicted upon us when we were in your hands.

According to your counsel and that of others who harbor no hatred for us and according to that of religious men, we are also prepared to make amends to our son, if we have offended him in any way, as well as to anyone else in the kingdom. Moreover, just as we were prepared earlier to render obedience to the Lord Pope before you and his legate so are we even now prepared sincerely and devoutly to show him in his very presence all due reverence and obedience. We are willing by your counsel, by that of our spiritual father, Hugh, abbot of Cluny, and by that of other religious men, as far as we can, to make dispositions concerning the state of the Church and the honor of the kingdom.

Since, therefore, we are prepared ourself for all these things, we ask—indeed, we earnestly pray—that you persistently admonish our son for the sake of God and for the honor of the kingdom and your own honor (since according to the stated position, he is left no reason for opposing us). Admonish him to desist from persecuting us and our vassals and to permit us to live quietly and peaceably so that the above-mentioned things may be accomplished wholly and with tranquillity. But if he is dissident, we ask you by the authority of the Roman Church, to which we commit ourself, and by the honor of the kingdom, not to persecute us and our vassals, since it is clear that he has undertaken this [activity] not through zeal for divine law or love of the Roman

[190] Richard of Albano.

Church, but through lust for the kingly power, having unjustly deprived his father of it. If your intercession and other intervention likewise can not succeed with him at the present time, we appeal to the Roman pontiff and to the holy universal Roman See and Church.

42 Henry protests to the princes against the terms of the truce they have offered and describes the terms he thinks acceptable. He appeals to God for justice, as well as to the Saints, to all Christians, and particularly to the princes. Should the princes not heed his appeal, he turns to Pope Paschal and to the Roman Church (1106).

Henry, by the grace of God Emperor Augustus of the Romans, sends to the archbishops, bishops, dukes, counts, and the other princes of the realm, grace and love to those worthy to receive it:

We have asked our son and you—in fact, we have often entreated you—that we dismiss our armies and arrange terms according to which we could come together peacefully to make with dignity and decency a final settlement redounding to the honor of the realm. Thus we could resolve the question of the wrong done us and that of the peace still to be concluded.

You have seen fit to make a reply which has given rise to a complaint far graver to us than the former one. Granting a truce of eight days, you wish to lift the siege of Cologne and then, under the guise of a conference, to come to us and our vassals with an army. As you know well, to this day, such terms have never been given by divine or human law or even by the usage of men to a man of any position for the legal settlement of any minor business, much less for that of so great an affair. We ought to have, if it pleases you, at least a truce such that during it we could summon and invite with prayers to be with us for this affair the archbishops of Mainz,[191] Trier,[192] and Bremen[193] and the bishops of Freising,[194] Augsburg,[195] Chur,[196] and Basel,[197] Duke Magnus[198] with Duke Theodoric,[199] the Duke of Bohemia[200] and the Count of Flanders,[201] with Count William of Burgundy and others who are highly needful, as you well know, to the stated business.

Wherefore, as we asked before, so also we pray and earnestly ask now again that for God's sake, for the sake of your own souls, and with

[191] Ruthard.   [192] Bruno.   [193] Frederick.   [194] Henry.   [195] Herman.   [196] Wido.
[197] Burchard.   [198] Of Saxony.   [199] Of Upper Lorraine.   [200] Boriwoi.
[201] Robert.

regard for the appeal of the Roman pontiff, Lord Paschal and of the Roman Church, and for the sake of the honor of the kingdom, you may see fit so to work with our son that he will disband his army and cease to persecute us. We also ask that terms be arranged by which securely and with undisputed authority, we can convene you quietly and peaceably with the others mentioned above to take action about the wrong done us and about the peace to be concluded in the realm.

But in the event that he is absolutely unwilling to cease, we make our appeal, and we make it constantly, to God, to Saint Mary, and to Saint Peter, our guardian, and to all the saints, and to all Christians, and particularly to you, praying with all devotion that you may see fit to cease following him in the perpetration of such great injustice. And to the end that he cease to persecute us and that you cease to follow his example, we have appealed, and now for the third time we do appeal, to the Roman pontiff, Lord Paschal, and to the holy and universal Roman See and Church.

But if all our efforts are of no avail, we commit ourselves to God, the Omnipotent Father, and to the Son, and to the Holy Spirit, the Paraclete, and to Saint Mary, Perpetual Virgin, and to Saint Peter and Paul and Saint Lambert,[202] and to all the saints, that Divine Mercy and the intercession of all the saints may deign to regard our low estate and to defend us against so great and so wrongful an onslaught.

[202] Patron Saint of Liége.

APPENDIX

In his article "Deutsche Könige, Kaiser, Päpste als Kanoniker an deutschen und römischen Kirchen," *Historisches Jahrbuch*, LV (1934), 137–77, A. Schulte assembled the most significant data which suggests that the Salian kings served as canons. This evidence is strong, but unfortunately it is not impeccable; without discounting it entirely, one may suggest that it needs to be re-evaluated. Schulte maintained that the earliest definite statement that a Salian king was also a canon was a confirmation of privileges issued in 1107 by Henry V to the cathedral chapter of Liége in which the issuer says that he "was made a brother in the congregation of the brethren." (The text is printed in S. Bormans and E. Schoolmasters, *Cartulaire de l'Eglise Saint Lambert de Liége* [Brussels, 1893], I, 48 ff., no. 30. A variant reading is in K. F. Stumpf-Brentano, *Die Reichkänzler*, Vol. II, no. 3021. See also G. Meyer von Knonau, *Jahrbücher des Deutschen Reiches unter Heinrich IV und Heinrich V* [Leipzig, 1907], VI, 71 f.) However, several characteristics of the document in its present edition suggest the desirability of an exacting investigation of its authenticity, or at least of a clarification of the text. For example, the form of the document is curious in that, perhaps through errors of the copyist, the *aregna* (the preliminary statement of the general motives of the act) seems to have been fused into one with the *narratio* (the statement of the particular circumstances surrounding the enactment) and the *promulgatio* (the order of promulgation). (The usual forms may be represented by *MGH Diplomata Heinrici IV*, p. 393, no. 299 and p. 645 no. 474. See also H. Bresslau, *Handbuch der Urkundenlehre für Deutschland und Italien*, 3d ed. [Berlin, 1958], I, 47.) Second, "Henry" is made to speak of himself in the first person singular instead of the first person plural, as was conventional in documents of this nature. And finally, the document is dated "in the second year" of Henry's reign. This is unusual, since until the thirteenth century (the period in which the earliest known exemplar of this charter was made) practice dictated dating documents from the coronation, rather than from the beginning of personal rule. In the orthodox fashion, the charter should have been dated from Henry's "ordinatio" in 1098, rather than from the beginning of his personal reign. (See Bresslau, *Handbuch*, II, 422 ff.) Of the other evidence suggesting the king-canon, very little can not be questioned seriously. For example, Schulte puts altogether too much value on the words "fratres nostri" when used by kings in reference to collegiate chapters. (See Schulte, "Deutsche Könige," pp. 147, 154, 157 and *passim*.) It would have been perfectly natural for the lord of a proprietary church to refer to its chapter as "fratres nostri" just as he might refer to its bishop as "episcopus noster" or "fidelis noster." Indeed, in a confirmation issued by Henry IV to the canons of Speier, the canons were not only referred to as "fratres nostros" (*MGH Diplomata Heinrici IV*, p. 631, 25), but also as "nostros in Spirensi ecclesia canonicos" (*ibid.*, p. 630, ll. 34 f.) In short, the word "fratres" may be used objectively, and consequently its use may allude only to the relation between a proprietary lord and "our clergy." It does not prove conclusively that its user was a "frater." Schulte also draws heavily on collegiate necrologies. But in the absence of a critical edition of the Echternach necrology, which he believed proof that Henry IV, Henry V, and Henry VI were "fratres nostrae congregationis," one cannot say with perfect confidence whether the entries in question were written in the twelfth century or in the fifteenth, nor can one assess accurately its value as evidence. (See E. Sackur, "Handschriftliches aus Frankreich," *Neues Archiv*, XV [1890], 135, 136; cf. p. 134.) And the Eichstätt necrology, which names Conrad II under the heading "Haec sunt nomina fratrum canonicorum nostrae recordationis tempore ex Eistentensi congregatione defunctorum" (*MGH SS.*, VII, 249 f.) also names Conrad's wife, the Empress Gisela, and three *conversae*. It is impossible that these last four should have been *canonici*, and one cannot accept entirely Schulte's supposition that these names were extracted from the midst of a rather long list to be used in special prayers of rogation while those names about them were simply the names of deceased canons. Clearly, there was some confusion in compiling the list; perhaps it was begun as a list of deceased canons and continued without a new title as a list of those for whom special prayers were to be made. At any rate, one may not conclude definitely on this evidence that "King Conrad II certainly belonged to the cathedral chapter of Eichstätt". (Schulte, "Deutsche Könige," p. 155.) To be sure, tradition supports the figure of the eleventh-century king-canon; but only the appearance of new documents and editions can make it possible to draw firm conclusions.

BIBLIOGRAPHY

Excellent bibliographies of works on the Investiture Controversy in general, and in particular on the German kingdom in the period covered by the works in this volume, exist in the following books: A. Fliche, *La réforme grégorienne et la reconquête chrétienne (1059-1123)*, Paris, 1940; B. Gebhart, *Handbuch der deutschen Geschichte*, 8th ed., by H. Grundmann et al., Vol. I, Stuttgart, 1954; K. Hampe, *Deutsche Kaisergeschichte in der Zeit der Salier und Staufer*, 10th ed., by F. Baethgen, Heidelberg, 1949. For works more recent than those cited in Gebhardt, consult the issues of the *Deutsches Archiv* for 1954 onwards and the annual bibliographical volumes of the *Revue d'histoire ecclésiastique*. While including many works of a general nature, the following bibliography is not exhaustive and is restricted to those writings used in preparing the introduction and annotations for the translations in this volume.

Barker, E. From Alexander to Constantine. Oxford, 1956.

Baynes, N. A. Byzantine Studies and Other Essays. London, 1955.

Becker, F. Der römische König zu Lebzeiten des kaiserlichen Vaters. Rostock (Diss.), 1913.

Bernheim, E. Mittelalterliche Zeitanschauungen, Teil I. Tübingen, 1918.

Bloch, H. "Monte Cassino, Byzantium, and the West in the Earlier Middle Ages," Dumbarton Oaks Papers, No. 3 (Harvard, 1946), pp. 163–224.

Blum, O. J. St. Peter Damian. Washington, 1947.

Boeckler, A. Deutsche Buchmalerei vorgotischer Zeit. Königstein im Taunus, 1953.

Braak, M. T. Kaiser Otto III: Ideal und Praxis im frühen Mittelalter. Amsterdam, 1928.

Bresslau, H. Jahrbücher des deutschen Reiches unter Konrad II. 2 vols. Leipzig, 1879, 1889.

—— Handbuch der Urkundenlehre für Deutschland und Italien, 3d ed., 2 vols. Berlin, 1958.

Brezzi, P. Roma e l'impero medioevale (774–1252). Bologna, 1947.

Brooke, Z. N. "Lay Investiture and Its Relation to the Conflict of Empire and

Papacy," *Proceedings of the British Academy*, XXV (1939), 217–247.

Canney, M. A. "Ancient Concepts of Kingship," Oriental Studies in Honor of Curdetji Erachji Pavry. London, 1933.

Carlyle, R. W., and A. J. Carlyle, A History of Medieval Political Theory in the West, 6 vols. London, 1950.

Cerfaux, L., and J. Tondriau, Un concurrent du christianisme: le culte des souveraines dans la civilization Gréco-Romaine. Paris, 1957.

Cavenaugh, Sister A. B. Pope Gregory VII and the Theocratic State. Washington, 1934.

Corpus Nummorum Italicorum, Rome, vol. IV, 1913; vol. X, 1927.

Dannenberg, H. Die deutschen Münzen der sächsischen und fränkischen Kaiserzeit, 4 vols. Berlin, 1876–1905.

Dümmler, E. Anselm der Peripatetiker. Halle, 1872.

Eckel, A. Charles le Simple, Paris, 1899.

Eichmann, E. "Das Exkommunikationsprivileg des deutschen Kaisers im Mittelalter," *ZfRG KA*, I (1911), 160–194.

—— "Königs- und Bischofsweihe," Sitzungsberichte der bayerischen Akademie der Wissenschaften, phil.-hist. Kl., No. 6. Munich, 1928.

Ensslin, W. "Das Gottesgnadentum des autokratischen Kaisertums der frühbyzantinischen Zeit," *Studi bizantini e neoellenici*, V (1939), 154–166.

—— "Die Religionspolitik des Kaisers Theodosius des Grossen," Sitzungsberichte der bayerischen Akademie der Wissenschaften, phil.-hist. Kl. 1953, Heft 2.

Erdmann, C. "Die Aufrufe Gerberts und Sergius IV für das Heilige Land," *Quellen und Forschungen aus italienischen Archiven und Bibliotheken*, XXIII (1931/2), 1–21.

—— "Endkaiserglaube und Kreuzzugsgeschichte im 11. Jahrhundert," *Zeitschrift für Kirchengeschichte*, 3. Folge, LI (1932), 384–414.

—— "Kaiserliche und päpstliche Fahnen im hohen Mittelalter," *Quellen und Forschungen aus italienischen Archiven und Bibliotheken*, XXV (1933), 1–48.

—— Die Entstehung des Kreuzzugsgedankens. Stuttgart, 1935. Reprinted, 1955.

—— "Die Anfänge der staatlichen Propaganda im Investiturstreit," *Historische Zeitschrift*, CLIV (1936), 491–512.

—— Studien zur Briefliteratur Deutschlands im elften Jahrhundert. Leipzig, 1938.

—— "Untersuchungen zu den Briefen Heinrichs IV," *Archiv für Urkundenforschung*, XVI (1939), 184–253.

—— and D. v. Gladiss, "Gottschalk von Aachen im Dienste Heinrichs IV," *Deutsches Archiv*, III (1939), 115–174.

—— F. Baethgen, ed., Forschungen zur politischen Ideenwelt des Frühmittelalters, Berlin, 1951.

Feierbach, H. Die politische Stellung der deutschen Reichsabteien während des Investiturstreits. Bresslau, 1913.

Gundlach, W. "Die Vita Heinrici IV und die Schriften des Sulpicius Severus," *Neues Archiv*, XI (1886), 289–309.

Haefele, Hans. Fortuna Heinrici IV Imperatoris, Cologne, 1954.

Hampe, K. Deutsche Kaisergeschichte in der Zeit der Salier und Staufer, 10th ed., by F. Baethgen. Heidelberg, 1949.

Harnack, A. v. "Christus praesens—Vicarius Christi," Sitzungsberichte der preussischen Akademie der Wissenschaften, 1927, phil.-hist. Kl., 415–446.

Hauck, A. Kirchengeschichte Deutschlands, 3rd–4th ed., 5 vols, Leipzig, 1922–1929.

Hellmann, S. "Die Vita Heinrici IV und die kaiserliche Kanzlei," *Historische Vierteljahrschrift*, XXVIII (1934), 213–334.

—— "Zur Benutzung der Vulgata in der Vita Heinrici IV," *Neues Archiv*, XXVIII (1903), 239–243.

Joachimson, P. "The Investiture Contest and the German Constitution," in G. Barraclough, ed. and trans., Medieval Germany, 911–1250, II, 95–130. Oxford, 1938,

Joranson, E. "The Great German Pilgrimage of 1064–1065," in The Crusades: Essays Presented to Dana C. Munro. New York, 1928.

Kampers, F. "Rex et Sacerdos," *Historisches Jahrbuch*, XLV (1925), 495–515.

Kantorowicz, E. Laudes Regiae. Berkeley, 1946.

—— "Mysteries of State," *Harvard Theological Review*, XLVIII (1955), 65–92.

—— The King's Two Bodies. Princeton, 1957.

Kellner, O. Das Majestätsverbrechen im deutschen Reich bis zur Mitte des 14. Jahrhunderts. Halle (Diss.), 1911.

Kern, F. Gottesgnadentum und Widerstandsrecht im frühen Mittelalter, 2d ed., by R. Buchner. Münster, 1954.

—— S. B. Chrimes, trans. Kingship and Law in the Middle Ages. Oxford, 1939.

Kirchberg, J. Kaiseridee und Mission unter den Sachsenkönige und den ersten Saliern von Otto I bis Heinrich III. Berlin, 1934.

Klewitz, H. W. "Die Festkrönungen der deutschen Könige," *ZfRG KA*, XXVIII, (1939), 48–95.

—— "Königtum, Hofkapelle, und Domkapitel im 10 und 11 Jahrhundert," *Archiv für Urkundenforschung*, XVI (1939), 102–156.

Lehmgrübner, H. Benzo von Alba, Ein Verfechter der kaiserlichen Staatsidee unter Heinrich IV. Berlin, 1887.

Lerner, F. Kardinal Hugo Candidus. Munich, 1931.

Manitius, M. Geschichte der lateinischen Literatur des Mittelalters, vols II, III. Munich, 1923, 1931.

Meyer von Knonau, G. Jahrbücher des deutschen Reiches unter Heinrich IV und Heinrich V. 7 vols. Leipzig, 1890–1909.

Mikoletzky, H. L. Kaiser Heinrich II und die Kirche. Vienna, 1946.

Mirbt, C. Die Stellung Augustins in der Publicistik des gregorianischen Kirchenstreits. Leipzig, 1888.

—— "Absetzung Heinrich IV durch Gregor VII in der Publicistik jener Zeit," in Kirchengeschichtliche Studien (Festschrift Hermann Reuter), 95–144. Leipzig, 1890.

—— Die Wahl Gregors VII. Marburg, 1892.

—— Die Publizistik im Zeitalter Gregors VII. Leipzig, 1894.

Munding, E., ed. *Königsbrief Karls den Grossen an Papst Hadrian*, Texte und Arbeiten herausgegeben durch die Erzabtei Beuren, I. Abt. Hft 6. Beuren, 1920.

Nottharp, H., "Ehrenkanoniker und Honorkapital," *ZfRG KA*, XIV (1925), 174–335.

Overall, J. Convocation Book. Oxford, 1844.

Previté-Orton, C. W. The Early History of the House of Savoy (1000–1233). Cambridge, 1912.

Rassow, P. "Der Kampf Kaiser Heinrichs IV mit Heinrich V," *Zeitschrift für Kirchengeschichte*, XLVII (1928), 451–465.

Rörig, R. "Heinrich IV und der Weltherrschaftsanspruch des mittelalterlichen Kaisertums," *Deutsches Archiv* VII, (1944), 200–203.

Runciman, S. A History of the Crusades, vol. I. Cambridge, 1951.

—— The Eastern Schism. Oxford, 1955.

Ryan, J. J. St. Peter Damiani and His Canonical Sources. Toronto, 1956.

Sackur, E. "Handschriftliches aus Frankreich," *Neues Archiv*, XV (1890), 103–139.

Santifaller, L. "Zur Geschichte des ottonisch-salischen Reichskirchensystems," Sitzungsberichte der Oesterreichischen Akademie der Wissenschaften, phil.-hist. Kl. 229 Bd. 1, 1954.

Schieffer, T. "Heinrich II und Konrad II," *Deutsches Archiv*, VIII (1951), 384–437.

Schirmer, E. Die Persönlichkeit Kaiser Heinrichs IV im Urteil der deutschen Geschichtsschreibung. Jena (Diss.), 1930.

Schmeidler, B. "Heinrichs IV Absetzung 1105/6, kirchenrechtlich und quellenkritisch untersucht," *ZfRG, KA*, XII (1922), 168–221,

—— "Über den wahren Verfasser der Vita Heinrici IV imperatoris," in Papsttum und Kaisertum (Festschrift P. Kehr). Munich, 1926.

—— Kaiser Heinrich IV und seine Helfer im Investiturstreit. Leipzig, 1927.

—— "Franconia's Place in the Structure of Medieval Germany," in G. Barraclough, ed. and trans., Medieval Germany: 911–1250, II, 71–94. Oxford 1938.

Schramm, P. E. Kaiser, Rom und Renovatio, Part I. Berlin, 1929.

—— "Die Ordines der mittelalterlichen Kaiserkrönung," *Archiv für Urkunden-forschung*, XI (1930), 285–390.

—— "Die Krönung in Deutschland bis zum Beginn des Salischen Hauses (1028)", *ZfRG KA*, XXIV (1935), 184–332.

—— "Der 'Salische Kaiserordo' und Benzo von Alba,"*Deutsches Archiv*,I (1937), 389–407.

—— "Sacerdotium und Regnum im Austausch ihrer Vorrechte," *Studi Gregoriani*, II (1947), 403–457.

—— Herrschaftszeichen und Staatssymbolik, 3 vols. Stuttgart, 1954–1956.

Schulte, A. "Deutsche Könige, Kaiser, Päpste als Kanoniker an deutschen und römischen Kirchen," *Historisches Jahrbuch*, LIV (1934), 137–177.

Schwerin, U. Die Aufrufe der Päpste zur Befreiung des Heiligen Landes von den Anfängen bis zum Ausgang Innozenz IV. Berlin, 1937.

Spangenberg, H. "Die Königskrönung Wratislavs von Böhmen und die angebliche Mainzer Synode des Jahres 1086," *MIÖG*, XX (1899), 381–396.

Stutz, U. "The Proprietary Church as an Element of Medieval Germanic Ecclesiastical Law," in G. Barraclough, ed. and trans., Medieval Germany: 911–1250, II, 35–70,Oxford, 1938.

Tellenbach, G., trans. R. F. Bennett. Church, State and Christian Society at the Time of the Investiture Contest. Oxford, 1948.

Waitz, G. Deutsche Verfassungsgeschichte, 8 vols, 1st–3d ed. Kiel, 1874–1885.

Wallach, L. "Onulf of Speier," *Medievalia et Humanistica*, fasc. 6 (1950), 35–56.

—— Alcuin and Charlemagne. Ithaca, N.Y., 1959.

Wattenbach, W., and R. Holtzmann. Deutschlands Geschichtsquellen im Mittelalter, vol. 1. Tübingen, 1948.

Weise, A. Die Bamberger Domskulpturen. 2 vols. Strassburg, 1914.

Ziegler, A. K. "Pope Gelasius I and His Teaching on the Relation of Church and State," *Catholic Historical Review*, XXVII (1942), 3–28.

INDEX